Also by FRANÇOIS TRUFFAUT:

The Adventures of Antoine Doinel:
  Four Autobiographical Screenplays
Day for Night
Four by Truffaut
The 400 Blows
Hitchcock
Jules and Jim
Small Change
The Story of Adele H
The Wild Child

THE
FILMS
IN MY LIFE

by
François Truffaut

translated by
Leonard Mayhew

SIMON AND SCHUSTER
New York

DESIGNED BY EVE METZ
MANUFACTURED IN THE UNITED STATES OF AMERICA

2 3 4 5 6 7 8 9 10
1 2 3 4 5 6 7 8 9 10 Pbk.

LIBRARY OF CONGRESS CATALOGING IN PUBLICATION DATA
TRUFFAUT, FRANÇOIS.

THE FILMS IN MY LIFE.

TRANSLATION OF LES FILMS DE MA VIE.
INCLUDES INDEX.
1. MOVING-PICTURES—REVIEWS. I. TITLE.
PN1995.T713   791.43'7   77–29036
ISBN 0–671–22919–2

ISBN 0–671–24415–9 Pbk.

FOR JACQUES RIVETTE

CONTENTS

III • THE GENERATION OF THE TALKIES: The French

CONTENTS

IV • HURRAH FOR THE JAPANESE CINEMA

V • SOME OUTSIDERS

*I believe a work is good to the degree that it expresses the man
who created it.*
ORSON WELLES

These books were alive and they spoke to me.
HENRY MILLER,
The Books in My Life

WHAT DO CRITICS DREAM ABOUT?

One day in 1942, I was so anxious to see Marcel Carné's *Les Visiteurs du Soir*, which at last had arrived at my neighborhood theater, the Pigalle, that I decided to skip school. I liked it a lot. But that same evening, my aunt, who was studying violin at the Conservatory, came by to take me to a movie; she had picked *Les Visiteurs du Soir*. Since I didn't dare admit that I had already seen it, I had to go and pretend that I was seeing it for the first time. That was the first time I realized how fascinating it can be to probe deeper and deeper into a work one admires, that the exercise can go so far as to create the illusion of reliving the creation.

A year later, Clouzot's *Le Corbeau* turned up; it fascinated me even more. I must have seen it five or six times between the time of its release (May 1943) and the Liberation, when it was prohibited. Later, when it was once again allowed to be shown, I used to go to see it several times a year. Eventually I knew the dialogue by heart. The talk was very adult compared to the films I had seen, with about a hundred words whose meaning I only gradually figured out. Since the plot of *Le Corbeau* revolved around an epidemic of anonymous letters denouncing abortion, adultery and various other forms of corruption, the film seemed to me to be a fairly accurate picture of what I had seen around me during the war and the postwar period—collaboration, denunciation, the black market, hustling, cynicism.

I saw my first two hundred films on the sly, playing hooky and slipping into the movie house without paying—through the emergency exit or the washroom window—or by taking advantage of my parents' going out for an evening (I had to be in bed, pretending to be asleep, when they came home). I paid for these great pleasures with stomachaches, cramps, nervous headaches and guilty feelings, which only heightened the emotions evoked by the films.

I felt a tremendous need to enter *into* the films. I sat closer and closer to the screen so I could shut out the theater. I passed up period films, war movies and Westerns because they were more difficult to identify with. That left mysteries and love stories. Unlike most moviegoers my own age, I didn't identify with the heroes, but with the underdog and, in general, with any character who was in the wrong. That's why Alfred Hitchcock's movies, devoted to fear, won me over from the start; and after Hitchcock, Jean Renoir whose work is directed toward understanding . . . "The terrible thing is that everyone has his own reasons" *(La Règle du Jeu)*. The door was wide open, and I was ready for Jean Vigo, Jean Cocteau, Sacha Guitry, Orson Welles, Marcel Pagnol, Ernst Lubitsch, Charlie Chaplin, of course, and all the others who, without being immoral, "doubt the morality of others" *(Hiroshima, mon amour)*.

I am often asked at what point in my love affair with films I began to want to be a director or a critic. Truthfully, I don't know. All I know is that I wanted to get closer and closer to films.

The first step involved seeing lots of movies; secondly, I began to note the name of the director as I left the theater. In the third stage I saw the same films over and over and began making choices as to what I would have done, if I had been the director. At that period of my life, movies acted on me like a drug. The film club I founded in 1947 was called—somewhat pretentiously but revealingly— the Movie-mania Club. Sometimes I saw the same film four or five times within a month and could still not recount the story line correctly because, at one moment or another, the swelling of the music, a chase through the night, the actress's tears, would intoxicate me, make me lose track of what was going on, carry me away from the rest of the movie.

In August 1951, ill and a prisoner of the Service des Détenus in a military hospital (they handcuffed us even when we went to the shower or to pee), I flew into a rage when, lying in my bed, I read in a newspaper that Orson Welles had been forced to withdraw his *Othello* from the Venice competition because, at the insistence of his backers, he wasn't allowed to risk losing to the British superproduction of Laurence Olivier's *Hamlet*.

A lovely time of life—when one cares more about the fate of those we admire than about one's own. More than two decades later, I still love movies, but no film can occupy my mind more than the one I'm writing, preparing, shooting, editing. I've lost the film-lover's generosity, so arrogant and overwhelming that at times it can fill one with embarrassment and confusion.

I have not been able to find my first article, published in 1950 in the *Bulletin of the Film Club of the Latin Quarter.* I remember it was about *La Règle du Jeu.* The original version of this film—including fourteen scenes we had never seen—had just been discovered and shown. In my article I carefully enumerated the differences between the two versions, which was probably what led André Bazin to suggest that I help him research a book on Renoir that he was planning.

By encouraging me from 1953 on to write, Bazin did me a great favor. Having to analyze and describe one's pleasure may not automatically change an amateur into a professional, but it does lead one back to the concrete and . . . to that ill-defined area where the critic works. The accompanying risk is that one may lose one's enthusiasm; fortunately, that didn't happen to me. In a piece on *Citizen Kane* I was at pains to explain how the same film might be viewed differently by a movie lover, a journalist, a filmmaker. This was as true of Renoir's work as it was of the big American movies.

Was I a good critic? I don't know. But one thing I am sure of is that I was always on the side of those who were hissed and against those who were hissing; and that my enjoyment often began where that of others left off: Renoir's changes of tone, Orson Welles's excesses, Pagnol's or Guitry's carelessness, Bresson's nakedness. I think there was no trace of snobbery in my tastes. I always agreed with Audiberti: "The most obscure poem is addressed to everybody." Whether or not they were called commercial, I knew that all movies were commodities to be bought and sold. I saw plenty of differences in degree, but not in kind. I felt the same admiration for Kelly and Donen's *Singin' in the Rain* as for Carl Dreyer's *Ordet.*

I still find any hierarchy of kinds of movies both ridiculous and despicable. When Hitchcock made *Psycho*—the story of a sometime thief stabbed to death in her shower by the owner of a motel who had stuffed his mother's corpse—almost all the critics agreed that its subject was trivial. The same year, under Kurosawa's influence, Ingmar Bergman shot exactly the same theme *(The Virgin Spring)* but he set it in fourteenth-century Sweden. Everybody went into ecstasy and Bergman won an Oscar for best foreign film. Far be it from me to begrudge him his prize; I want only to emphasize that it was exactly the same subject (in fact, it was a more or less conscious transposition of Charles Perrault's famous story "Little Red Riding

Hood"). The truth is that in these two films, Bergman and Hitchcock each expressed part of his own violence with skill and freed himself of it.

Let me also cite the example of Vittorio De Sica's *Bicycle Thief,* which is still discussed as if it were a tragedy about unemployment in postwar Italy, although the problem of unemployment is not really addressed in this beautiful film. It shows us simply—like an Arabic tale, as Cocteau observed—a man who absolutely *must* find his bicycle, exactly as the woman of the world in *The Earrings of Madame de . . . must* again find her earrings. I reject the idea that *The Virgin Spring* and *Bicycle Thief* are noble and serious, while *Psycho* and *Madame de . . .* are "entertainments." All four films are noble and serious, and all four are entertainment.

When I was a critic, I thought that a successful film had simultaneously to express an idea of the world and an idea of cinema; *La Règle du Jeu* and *Citizen Kane* corresponded to this definition perfectly. Today, I demand that a film express either the *joy of making cinema* or the *agony of making cinema.* I am not at all interested in anything in between; I am not interested in all those films that do not pulse.

The time has come to admit that it seems much more difficult to be a film critic today that it was in my time. A boy such as I was, who is learning on the job to be a professional writer, who is working by instinct rather than out of any real cultural base, probably would not be able to get his first articles printed.

André Bazin could not write today that "All films are born free and equal." Film production, like book publishing, has become diversified and specialized. During the war, Clouzot, Carné, Delannoy, Christian-Jaque, Henri Decoin, Cocteau and Bresson addressed the same public. This is no longer true. Today few films are conceived for the "general" public—people who wander into a movie theater by chance, attracted simply by the stills at the entrance.

Today, in America, people make films that are directed to minorities—blacks, Irish; there are karate films, surfing films, movies for children and for teen-agers. There is one great difference between the productions of today and those of former days: Jack Warner, Darryl F. Zanuck, Louis B. Mayer, Carl Laemmle and Harry Cohn loved the films they produced and took pride in them; today the owners of major companies are often disgusted by the sex-and-violence films they throw into the market so they won't be left behind by the competition.

When I was a critic, films were often more alive though less "intelligent" and "personal" than today. I put the words in quotes precisely because I hold that there was no lack of intelligent directors at that time, but that they were induced to mask their personalities so as to preserve a universality in their films. Intelligence stayed behind the camera; it didn't try to be in evidence on the screen. At the same time, it must be admitted that more important and profound things were said around the dinner table in real life than were reflected in the dialogue of the films that were being made, and that more daring things took place in bedrooms and elsewhere than in the movies' love scenes. If we had known life only through the movies, we could quite believe that babies came from a kiss on the lips with the mouth closed.

All that is changed; not only has cinema caught up with life in the past fifteen years, sometimes it seems to have gone beyond it. Films have become more intelligent—or rather, intellectual—than those who look at them. Often we need instructions to tell whether the images on the screen are intended as reality or fantasy, past or future; whether it is a question of real action or imagination.

As for erotic or pornographic films, without being a passionate fan I believe they are in expiation, or at least in payment of a debt that we owe for sixty years of cinematographic lies about love. I am one of the thousands of his readers who was not only entranced but helped through life by the work of Henry Miller, and I suffered at the idea that cinema lagged so far behind his books as well as behind reality. Unhappily, I still cannot cite an erotic film that is the equivalent of Henry Miller's writing (the best films, from Bergman to Bertolucci, have been pessimistic), but, after all, freedom for the cinema is still quite new. Also, we must consider that the starkness of images poses far more difficult problems than those posed by the written word.

As film production has continued to diversify, criticism has tended to specialize; one critic understands and is skillful at analyzing political films, another, literary films, a third, plotless or experimental films, etc. The quality of films has indeed progressed but sometimes less than they aspired to. There is often a large gap between a film's intentions and its achievement. If the critic considers only a film's intentions, he will praise it to the heavens; if he is conscious of form and demanding about its execution, he will criticize the achievement in proportion to its ambitions, which he may find pretentious.

It used to be much easier to achieve unanimity among both critics and the public. Out of ten films, only one had artistic ambitions, and it was hailed by all the critics, though not always by the public. The other nine were pure entertainment and the critics would praise two or three, for the demand (both for pleasure and quality) was greater than the supply. Today, almost all films are ambitious, and their producers are often unconcerned about profits because those who think only of profits (I speak of Europe) have turned to other activities, such as real estate.

So today the critic's function is delicately balanced, and frankly I am not sorry to have moved to the other side of the barricade, to be among those judged. But what is a critic?

They say in Hollywood, "Everyone has two trades—his own and reviewing movies." We can either rejoice in that or complain about it. For some time I have rejoiced, for I prefer this state of affairs to the solitude and indifference in which musicians and painters live and work.

Anyone can be a film critic. The apprentice supposedly need not possess a tenth of the knowledge that would be demanded of a critic of literature, music or painting. A director must live with the fact that his work will be called to judgment by someone who has never seen a film of Murnau's.

Every person on the editorial staff of a newspaper feels he can question the opinion of the movie columnist. The editor-in-chief, who shows careful respect to his music critic, will casually stop the movie critic in the corridor: "Well, you really knocked Louis Malle's last film. My wife doesn't agree with you at all; she loved it."

Unlike the American reviewer, the French critic counts himself a man with a mission to dispense justice; like God—or Zeus, if he is an unbeliever—he wants to humble the powerful and exalt the weak. First, there is the typical European phenomenon of a distrust of success. In addition, the foremost concern of the French critic to justify his function in his own eyes induces in him a strong desire to be useful. Sometimes he manages to be so.

Today, since the "new wave" and its extension, good films come not only from five or six countries but from everywhere in the world. The critic must strive to give the widest possible exposure to all important films. One film may be showing in twenty theaters in Paris;

another in a studio with ninety seats. One film has an advertising budget of $100,000; another will have one-tenth of that. The situation creates great injustices, and it is understandable that critics take this fact into account so seriously, even at the risk of irritating people in the movie industry.

I am very familiar with the French critic as protester, off to tilt at the windmills of the Gaumont Théâtre chain; the constant spoiler who breaks up the game. I know him very well: I was he, or at least one of them, from 1954 to 1958, always ready to defend the widow Dovzhenko, Bresson the orphan. I had noticed, for example, at the Cannes Festival in 1958 that the flower vases placed in front of the screen to add a festive air were arranged to offer the best effect for the official spectators in the balcony, but that they blocked the subtitles for the mere movie lovers in the first ten rows of the orchestra. That was all I needed to call the directors of the Festival a lot of bad names. They grew so tired of my incessant attacks that eventually they asked my editor-in-chief to send another reporter the following year. I was back in Cannes in 1959 for the Festival, but I was seated in the balcony for *Les Quatre Cents Coups (The 400 Blows)*. From that perspective I could appreciate unreservedly the lovely effect of the flowers in front of the screen. . . .

Since I've been a director I have made it a point not to go too long without writing about films. Doubling in brass as a critic-movie-maker has given me the boldness to examine the situation from the heights, like a Fabrice who might have had the luck to fly over Waterloo in a helicopter.

American critics seem better to me than the European critics. But, even as I advance such a hypothesis, I ask the reader to keep me from bad faith. By a simple law of life, we quite easily adopt notions that serve our purpose. And it is true that American critics have been more positive about my films than my compatriots have been. So watch out. In any case, I shall push the point forward. The American critic is usually a graduate of a journalism school and is more visibly professional than his French counterpart. You can see it in the methodical way he conducts an interview. Because of the wide distribution of American newspapers, the American critic is well paid. That is a not inconsiderable point. He doesn't feel that he has to live by his wits. Even if he doesn't publish books, or have a second trade, he can manage, and he doesn't feel as if he belongs to a different social class from those in the film industry. As a consequence, he is not tempted as a matter of course to distance himself from a mammoth production like *The Godfather,* to identify himself automatically with the marginal author who is struggling against the disdain of the large Hollywood studios. Having a certain peace of mind, he is able to simply relate what he sees. In France it has become customary to see the director attend press screenings of his film and wait calmly at the exit after the showing. This would be unthinkable in New York; it would have the makings of a public scandal.

What the Hollywood filmmakers generally complain about in the New York critics is that they give preference over domestic productions to little films from Europe that in their original subtitled versions will generally reach only students and cultivated people in the major cities.

There is some merit to the complaint, but the preference is quite understandable. And, indeed, many American moviemakers benefit from the reverse impulse when they arrive in Europe, as I have tried to demonstrate elsewhere in this book when I recall the fanaticism all of us French movie lovers displayed when the first American films reached us after the Liberation. It is still true today, and I believe it is a normal reaction. We always appreciate better what comes to us from afar, not only because of the attraction of the exotic but because the absence of everyday references reinforces the prestige of a work. A new movie by Claude Chabrol will not be seen in the same light in New York as in Paris. The Paris critic brings impressions with him that are extrinsic to the film. Writers will refer to the filmmaker's appearances on television, the critical and commercial success, or lack of it, of his last film, gossip about his private life, maybe his politics. Six months later, the same Chabrol film will arrive in New York unencumbered by these peripheral considerations, and the American critics will judge the film and *only* the film. We don't have to look any further for reasons why we always feel better understood outside our own country.

"People of the world are so imbued with their own stupidity that they can never believe that one of their own has talent. They appreciate only people of letters who are not of their world." So Marcel Proust wrote to Mme. Straus.

What this amounts to is that if we are uninvolved with the artist, we judge with considerably more sympathy what he does rather than what he is; more exactly, if we are involved, what he is—and what we know about him—intrudes itself between his work and our judgment. It must also be added that a film seldom arrives all on its own; it is part of a larger environment, maybe a style, or a seeming series. If three films come out in Paris in the same month, and all are set in the same period—for example, the Occupation—or in the same place—Saint Tropez—woe to the one that follows the first two, even if it is the best of the lot.

By the same token, I had to live in America for a while to understand why Alfred Hitchcock had been so underestimated there for so long. From morning to night, on American television, there is murder, brutality, suspense, espionage, guns, blood. None of these gross and manipulative productions approaches a fraction of the beauty of a film by the maker of *Psycho,* but it is the *same material,* and so I can understand in that violent atmosphere what a breath of fresh air an Italian comedy, a French love story, a Czechoslovak intimist film must be.

No artist ever accepts the critic's role on a profound level. In his early period he avoids thinking about it, probably because criticism is more useful to and also more tolerant of beginners. With time, artist and critic settle into their respective roles; maybe they grow to know each other, and soon they consider each other, if not exactly adversaries, in some simplistic image—cat and dog.

Once an artist is recognized as such, he stubbornly refuses to admit that criticism has a role to play. If he does admit it, he wants it to draw closer to him, to make use of it. He is wrong. The artist reproaches critics with bad faith, but he is often guilty of the same bad faith. I found the repeated attacks of General de Gaulle and Georges Pompidou on the press too awful not to apply the lessons to artistic criticism. The most regrettable ploy of the public man consists in trying to have it both ways: "First of all, I despise the press; secondly, I don't read it."

The susceptible person is so eaten up by egoism that he would likely be unsatisfied even with a favorable review, if it also showed indulgence to others. There is no great artist who has not given in, at one time or another, to the temptation of attacking criticism of his work, but I believe that this has been held to be a fault, a weakness, even when it comes from Flaubert: "There has never been a good review since the day the first one was written." Or from Ingmar Bergman, who once slapped a Stockholm reviewer.

It took a certain daring for Sainte-Beuve to write, as Sacha Guitry reminds us, "Monsieur de Balzac seems determined to end as he has begun: with one hundred volumes that no one will read." But we see how time has dealt with Sainte-Beuve and Balzac.

I would consider an artist courageous when, without disparaging the role of criticism, he could disagree with it even when it favored him. That is opposition on principle; it clarifies. That artist could wait for attacks without flinching, and could respond to them with the same openness. Instead, we note a depressing situation where artists begin the dispute only when they have been disagreed with. Bad faith, if there is bad faith, is never all on one side. When a very gifted French filmmaker presents each of his films as his "first real film," and states that those that preceded it were merely tentative exercises of which he is now ashamed, how is the critic who has supported his work from the beginning supposed to feel?

A simple question to those who rail against unfavorable reviews: Would you prefer to take your chances that the critics will never mention you, that your work will not be the subject of a single printed line? Yes or no?

We must not make exaggerated demands on critics, and particularly we must not expect that criticism can function as an exact science. Art is not scientific; why should criticism be?

The main complaint against some critics—and a certain type of criticism—is that too seldom do they speak about *cinema* as such. The scenario of a film is not *the* film; all films are not *psychological.* Every critic should take to heart Jean Renoir's remark, "All great art is abstract." He should learn to be aware of form, and to understand that certain artists, for example Dreyer or Von Sternberg, never sought to make a picture that resembled reality.

When I met Julien Duvivier a little while before his death, and after I had just shot my first film, I tried to get him to admit—he was always complaining—that he had had a fine career, varied and full, and that all things considered he had achieved great success and ought to be contented. "Sure, I would feel happy . . . if there hadn't been any reviews." This remark, undeniably sincere, stupefied me. I told Duvivier that when I had been a critic and had insulted Yves Allégret, Jean Delannoy, André Cayatte, even Duvivier himself, I was always aware, deep down, that I was like a cop directing traffic on the Place de l'Opéra as the shells fell on Verdun.

This was the image that came to me, because the expression "trial by fire" is justly applied to each artist on the day his work, which is part of himself, is handed over to the public for judgment.

The artist, in a sense, creates himself, makes *himself* interesting, and then places himself on display. It is a fabulous privilege, but only provided he accepts the opposite side of the coin: the risk involved in being studied, analyzed, notated, judged, criticized, disagreed with.

Those who do the judging—I testify from experience—are cognizant of the enormous privilege of the act of creation, of the risks incurred by the one who exposes himself thus, and in turn feel a *secret* admiration and respect which would at least partially restore the artist's peace of mind if he could know it. "You cannot write a great article on what someone else has created; that's criticism," said Boris Vian.

In the relations between artist and critic, everything takes place in terms of power, and curiously, the critic never loses sight of the fact that in the power relationship he is the weaker even if he tries to hide the fact with an aggressive tone; while the artist constantly loses sight of his metaphysical supremacy. The artist's lack of perspective can be attributed to emotionalism, sensitivity (or sentimentality), and certainly to the more or less powerful dose of paranoia that seems to be his lot.

An artist always believes that the critics are against him—and have always been against him—because his selective memory benignly favors his persecution complex.

When I went to Japan to present one of my films, a number of reporters talked to me about Julien Duvivier, because his *Poil de Carotte* had remained one of their favorite films over the years. When I was in Los Angeles in 1974, a great Hollywood actress told me that she would give anything to have the music of *Carnet de Bal* on a cassette. I wish I could have told Duvivier this, while he was still alive.

The artist should also keep another consideration in mind—reputation. He should not confuse the criticism of one film with the reputation it gains over the years. Aside from *Citizen Kane*, all of Orson Welles's films were severely criticized in their day, too poor or too baroque, crazy, too Shakespearean or not sufficiently so. Nevertheless, in the end, Welles's reputation throughout the world is secure. The same goes for Buñuel and Bergman, who were often unjustly criticized both at home and abroad.

Daily or weekly criticism is egalitarian, and this is to be expected. Anatole Litvak is as important as Charlie Chaplin; since they are equal before God, they must also be so before Criticism. But time is the element that will put all that right. And movie lovers will come to see films at the Museum of Modern Art in New York and the Cinémathèque in Paris, as well as at thousands of art and experimental movie houses throughout the world. So things are all right after all, and I shall wind up my defense of criticism by observing that excessively kind notices, coming from all sides and lasting a career, can sterilize an artist more effectively than the cold shower that wakes one up to real life. That must have been what Jean Paulhan had in mind when he wrote, "Bad reviews preserve an author better than alcohol preserves a piece of fruit."

Until the day he dies, an artist doubts himself deeply, even while he is being showered with his contemporaries' praise. When he tries to protect himself from attack or indifference, is it his work he defends or treats as if it were a threatened child or is it himself? Marcel Proust answered it this way: "I am so convinced that a work is something that, once it has come forth from us, is worth more than we are, that I find it quite natural to sacrifice myself for it as a father would for his child. But this idea must not lead me to address others about what can, unfortunately, only interest me."

The truth is that we are so vulnerable at the moment that we expose the result of a year's work to scrutiny that it would take nerves of steel to accept a hailstorm of bad reviews with equanimity, even if, in two or three years, our own perspective will bring us closer to the critics' verdict and make us aware that we failed to blend the mayonnaise. I use the word "mayonnaise" deliberately. When I was twenty, I argued with André Bazin for comparing films to mayonnaise—they either emulsified or did not. "Don't you see," I protested, "that all Hawks's films are good, and all Huston's are bad?" I later modified this harsh formula when I had become a working critic: "The worst Hawks film is more interesting than Huston's best." This will be remembered as "la politique des auteurs" (the *auteur* theory); it was started by *Cahiers du Cinéma* and is forgotten in France, but still discussed in American periodicals.

Today many of these Hawksians and Hustonians are movie directors. I don't know what any of them think of that ancient argument any more, but I feel sure we've all adopted Bazin's mayonnaise theory because actually making films has taught us a lot:

It is as much trouble to make a bad film as a good one.

Our most sincere film can seem phony.

The films we do with our left hands may become worldwide hits.

A perfectly ordinary movie with energy can turn out to be better cinema than a film with "intelligent" intentions listlessly executed.

The result rarely matches the effort.

Cinematic success is not necessarily the result of good brain work, but of a harmony of existing elements in ourselves that we may not have even been conscious of: a fortunate fusion of subject and our deeper feelings, an accidental coincidence of our own preoccupations at a certain moment of life and the public's.

Many things.

We think that criticism should play an *intermediary* role between the artist and the public, and that is sometimes the case. We think that criticism should play a *complementary* role, and that is sometimes the case. But most of the time, criticism is only one element among others: advertising, the general atmosphere, competition, timing. When a film achieves a certain amount of success, it becomes a sociological event and the question of its quality becomes secondary. An American critic wrote that "To review *Love Story* would be like reviewing vanilla ice cream." The frankest words about this kind of movie come definitively from Hollywood. When a director has a great success with a film that has been panned, he tells the critics: "Gentlemen, I cried all the way to the bank."

The public's desire to see a film—its power to attract—is a stronger motivation than the power of any criticism. Universally favorable reviews couldn't get people into the theaters to see Alain Resnais' *Nuit et Brouillard* (about deportation), Nelson Pereira dos Santos' *Vidas Secas* (about the famine and drought in Brazil), or Dalton Trumbo's *Johnny Got His Gun* (about a soldier who has lost his legs, arms, sight and speech). These examples suggest two interpretations: The filmmaker is wrong in believing his enemy to be the producer, the theater manager, or the critic; these genuinely want the film to be successful. The real enemy is the public, whose resistance is so hard to overcome. This theory has the merit of being nondemagogic, for it's always easy to flatter the public, the mysterious public that nobody can identify, and it is easy to inveigh against people of wealth who love to produce, distribute, and exploit all the films they are involved with, including the above.

The second interpretation holds that there exists, in the very idea of cinematic spectacle, a promise of pleasure, an idea of exaltation that runs counter to the downward spiral of life that goes through infirmity and old age to death. I am using shorthand and, of course, oversimplifying: the spectacle moves upward, life downward. If we accept this vision, we will say that the spectacle, as opposed to journalism, has a mission to deceive, but that the greatest of those who create such spectacles do not resort to lies but instead get the public to accept their truth, all without breaking the law that the spectacle must represent the rising movement. Both their truth and their madness are accepted, for we must never forget that an artist imposes his madness on an audience less mad, or at least unaware of its madness.

It might help to cite an example. Ingmar Bergman's *Cries and Whispers* was a worldwide success though it had all the elements of failure, including the sight of the slow torture of a woman dying of cancer—everything the public refuses to look at. But the film's formal perfection, especially the use of red in the decor of the house, constituted the element of exaltation—I would even say the element of pleasure—so that the public immediately sensed that it was watching a masterpiece. And it made up its mind to look at it with an artistic complicity and admiration that balanced and compensated for the trauma of Harriet Andersson's cries and her groans of agony. Others of Bergman's films, no less beautiful, were treated coolly by the public—and perhaps all they lacked were the red walls. For an artist like Bergman there will always be a core of faithful viewers in every great city of the world—an encouragement for him to continue his work.

Now, I must come to the content of this book. It contains a selection of articles I have written since 1954 for various newspapers and magazines. In the period between 1954 and 1958, there are, first, articles I wrote as a journalist and then articles I wrote as a director. The distinction is important. Once I became a director, I did not criticize my colleagues' work but only wrote about it as desire and opportunity dictated.

This book contains about a sixth of what I have written. The choice can be criticized, but it is my own. I have included very few bad reviews, even though I had the reputation at that time of being the "demolisher of French cinema." What purpose would be served by publishing diatribes against forgotten films? Let me quote Jean Renoir:

"I considered that the world, and especially the cinema, was burdened with false gods. My task was to overthrow them. Sword in hand, I was ready to consecrate my life to the task. But the false gods are still there. My perseverance during a half-century of cinema has perhaps helped to topple a few of them. It has likewise helped me to discover that some of the gods were real, and had no need to be toppled."

I have preferred to publish favorable or enthusiastic articles, even when they are less good, about films that are still shown or that were made by important directors.

Some of these articles have never been previously published; happily, I have always written for my own pleasure or to clarify my ideas. Others are syntheses of different texts on the same film because at a certain time I wrote regularly, under my own name and various pseudonyms, for a number of publications: weeklies such as *Arts, Radio-Cinéma, Le Bulletin de Paris;* monthlies such as *Les Cahiers du Cinéma, La Parisienne;* and a marginal daily, *Le Temps de Paris.* It was the first happy period of my life; I was going to the movies and talking about them, and somebody was paying me to do it. I was finally earning enough money to do nothing from morning to night but what I enjoyed, and I appreciated it all the more because I had just gone through seven or eight years of trying to find enough money to eat every day and pay my rent.

Part One, "The Big Secret," is devoted to directors who began with silent films and continued into the era of talking pictures. They have something *extra.* Jean Renoir, in *Ma Vie et mes Films,* describes the fascination this generation holds for its juniors. "I am pursued by the insistent questions of young colleagues for whom everything that preceded the talking film seems as distant and mysterious as the movement of the great glaciers in the prehistoric period. We elders enjoy a respect analogous to what the modern artist feels in front of the graffiti of the caves of Lascaux. The comparison is flattering and brings us the satisfaction of knowing that we weren't wasting film."

Some texts in this chapter are obituaries and have not been previously published: Carl Dreyer, John Ford. About Ford I have had a complete turnabout. When I was a critic, I hardly liked anything of his and I wrote two or three vicious articles about him. I had to become a director and watch *The Quiet Man* on television to realize one day how blind I had been. Then I saw, or saw again, many of his films, and today I have the same respect for Ford as I have for Jean Giono.

The articles on Jean Renoir and Luis Buñuel are also previously unpublished. The long piece on Jean Vigo was intended as a preface to an edition of his complete works—this has not yet been published. The article on Frank Capra was written for an American collection.

In "The Generation of the Talkies" (Parts Two and Three), once again I had to make a choice. In order not to disappoint those who like negative reviews, I kept a few in Part Three that seemed well thought through: *Monsieur Ripois, Le Ballon Rouge, Arsène Lupin*— though today I prefer the articles that are full of praise. They are infinitely more difficult to write and more interesting after the passage of time. When I was enthusiastic about a film, I often wrote about it in different journals under various pseudonyms. It has been an interesting task to synthesize them. That explains the length of the texts devoted to *Un Condamné à Mort s'est échappé (A Man Escaped)* and *Lola Montès,* and to Jean Cocteau.

I included in Part Two, devoted to American filmmakers like Billy Wilder, George Cukor, and Nicholas Ray, all of whom I admire, films that are either not well known or have been forgotten, but which were, nevertheless, important for me—*Love Me or Leave Me* by Charles Vidor and *The Naked Dawn* by Edgar G. Ulmer; the latter marked an important date in my life. I mentioned in the course of an article on *The Naked Dawn* a novel called *Jules et Jim.* Its author, Henri-Pierre Roche, wrote me a note, I went to meet him, and the rest of the story is well known.

In Part Five,* "Some Outsiders," I have included Ingmar Bergman because he is Swedish; Luis Buñuel, a Spaniard who has worked in Mexico and France; Norman MacLaren, a Scot living in Canada and one of the greatest filmmakers in the world, even though his films are only three and seven minutes long; two of the great Italians (there are more), Fellini and Rossellini. I have also put Orson Welles in this chapter—although he could have been included in Part Two— "The Americans"—because I consider him a director-citizen of the world. (The article on *Citizen Kane* is published here for the first

* The section on the Japanese directors (Part Four, "Hurrah for the Japanese Cinema") was not included in the French version of this book.

time.) Finally, I have included two portraits of actors whose deaths touched me: James Dean, who was already the object of a cult while alive, and Humphrey Bogart, a different kind of actor whose posthumous fame has continued to grow.

"My Friends in the New Wave": The title of Part Six may be a surprise. First of all, I wanted to affirm my position as a "new wave" director, because in the chronicles of French writers, the expression has in the last ten years become an arbitrary insult. To denigrate the new wave, without naming names or films is all too easy and risks no contradiction.

The new wave, which was never a school or a tight group, was a spontaneous and important movement that spread rapidly beyond our borders. I feel myself very much a part of it; I expressed in my articles the fervent wish for its coming, so much so that I could write, in 1957, a naïve but sincere profession of faith: "The film of tomorrow appears to me as even more personal than an individual and autobiographical novel, like a confession, or a diary. The young filmmakers will express themselves in the first person and will relate what has happened to them: it may be the story of their first love or their most recent; of their political awakening; the story of a trip, a sickness, their military service, their marriage, their last vacation . . . and it will be enjoyable because it will be true and new. . . . The film of tomorrow will be an act of love."

Depending on one's point of view, the new wave can be dated from *Et Dieu créa la Femme* by Vadim (the first French film by a young filmmaker to win international acclaim) or, even earlier, from *Les Mauvaises Rencontres* by Alexandre Astruc, a fine example of a first "*auteur's*" film." I have chosen to begin with *Nuit et Brouillard* because of the importance of the film and its author, Alain Resnais. The best information on the formation of the new wave is in the piece on Jacques Rivette's *Paris nous appartient*.

In this section I have gathered texts which are not really reviews but occasional pieces; they are honest, but it's a fact that they were written to draw attention to certain difficult films, to help launch them. It wasn't a matter of taking care of my friends: I met several of them only after I had written about them. Nevertheless, since the pieces were written with a kind of complicity, I thought it best to call Part Six "My Friends in the New Wave."

I think that these filmmakers, and many others about whom I

have not had occasion to write, brought more richness and variety to film production in France in one year than in all the previous years I had functioned as critic. In those days we saw all the good films, as well as many of the bad ones, because our love for cinema was like the explorer's thirst which moves him to drink even contaminated water. Today a film lover sees only a few bad films and a portion of the good ones. I think of my friend, Professor Jean Domarchi. He has watched 350 films a year passionately for the past thirty years and every time I meet him he says, "Tell me, old friend, it's nice to have something to see, isn't it?"

I have dedicated this volume to my friend Jacques Rivette, because it was with him that I saw most of the films I have written about in this book.

—1975

I
THE BIG SECRET

JEAN VIGO IS DEAD AT TWENTY-NINE

I had the huge pleasure of discovering Jean Vigo's films in a single Saturday afternoon session in 1946, at the Sevres-Pathé, thanks to the Ciné-Club "La Chambre Noire," organized by André Bazin and other contributors to *La Revue du Cinéma*. When I entered the theater, I didn't even know who Jean Vigo was. I was immediately overwhelmed with wild enthusiasm for his work, which doesn't take up two hundred minutes of projection time.

At first, I liked *Zéro de Conduite* best, probably because I identified with Vigo's collegians, as I was only three or four years older than they. Later, after I'd seen both films again and again, I definitely came to prefer *L'Atalante*, which I never leave out when I'm asked: "What, in your opinion, are the ten best films of all time?"

In a way, *Zéro de Conduite* seems to represent something rarer than *L'Atalante* because masterpieces devoted to childhood, in literature and in film, can be counted on the fingers of one hand. They knock us out on two grounds: besides the esthetic response, there is the autobiographical, the personal response. All films about children are period films because they send us back to short pants, school days and the blackboard, summer vacations, our beginnings.

Like all "first films," *Zéro de Conduite* has its experimental aspect. Lots of ideas that are more—or less—integrated into the scenario are shot through with a kind of "let's try it and see what happens" attitude. I am thinking of the college celebration when dummies are mixed with real people on the platform, which is also a fairground booth. That could be out of René Clair of the same period; in any case, it is a dated idea. But for one set piece like that, there are nine superb inventions, droll, poetic, or shocking, but all possessing great visual power and a still-unequalled bluntness.

When he shot *L'Atalante* shortly afterward, Vigo had clearly learned his lessons. This time, he achieved perfection, he made a masterpiece.

He still used slow motion to draw out poetic effects, but he didn't try for comic effects by speeding up the action. He no longer had recourse to dummies; he focused his lens only on the real and transformed it into fairy tales. Filming prosaic words and acts, he effortlessly achieved poetry.

The lightning-like career of Vigo is like Radiguet's on the surface. Both were young authors who died prematurely and left only two works. In both cases, the first work is openly autobiographical and the second seems further removed from its author, based more on external material. To underestimate L'Atalante, because it was created to order, is to forget that second works are almost always that. Le Bal du Comte d'Orgel is an order of Cocteau to Radiguet, or of Radiguet to himself. As a matter of principle, every second work is important because it allows us to determine whether the artist had only one work in him, that is, whether he was a gifted amateur, or a creator, whether he was someone who had a lucky break or someone who is going to develop. Finally, there is the same line of development, the passage from realism and revolt to preciousness and estheticism. (I use these terms in their most favorable sense.) Even though we can dream of what a marvelous Diable au Corps Jean Vigo would have directed, I don't want to stretch the comparison between the writer and the filmmaker. But studies of Jean Vigo often cite Alain-Fournier, Rimbaud, Céline, and with good reasons.

L'Atalante has all the qualities of Zéro de Conduite, along with maturity and artistic mastery. Two of the major tendencies of cinema—realism and estheticism—are reconciled in the film. In the history of cinema, there have been great realists like Rossellini, and great esthetes like Eisenstein, but few filmmakers have been interested in combining these two tendencies—most have treated them as if they were contradictory. For me, L'Atalante grasps the essence of both Godard's A Bout de Souffle (Breathless) and Visconti's White Nights—two films which can't be compared, which are diametrically opposite, but which represent the best in each genre. Godard accumulates bits of truth and binds them together to make a kind of modern fairy tale; Visconti begins with a modern fairy tale in order to rediscover a universal truth.

I believe that L'Atalante is often underestimated as being concerned with a small subject, a "particular" subject, as opposed to the great "general" subject of *Zéro de Conduite*. In reality, *L'Atalante* deals with a major theme, and one that has seldom been treated in films, the beginnings of a young couple's life together, their difficulty in adapting to each other, the early euphoria of coupling (what Maupassant calls "the brutal physical appetite that is quickly extinguished"), then the first wounds, rebellion, flight, reconciliation, and finally acceptance. *L'Atalante* doesn't treat any less a subject than *Zéro de Conduite*.

If you look at the history of French movies as the talkies began, you find that between 1930 and 1940 Jean Vigo was almost alone with Jean Renoir the humanist, and Abel Gance the visionary, although the importance of Marcel Pagnol and Sacha Guitry has been underestimated by historians of cinema.

Clearly, Vigo was closest to Renoir, but he forged further into bluntness and surpassed him in his love of the image. Both were brought up for the task in an atmosphere that was both rich and poor, aristocratic and common. But Renoir's heart never bled. The son of a painter who was a recognized genius, Renoir had the problem of doing nothing to blemish the name he bore. He came to the cinema after giving up ceramics, which he thought was too close to painting.

Jean Vigo was also the son of a famous but controversial man, Miguel Almereyda, an anarchist militant who died in prison under mysterious and sordid circumstances. An orphan who was bounced from one institution to another under an assumed name, Vigo suffered so much that his work cries out of necessity. Every biographical detail chronicled in P. E. Salès Gomès' admirable book on him confirms what we imagine about Vigo from watching his films. His great grandfather, Bonaventure de Vigo, was a magistrate in Andorra in 1882. His son, Eugene, died at twenty of tuberculosis, leaving one son, Miguel. Miguel's mother, Aimée Salles, remarried—she married Gabriel Aubès, a photographer in Sète; later, she went insane and in 1901 had to be institutionalized. The young Miguel took the name Almereyda, both because it sounded like the name of a Spanish grandee and because it contained all the letters of the word *merde* (shit). Miguel Almereyda married Emily Clero, a young anarchist militant, who already had five children from an earlier informal relationship. All the children died young, one by falling out of a window. In 1905 she gave birth to Jean, who was born to a hard life. Orphaned, he had for his whole inheritance his paternal great grandfather's motto:

"I protect the weakest." His films were a faithful, sad, funny, affectionate and brotherly, sharp illustration of that motto.

The motto indicates a fundamental point shared by Vigo and Renoir: their passion for Chaplin. Since the "histories of the cinema" do not pay much attention to the chronology of films and the influences of filmmakers on one another, it is impossible to prove what I believe to be true—that the construction of *Zéro de Conduite* (1932), with scenes divided by titles that comment humorously on life in the dormitory and the refectory, was very much influenced by Renoir's *Tire au Flanc* (1928), which was itself directly inspired by Chaplin, most particularly by *Shoulder Arms* (1918). By the same token, when he called on Michel Simon for *L'Atalante* (1933), Vigo must have had in mind Simon's role in Renoir's *Boudu sauvé des Eaux (Boudou Saved from Drowning)* the previous year.

When we read the recollections of the moviemakers of the silent generation, we notice that almost all of them came to films accidentally. A friend had asked them to be extras, or an aged uncle had taken them to visit a studio. This was not, however, the case with Jean Vigo, who was one of the first filmmakers by *vocation*. He was a spectator who fell in love with films, began to see more and still more movies, established a film club to bring better films to Nice, and was soon making them. He wrote to absolutely everybody, asking for a job as an assistant: "I'm willing to sweep up the stars' crap." He bought a camera and produced on his own his first short subject, *À propos de Nice*.

It has often been remarked that the line of *Zéro de Conduite* is broken by gaps that are usually blamed on the hellish working schedule. I think these gross ellipses can also be explained by Vigo's feverish haste to get at what was essential, and by the state of mind of the filmmaker who has just been given his first chance. He can't believe it; it's too good to be true. He shoots the film wondering whether it will ever see the light of day. When he had been merely a spectator, he thought he knew what was good and what was bad. Now that he is a filmmaker he is assailed by doubt. He thinks that what he is doing is too special, too far from the old norms, he wonders whether his film will even be shown. That's why I imagine that Vigo, learning that *Zéro de Conduite* was forbidden totally by the censors, and once the moment of shock was past, might have seen it as a confirmation of his own doubts. Perhaps he thought, "I knew I hadn't made a real film, like the others. . . ."

Later, when he presented *Zéro de Conduite* in Brussels, anticipating the eventual criticism of those famous "gaps" in the story line, Vigo allowed a misunderstanding to develop in the mind of the public: not only that the film had been prohibited by the censors but that it had also been tampered with—which is not true. So, Jean Vigo doubted himself, despite the fact that he had scarcely exposed 150 feet of film when, without realizing it, he became a great filmmaker, the equal of Renoir, Gance and Buñuel, who also began at the same time. Just as we say a person is fully formed between the ages of seven and twelve, so we can also say that a filmmaker shows what his career will be in his first 150 feet of film. His first work is himself, and what he does later will also be himself, always the same thing, sometimes a masterpiece, sometimes something less good, even some failures. All of Orson Welles is in the first reel of *Citizen Kane*, Buñuel in *Un Chien Andalou*, Godard in *Une Jeune Coquette;* and all of Jean Vigo is in *À propos de Nice*.

Like all artists, filmmakers search for realism in the sense that they search for their own reality, and they are generally tormented by the chasm between their aspirations and what they have actually produced, between life as they feel it and what they have managed to reproduce of it.

I think that Vigo would have more reasons to be satisfied with his work than his contemporaries had. He was far more advanced in evoking different realities: objects, surroundings, personalities, feelings, and above all the physical circumstance. I wonder whether it would be an exaggeration to speak of Vigo's work as the cinema of smells. The idea came to me when a reviewer, putting down a film I liked, *Le Vieil Homme et l'Enfant (The Two of Us)*, said to me, "It's a film that smells like dirty feet." I didn't answer at the time but I thought about it again and said to myself, "Here's an argument that smells reactionary and might easily have been used by the censors who prohibited *Zéro de Conduite*." Salès Gomès points out that many articles hostile to Vigo's films contain expressions like "It's like water out of the bidet" or "It verges on scatology," etc. In an article on Vigo, André Bazin employs a most felicitous phrase when he refers to his "almost obscene taste for the flesh." It's true that no one has filmed people's skin, human flesh, as bluntly as Vigo. Nothing that has been seen for the past thirty years has equaled the professor's fat paw on the tiny white hand of the child in *Zéro de Conduite*, or the physical embraces of Dita Parlo and Jean Dasté as they prepare to make love, even more so when they have finished and parallel shots show them each returning to his own bed, he to his barge, she to her hotel room, both still in the grip of passion. The prodigious score of Maurice Jaubert plays a role of the first importance in this scene. It is a sequence both carnal and lyrical, an exact rendition of lovemaking at a distance.

As both a realist and an artistic filmmaker, Vigo avoided the traps of realism and estheticism. He managed explosive material, for example, Dita Parlo in her wedding gown on the barge in the fog; the jumble of dirty clothing in Jean Dasté's closet. In both, he steered clear of trouble thanks to his own delicacy, his refinement, his humor, his elegance, intelligence, intuition, and sensitivity.

What was Vigo's secret? Probably he lived more intensely than most of us. Filmmaking is awkward because of the disjointed nature of the work. You shoot five to fifteen seconds of film and then stop for an hour. On the film stage there is seldom the opportunity for the concentrated intensity a writer like Henry Miller might have enjoyed at his desk. By the time he had written twenty pages, a kind of fever possessed him, carried him away; it could be tremendous, even sublime. Vigo seems to have worked continuously in this state of trance, without ever losing his clearheadedness. We know he was sick when he made his two films and that he directed some sequences of *Zéro de Conduite* lying on a cot. It is easy to conclude that he was in a kind of fever while he worked. It is very possible, indeed plausible. It is certainly true that one can be considerably more brilliant, more intense, and stronger when one has a "temperature." When one of his friends advised him to husband his strength, to hold himself back, Vigo answered that he felt he lacked the time and that he had to give everything right away. It seems likely that Jean Vigo, knowing the game was almost up, was stimulated by this measured time. Behind his camera he must have been in the state of mind Ingmar Bergman referred to when he said, "One must make each film as if it were the last."

—1970 (unpublished)

ABEL GANCE

Napoléon

This time "the film of the week" is twenty-eight years old. It isn't every week that one has the opportunity to criticize a film like *Napoléon*. Not every month, either . . . nor, alas, every year. Therefore it would be a bit ridiculous to analyze it like a current production, sorting out the good elements from the less good, looking for some flaw in Abel Gance's main structural support. *Napoléon* must be discussed as a whole, an unassailable monument. It must also—this is essential—be spoken of with humility. What contemporary film, French or foreign, that has been praised unanimously by the press and public, will be shown in twenty-eight years and arouse the applause of a theater filled with filmmakers and critics as *Napoléon* did yesterday evening?

Gance first thought about making *Napoléon* in 1921. He had just completed *La Roue* and was in New York to present the first version of *J'accuse*, which Griffith was going to have distributed in America by Allied Artists, whose membership included Charlie Chaplin, Mary Pickford, Douglas Fairbanks, and Griffith himself. Preparations began in 1923, and in 1924 the Société Napoléon was established. The world premiere took place April 7, 1927, at the Paris Opéra on a triple screen.

Napoléon took four years of work, three for the shooting alone. Before writing his scenario, Abel Gance read more than three hundred books and other documentation on Bonaparte: the Memorial, the correspondence, the proclamations, the works of Thiers, Michelet,

Lamartine, Frédéric Masson, Lacour-Gayet, Stendhal, Elie Faure, Schuermans, Aulard, Louis Madelin, Sorel, Arthur Lévy, Arthur Chuquet, and others.

The film cost eighteen million francs, an enormous sum for that time. Two hundred technicians were employed: operators, photographers, architects, decorators, painters, assistants, assistant directors (stage managers), electricians, explosives experts, gunsmiths, makeup artists, historical advisers, etc. Forty stars act in the film. Certain scenes contain as many as six thousand extras. One hundred and fifty sets were constructed either in the studio or outdoors and the scenes were shot on location in Brienne, Toulon, at Malmaison, on Corsica, in Italy, at Saint-Cloud and in Paris. The film was to have had three episodes: Bonaparte's youth; Bonaparte and the Terror; and the Italian campaign. Only the first two were made. During the preparation for the film eight thousand costumes, four thousand rifles and other weapons, tents and banners were stockpiled at Billancourt. At the same time a whole area of Paris with its twisting streets was reconstructed.

For the role of Bonaparte, Abel Gance tried out René Fauchois, a playwright; Pierre Bonardi, a writer; a singer, Jean Bastia; and two actors, Van Daële (who, in the end, played Robespierre) and Ivan Mosjoukine. The last refused the part because he was Russian and he felt that Bonaparte could only be interpreted by a Frenchman. In the end, Albert Dieudonné was chosen. He was a writer, an actor, and a director. Antonin Artaud was chosen for the part of Marat, fated to perish under the dagger of Eugénie Buffet, the beautiful Charlotte Corday.

The first camera work took place in Brienne on January 15, 1925. Abel Gance was the first to use subjective images in an original way. He had supports constructed so that he could mount cameras on horses. Camera platforms were pulled along on dollies at a dizzying speed. During the shooting of horseback chases in Corsica, there were two tragic deaths from falls. During the famous snowball fight at Brienne, where the child Bonaparte proved his skill as a precocious tactician, Gance had a net installed to hoist loaded cameras into the air so that their trajectory could follow the snowballs.

In Corsica, at the end of a chase, Dieudonné had to leap from his horse into a boat. He fell alongside into the water. Like Bonaparte, the actor didn't know how to swim. He cried out, "Save Bonaparte, save Bonaparte." The end of shooting in Corsica coincided with the local elections, and the native population was so fired up that the Bonapartist party won over the Republicans.

For the scenes of storms at sea, in which Bonaparte fights the elements with only the tricolor for a sail, the Mediterranean Sea had to be created inside a studio.

Although there was no sound, Gance chose a singer to play Danton, who sang the "Marseillaise" in the Constitutive Assembly. The extras had to chant the national anthem twelve times in a row. Emile Vuillermoz described this memorable day of shooting in *Le Temps:*

These improvised actors had taken their role terribly seriously. Their costumes had given them a new soul and mentality. The current from Abel Gance, that admirable conductor of people, electrified the mass. . . . These men and women of the people instinctively rediscovered their ancestors' feelings. . . . The director played on their nerves as a conductor plays on his musicians. . . . At one point, when he went to a lectern to give them a few technical explanations in his gentle, soft voice, he was greeted spontaneously by an admiring cheer as these tamed human beings gave themselves over entirely to their leader.

Watching the production of this tiny revolution, one understood the mechanics of the great revolution itself. If Abel Gance had had ten thousand extras under his command that day, all intoxicated with history, their minds disoriented with the drunkenness of obedience, he could have sent them to attack any barricade, he could have mounted an invasion of the Palais Bourbon or the Elysée and had himself proclaimed dictator.

One day Gance and several others on the set were wounded by a small case of cartridges that exploded in a corner of the studio. Without a word, he took a taxi to the clinic, and a week later he was back at work while the others were still convalescing.

When they were shooting the taking of Toulon and the harbor was captured by the English, for a few hours the English flag replaced the French tricolor. One evening, a nurse told Gance, "We had forty-two injured today." He replied, "That's a good sign; the boys are putting their hearts into it; the movement in the film will be excellent." When Bonaparte passed to review his troops, the extras were supposed to cheer and shout "Vive Bonaparte," instead of which they cried out "Vive Abel Gance."

For some scenes it was impossible to hire enough extras. At such times production secretaries went into the streets of Paris to hire out-of-work laborers at the gates of factories, students in the Latin Quarter, and derelicts sleeping in the markets at night.

In 1934 Abel Gance added sound to *Napoléon*. He filmed a number of supplementary scenes, which allowed him to transform silent scenes. He also made many "insert" shots and created "eloquent" roles: Robespierre, Saint-Just, and above all Marat, played by the man who might have become the greatest French actor—Antonin Artaud. The critics of the time chose to put down the sound version of *Napoléon*, and I want to be careful to dissociate myself from them. Without it we would have been deprived of such extraordinary scenes as the long monologue of Théroigne de Méricourt (Sylvie Gance), and all the shots of Antonin Artaud, Vladimir Sokolov, and many others. I believe that Gance's prodigious gift for direction required the talking pictures in order to reach its full measure.

When he wrote the scenario for *Napoléon*, Abel Gance perceived for the first time that the screen was too narrow for the scale of the subject and so he invented the "triple screen"—nothing more or less than a combination of CinemaScope and Cinerama, which arrived from America thirty years later. The siege of Toulon and the departure of the army from Italy were filmed with three cameras, thus giving the viewer a 100-degree angle of vision. The side images are totally different from the central scene; acting as a frame, they comment on and support the main image. In the scenes of the departure of the army from Italy, we can watch about ten shots which give a sensation of bold relief and proximity unequaled by the twelve or fifteen CinemaScopes shown in Paris in the last year and a half.

"I filmed *Napoléon*, because he was a paroxysm in a period which was itself a paroxysm in time," Abel Gance said.

In fact, the film is a long lyric poem, a sheaf of paroxysms, a continuum of animated bas-reliefs. Only Griffith in *Orphans of the Storm* and Jean Renoir in *La Marseillaise* have reevoked the episode of the Reign of Terror as well.

There is not a single scene in *Napoléon* which does not make us think it is the key to the film, no shot that is not filled with emotion, no actor who does not give his best. Despite his years, Abel Gance remains the youngest of our directors.

—1955

La Tour de Nesle

There is nothing very original left to say about *La Tour de Nesle*. Everyone knows it is a film that was made to order on an absurd budget, the best part of which remained in the distributor's till. *La Tour de Nesle* is, if you will, the least good of Abel Gance's films. But, since Gance is a genius, it also is a film of genius. Gance does not *possess* genius, he *is possessed* by genius. If you gave him a portable camera and set him in the midst of twenty other newsreel makers outside the Palais Bourbon or at the entrance to the Parc des Princes, he alone would deliver a masterpiece, a few hundred inches of film in which each shot, each image, each sixteenth or twenty-fourth of a second would bear the mark of genius, invisible and present, visible and omnipresent. How would it have been done? Only he would know. To tell the truth, I think that even he would not know how he did it.

I observed Abel Gance during the making of *La Tour de Nesle*. He gave it eight hours of work a day. There is no doubt that the films on which he spent twenty-four hours a day are better. Still eight hours is eight hours. I remember the closeup of Pampanini gazing at herself in the mirror, at first talking to herself, then silent. Seven inches separated the mirror from the face, the face from the lens. Seven inches from the mirror and the face and the lens, off camera, stood Abel Gance. Leaning toward the motionless woman, Gance mouthed the words that a French substitute would dub for the Italian actress: "Look at yourself, Marguerite of Burgundy, look at yourself in the mirror; what have you turned into? You are nothing but a slut!" (I paraphrase from memory.) Gance read this absurd monologue in a kind of lyrical whisper. This was no longer direction, it was hypnotism! As I watched the film later, I waited for this scene. The result was magnificent—her face distorted, her eyes bulging, her mouth open in a gaping scar, the lines of nightly dissipation etched on her face, she was the greatest actress in the world, like Sylvie Gance in *Napoléon*, Micheline Presle in *Paradis Perdu*, Ivy Close in

La Roue, Line Noro in *Mater Dolorosa,* Jany Holt in *Beethoven,* Viviane Romance in *Vénus aveugle,* and Assia Noris in *Fracasse.* Go and see Pampanini in *La Tour de Nesle* and then go see her in something else and if you don't see immediately that Gance was a genius, you and I do not have the same notion of cinema (mine, obviously, is the correct one). People have said to me, "Pampanini? All I see is grimaces!" I will permit Jean Renoir to reply, "A well-done grimace can be magnificent."

When a great director has been without work for twelve years and is forced to make a movie based on such a scenario, there are two possible solutions: either parody or melodrama. Gance chose the second—a more difficult solution but also the more daring and, in the last analysis, more intelligent and profitable. "I wanted to make a cloak-and-dagger Western," the director admitted.

That aside, the film is extraordinarily sound and youthful. Gance moves *La Tour de Nesle* with hell-for-leather speed. There is a steady pace, sustained first of all within scenes and then from one scene to the other, thanks to very skillful editing. The shots that were made with the help of a pictograph are very beautiful, and recall the miniatures in Laurence Olivier's *Henry V.*

The Centrale Catholique, which takes upon itself the duty of rating the morality of films, was in a complete uproar. Erotically, *La Tour de Nesle* went far beyond what people were used to seeing. They had to invent a new code to warn parents whose children might wander in by accident. Recently, answering a question on eroticism, Gance said, "If we had had a free hand in terms of eroticism, we would have made the most beautiful films in the world." It is regrettable that once again censorship showed itself so stringent. The film does not fulfill the promises of the photos posted at the entrance to the movie theater. Our expectations are frustrated, we are deceived in our hopes. Surely cinema is *also* eroticism.

Gance has been spoken of as "failed," and recently even as a "failed genius." But we know that "failed" *(raté)* means "bitten and spoiled by rats." The rats swarmed around Gance but they were as unable to absorb his genius as they were to destroy it. The question now is whether one can be both a genius and a failure. I believe, to the contrary, that failure is talent. To succeed is to fail. I wish to defend the proposition that Abel Gance is the failed *auteur* of failed films. I am convinced that there is no great filmmaker who does not sacrifice something. Renoir will sacrifice anything—plot, dialogue, technique—

to get a better performance from an actor. Hitchcock sacrifices believability in order to present an extreme situation that he has chosen in advance. Rossellini sacrifices the connection between movement and light to achieve greater warmth in his interpreters. Murnau, Hawks, Lang sacrifice realism in their settings and atmosphere. Nicholas Ray and Griffith sacrifice sobriety. But a film that succeeds, according to the common wisdom, is one in which all the elements are equally balanced in a whole that merits the adjective "perfect." Still, I assert that perfection and success are mean, indecent, immoral, and obscene. In this regard, the most hateful film is unarguably *La Kermesse héroique* because everything in it is incomplete, its boldness is attenuated; it is reasonable, measured, its doors are half-open, the paths are sketched and only sketched; everything in it is pleasant and perfect. All great films are "failed." They were called so at the time, and some are still so labeled: *Zéro de Conduite, L'Atalante, Faust, Le Pauvre amour, Intolerance, La Chienne, Metropolis, Liliom, Sunrise, Queen Kelly, Beethoven, Abraham Lincoln, La Vénus aveugle, La Règle du Jeu, Le Carrosse d'Or, I Confess, Stromboli*—I cite them in no particular order and I'm sure I'm leaving out others that are just as good. Compare these with a list of successful films and you will have before your eyes an example of the perennial argument about official art.

It's good to go back and again see Abel Gance's *Napoléon* upstairs in Studio 28. Each shot is like a bolt of lightning that illuminates everything around it. The spoken scenes are marvelous and not—as is still being said today in 1955—unworthy of the original silent scenes. "Sir Abel Gance," as Jacques Becker says! We won't find again very soon in the world of cinema a man of his breadth, ready to take on the whole world, to mold it like clay, to fashion his own witnesses out of sky, sea, clouds, earth, and hold all in the hollow of his own hand. To put an Abel Gance to work, you have to look for a backer in the class of Louis XIV.

—1955

A JEAN RENOIR FESTIVAL

My judgment that Jean Renoir is the greatest filmmaker in the world is not based on a public opinion poll, but purely on my own feelings. It's a feeling, I might add, that is shared by many other filmmakers. And after all, Renoir is the quintessential movie-maker of the personal. The conventional division of films into dramas and comedies becomes meaningless when we consider Jean Renoir's films, which are dramatic comedies.

Some filmmakers think that they should put themselves "in the place" of the producer, or of the public, as they work. Jean Renoir always gives us the impression that he has put himself in the place of his characters. That's why he had been able to offer Jean Gabin, Marcel Dalio, Julien Carrette, Louis Jouvet, Pierre Renoir, Jules Berry, Michel Simon their most beautiful roles. Not to mention the numerous actresses that I'll speak about later, at the end of this speech (as one keeps the best dish for dessert).

At least fifteen of Jean Renoir's thirty-five films are drawn from others' work: Hans Christian Andersen, La Fouchardière, Simenon, René Fauchois, Flaubert, Gorky, Octave Mirbeau, Rumer Godden, Jacques Perret. Nonetheless, in each we inevitably rediscover Renoir's tone, music, style, without betraying the original author in the slightest. Renoir absorbs everything, understands everything, is interested in everything and everyone.

Our love for all of Jean Renoir's work—I speak for all my friends at *Cahiers du Cinéma*—has often led us to use the word "infallibility," which never fails to irritate lovers of "masterpieces," those people who demand a homogeneity of intention and execution that Renoir has never attempted—in fact, quite the contrary. His work unfolds as if he had devoted his most brilliant moments to fleeing from the masterpiece, to escape any notion of the definite and the fixed, so as to create a semi-improvisation, a deliberately unfinished "open" work that each viewer can complete for himself, comment on as it suits him, approach from any side.

As with Ingmar Bergman and Jean-Luc Godard, who are his heirs, each of Renoir's films marks a moment of his thought. The whole body of his films makes up his work. That's why it's really crucial to gather them together in a festival such as this to appreciate them better, as a painter collects and shows his older and more recent canvases together, covering several periods, each time he holds an exhibition.

A lecturer will have a success or a failure according to whether or not he is in form on any particular night. Renoir has never filmed speeches, just conversations. He has often avowed how easily he was influenced by other filmmakers like Stroheim or Chaplin, by his producers, his friends, the authors he adapted, his actors. Out of the grace of this continual exchange there came thirty-five natural and alive films, modest and sincere, as simple as saying hello. To use the word "infallible" about his work, which contains not one whit of pretense, is not an insult, whether we are discussing a tentative film like *La Nuit du Carrefour* or a completely realized one like *Le Carrosse d'Or*.

The first films in this retrospective all star Michel Simon, who was probably Jean Renoir's favorite actor: "His face is as passionate as the masks of ancient tragedy." Watching *La Chienne* (1931) you will be able to verify the truth of this judgment, but in *Boudu sauvé des Eaux* (1932) the same Michel Simon will show you how he can raise the comic to the level of fable. All the words that evoke laughter can be used about Boudu: droll, buffoon, burlesque, incongruous. The theme of *Boudu* is vagabondage, the temptation to try to pass from one class to another, the importance of the natural; Boudu was a hippie long before the word was invented. The fact that the film was taken from a banal vaudeville play by René Fauchois makes Renoir's success even more astonishing.

Watching Michel Simon, moviegoers have always felt that they were not just watching an actor play a role, but watching the actor himself. His best roles were double roles: Boudu is both a vagrant and a child discovering life; Père Jules in Vigo's *L'Atalante* is a frustrated barge captain and a refined collector; Irwin Molyneux, the businessman of *Drôle de Drame*, secretly writes bloody novels; and, to come back to Renoir, Maurice Legrand in *La Chienne* is an insignificant and docile cashier but also, without knowing it, a great painter. I am persuaded that filmmakers entrusted Simon with these difficult double roles—which he always played magnificently even when the films were weak—because they felt that this great actor incarnated life and the secret of life. Jean Renoir was the first to make this truth evident. When Michel Simon acts for us, we penetrate to the core of the human heart.

In 1934, when Jean Renoir undertook the production of *Toni,* he had already tried naturalism *(Une Vie sans Joie),* romanticism *(Nana),* burlesque *(Charleston, Tire au Flanc),* historic films *(Le Tournoi).* At the same time, French cinema was wrestling with the concepts of psychology, something Renoir was to turn his back on throughout his life.

Toni is a pivotal film, a departure in a new direction. Ten years before the Italians, Renoir invented neorealism, the painstaking narration of a truly random deed, told in an objective tone and without ever raising one's voice. In his *Histoire du Cinéma,* Georges Sadoul writes correctly that the crime in *Toni* is "an accident, not an end." The characters drink a glass of wine or die in the same manner; Renoir shows us each fact in the same way, without superimposing eloquence, lyricism, or tragedy. *Toni* is life as it comes. If the actors cannot keep from laughing in the middle of a scene, it is because everyone enjoys himself in front of Jean Renoir's camera. They seek real life so ardently that they end up finding it, even at the risk of a sequence that, having begun seriously, ends in merriment.

The work of the actors in *Toni* is pure pleasure: the little cries of Celia Montalvan when Blavette licks her back after she is stung by a bee, Delmont's remarks and Dalban's ebullient tricks, all of these share in the truth Jean Renoir tried to find by any and all means, a truth of gesture and feeling which he achieved more often than any other filmmaker.

Une Partie de Campagne (A Day in the Country—1936) is a film of pure sensation; each blade of grass tickles our face. Adapted from a story by Guy de Maupassant, it is the only true cinematic equivalent of the art of the short story. Without using a single line of commentary, Renoir offers us forty-five minutes of a poetic prose whose truth makes us shudder or gives us goose bumps at certain moments. This film, the most physical Renoir made, touches us physically.

La Grande Illusion (Grand Illusion—1937), the least contested of Renoir's films, is built on the idea that the world is divided horizontally by similarities, not vertically by frontiers. If World War II and especially the horrors of the concentration camps seem to have weakened Renoir's ennobling thesis, the present attempts at "Europeanization" show that the strength of his idea was ahead of the spirit of Munich. But *La Grande Illusion* is nonetheless a film of its own time, as *La Marseillaise* was, because in it men fought a war based on fair play, a war without atom bombs or torture.

La Grande Illusion is a film precisely about chivalry, a film about war considered, if not exactly as one of the fine arts, at least as a sport, or an adventure in which the question was to measure oneself as much as to destroy. German officers of Erich von Stroheim's stamp were soon dismissed from the Third Reich's army, and the French officers as portrayed by Pierre Fresnay died of old age. The great illusion was to believe that that war would be the last. Renoir seems to consider war as a natural scourge that has its own beauties, like storms or fire. It was a matter *of waging war politely* as Pierre Fresnay does in the film. For Renoir, the idea of the frontier must be abolished in order to destroy the spirit of Babel, to reconcile men who will always, nevertheless, be separated by birth. There is a common denominator among men: woman. Unquestionably, the most powerful moment of the film occurs after the announcement of the recapture of Douaumont by the French, when the "Marseillaise" is sung by an English soldier dressed as a woman who takes off his wig as he sings it.

If, in contrast to most of Renoir's films, *La Grande Illusion* was immediately received with enthusiasm by everyone everywhere, it may be because Renoir made it when he was forty-three years old, that is, the same age as his audience. Before *La Grande Illusion*, his films at first appeared aggressive and juvenile, then disenchanted and bitter. In addition, we have to admit that *La Grande Illusion* was, by 1937, somewhat behind the times when we realize that only a year later, in *The Great Dictator*, Chaplin was to give us a portrait of Nazism and of wars that does not respect the rules of the game.

The definitive print of *La Marseillaise* (1938) comes to us from far away, from Moscow to be exact, where the only complete version existed. Those who are young enough will discover a work that is the equal of *La Grande Illusion*, made the year before. The critics received it badly on the basis of the "law of alternation," which dictates that an artist may not produce two consecutive masterpieces.

Renoir's work was always guided by something that is rather like a secret—it might be called a professional secret: sympathy. In *La Marseillaise* this sense of sympathy enables him to escape the traps of historical recreations. His extraordinary gift for life allows him to give us a film which lives, which is inhabited by individuals who breathe and experience real feelings.

La Marseillaise is constructed like a Western, his only "trail" film. We follow the battalion of five hundred Marseilles volunteers who left their homes on July 2, 1792, and marched to Paris, where they arrived on the 30th, the eve of the publication of the Manifesto of Brunswick. The film ends shortly after August 10, just before the battle of Valmy. There is no central hero, no star roles as opposed to bit parts, but there are a half-dozen interesting, plausible, noble, and human characters representing the court, the Marseilles volunteers, the aristocrats, the army, the people.

To balance the Marseilles volunteers, the individuals we see growing noble and becoming poets as they come in contact with the revolutionary ideal, Renoir insists on the prosaic and everyday side of Louis XVI, magnificently played by Jean's brother, Pierre Renoir. This king, who gives concrete meaning to the expression "to be overtaken by events," is interested in dental hygiene: "I'd really like to try that brushing." Two hours before he flees from the Tuileries we see him eating for the first time the tomatoes the Marseilles volunteers have brought to Paris: "I say, they're excellent."

I referred to a historical Western. As in all good Westerns, we find the structure of an itinerant film; action-filled daytime scenes alternate with more static nighttime scenes, which are always convenient for discussions around a campfire, discussions about ideology or feelings. But whether they are about food, revolution, feet tired from marching, love, or the use of weapons, everything in *La Marseillaise* illustrates the idea of French unity and even makes it convincing. Just as Griffith's most illustrious film is called *Birth of a Nation*, this one might be called *La Naissance de la Nation*.

La Bête Humaine, made in 1938, is the story of an assistant station-master, Roubaud (Fernand Ledoux), who is afraid of being fired because he has quarreled with a superior. He asks his young wife, Séverine (Simone Simon), to intervene with a "big shot," a sort of godfather whom she knew as a teenager and who was a great friend of her mother's. When Séverine returns, everything has been fixed up, but when Roubaud realizes what the price is, he goes mad with jealousy and works out revenge which will end with him killing the godfather in front of Séverine on the Paris-LeHavre train.

On the train the murderous pair have been noticed by Jacques Lantier (Jean Gabin), a railroad employee. During the investigation, Roubaud sends Séverine to insure Lantier's silence, and again quite naturally, these two become lovers, after Lantier has figured out and confirmed by fragments what really happened. Séverine wants Lantier to kill Roubaud, with whom life has become impossible since the murder. Lantier cannot make up his mind to kill Roubaud, but while in a rage he strangles Séverine and the next day jumps to his death from the locomotive on which he was chief engineer.

In Emile Zola's novel, Jacques Lantier was in the countryside, watching a train pass, and saw the crime of Roubaud and his wife in a flash. It is Renoir who places Lantier in the corridor of the train and has him observe the accomplice in the crime. Renoir's version was adapted by Fritz Lang in 1954 when he directed a remake of *La Bête Humaine* in Hollywood under the title of *Human Desire*. Lang had already stepped into Renoir's shoes a few years earlier, when he directed *Scarlet Street (La Rue Rouge)*, a remake of *La Chienne*.

As we think about it, it seems that Jean Renoir and Fritz Lang had in common a taste for the same theme: an old husband, a young wife, and a lover (*La Chienne, La Bête Humaine, The Woman on the Beach* for Renoir; *Scarlet Street, The Woman in the Window, Human Desire* for Lang). They also have in common a predilection for catlike actresses, feline heroines. Gloria Grahame is the perfect American replica of Simone Simon, and Joan Bennett is a heroine in the films of both Renoir and Lang. There the comparisons stop. The director of *La Bête Humaine* and the director of *Human Desire* are not after the same thing. Renoir treated Zola's novel with what we customarily call asceticism. Recently he explained it this way: "What helped me to make *La Bête Humaine* are the hero's explanations of his atavism. I said to myself, it isn't very pretty, but if a man as handsome as Jean Gabin said that outdoors, with the horizon behind him and perhaps some wind, it might have a certain validity. This is the key that helped me to make this film."

That's how Renoir works, seeking constantly to find a balance, a comic detail to compensate for a tragic note: clouds float by behind

Gabin as he talks about his "illness," locomotives pass outside the window of the tiny bedroom where Fernand Ledoux begins to suspect his wife.

La Bête Humaine is probably Gabin's best film. "Jacques Lantier interests me as much as Oedipus Rex," Renoir has said, and Claude de Givray has described it to perfection: "There is the triangle film *(Le Carrosse d'Or)*, the circle film *(Le Fleuve)—La Bête Humaine* is a straight-line film, that is, a tragedy."

La Règle du Jeu (The Rules of the Game, 1939) is the credo of film lovers, the film of films, the most despised on its release and the most valued afterward, to the point that it became a commercial success on its third re-release in normal distribution and in its uncut version. In this "comedy drama," Renoir expresses a great number of both general and concrete ideas, without insisting on them, and in particular expresses his great love for women. Along with *Citizen Kane, La Règle du Jeu* is certainly the film that sparked the careers of the greatest number of directors. We look at this movie with a strong feeling of complicity; I mean that instead of seeing a finished product handed to us to satisfy our curiosity, we feel we are there as the film is made, we almost think that we can see Renoir organize the whole as we watch the film projected. For an instant, we think to ourselves, "I'll come back tomorrow and see if it all turns out the same way." It's why some of the best evenings of the year would be spent watching *La Règle du Jeu.*

After the failure of the film—which had been cut by fifteen minutes at the insistence of the distributors, and then had been prohibited by the authorities for fear it would demoralize the French (we were on the eve of the declaration of war)—Jean Renoir, probably very depressed, left for Hollywood, where he made five films in eight years. *The Woman on the Beach* (1946) is the last of his Hollywood films. It is a curious and interesting movie, but we don't find those exact qualities that are most often praised in Renoir's French work: a sense of familiarity, fantasy, what we call his humanism. It seems likely that Renoir decided deliberately to adapt himself to Hollywood and make a completely American film.

The main difference between European and Hollywood films—and this is true of Renoir's work on both sides of the Atlantic—is that our films are first of all films of personalities, and the American productions are primarily films about specific situations. In France, our instinct is toward verisimilitude and the psychological, while Americans prefer to deal strongly with what happens, with a place and time, and not to stray from the situation. Since a film is nothing more than a celluloid ribbon about 6,000 inches long that passes before our eyes, one can compare it to a journey. So, I could say that a French film moves forward like a light cart on a windy road while an American film rolls along like a train on its tracks. *The Woman on the Beach* is a train film. It is a film about sex, physical love, desire, all expressed without a single nude scene. Nonetheless, it won't do to say that Joan Bennett is sensual; actually, she is sexual. What I like about *The Woman on the Beach* is that we see two films in it. The first never mentions love, the characters only exchange polite remarks. But the meaning is not in what they say but in the looks they exchange, looks that express troubled, secret matters very precisely.

Cinema is never purer, never more itself, than when it uses dialogue like contrapuntal music to allow us to enter into the characters' thoughts. That's how I'd invite you to watch the three tremendous actors in *The Woman on the Beach:* Joan Bennett, Robert Ryan, Charles Bickford. Watch them as if they were animals, wild beasts stalking the shadowy jungle of repressed sexuality.

Le Carrosse d'Or (*The Golden Coach*, 1952) is a key film of Renoir's because it connects the themes of a number of his others, certainly the notion of sincerity in love and in one's artistic vocation. It is a film constructed like the "box game," one inside the other, a film *about* theater *in* the theater.

There was unfairness in the way the critics and public received *Le Carrosse d'Or*, which may be Renoir's masterpiece. In any case, it is the noblest and most refined film ever made. It combines all the spontaneity and inventiveness of the prewar Renoir with the rigor of the American Renoir. It is all breeding and politeness, grace and freshness. It is a film of gestures and attitudes. Theater and life are mingled in an action that is suspended between the ground level and the first floor, just as *commedia dell'arte* swings back and forth between respect for tradition and improvisation. Anna Magnani is the wonderful star of this elegant film; the color, rhythm, editing, and actors are all worthy of the soundtrack dominated by Vivaldi. *Le Carrosse d'Or* is itself absolutely beautiful, just as beauty itself is the subject of the film.

I described Renoir's other masterpiece, *La Règle du Jeu,* as an open conversation, a film in which we are invited to participate; it is quite a different matter with *Le Carrosse d'Or,* which is closed, a finished work—you look without touching. The film has already a definitive form; it is a perfect object.

French Cancan (1955) marked Renoir's return to French studios. I am not going to recount the plot; it simply concerns an episode from the life of a certain Danglard, who established the Moulin Rouge and created the cancan. Danglard devoted his life to the music hall, discovered young talent, dancers and singers, and "made" them stars. He becomes for a time their lover and they become possessive, jealous, capricious, unbearable. But Danglard never allows himself to become attached; he is married to the music hall and he cares only for the success of his spectacles. This single-minded love for his métier and the desire to inculcate it in the young artists he discovers and showcases is his whole reason for living.

You will recognize the parallel between this theme and that of *Le Carrosse d'Or:* the demands of the spectacle triumphing over sentiment. *French Cancan* is a homage to the music hall as *Le Carrosse d'Or* is to commedia dell'arte. But I must admit my preference for *Le Carrosse d'Or.* The weaknesses of *French Cancan,* although they are not Renoir's fault, are nonetheless harmful because for one thing they affected the cast. Gianni Esposito, Philippe Clay, Pierre Olaf, Jacques Jouanneau, Max Dalban, Valentine Tessier and Anik Morice are all excellent, but Jean Gabin and Maria Félix do not seem to give their utmost.

Still, *French Cancan* marks an important date in the history of color films. Jean Renoir did not want to make a merely pictorial film and so *French Cancan* is an anti-*Moulin Rouge* film. In the latter, John Huston mixed colors by the use of gelatine filters. In Renoir's film there are only pure colors. Each shot in *French Cancan* is a popular poster, a moving "Epinal image," with beautiful blacks, maroons, and beiges.

The final cancan is a tour de force, a long bravura scene which usually has the audience on its feet. If *French Cancan* does not have the importance of *La Règle du Jeu* or *Le Carrosse d'Or,* it is still a brilliant and spirited film in which we once again discover Renoir's power, wholesomeness, and youthfulness.

Eléna et les Hommes (1956) is Renoir in his greatest period; Jacques Jouanneau is magnificent playing with Ingrid Bergman, Jean Marais, and Mel Ferrer. In *Eléna* we can see the realization of Renoir's ideal: a rediscovery of the spirit of the primitives, the genius of the great pioneers of the cinema: Mack Sennett, Larry Semon, Picrat, and— why not? Charlie Chaplin. With *Eléna* cinema goes back to its origins as Renoir returns to his youth.

To answer those who argue that Renoir's last films are too far removed from the realities of the world we live in, I shall sum up *Eléna et les Hommes:* On the eve of the Great War, Bastille Day is being celebrated by a crowd wild with enthusiasm for a certain General Rollan. After a stupid diplomatic incident has created a war mentality, the general's entourage tries to take advantage of the occasion to overthrow the government. In the streets the people are singing, "And thus has destiny placed him on our path. . . ." Two years after *Eléna* was released, de Gaulle pronounced his famous "I have understood you," referring to the Algerian agitation being carried out by his partisans. So it is true, you see, there is always a general somewhere. Renoir's general (Jean Marais plays Rollan) has at least two advantages: he prefers women to power and he knows how to make us laugh.

Eléna tells the truth about the princes who govern us, who have made the decision to govern us and do what is good for us in spite of ourselves. If it seems surprising that this realistic film is also a fairy tale, let's listen to Renoir's reply: "Reality is always a fairy tale. To make it not a fairy tale, some authors take a great deal of trouble and present it in a downright odd light. If we leave reality alone, it is a fairy tale."

Le Testament du Docteur Cordelier (1959) is one of Renoir's ill-fated films, like his *Journal d'une Femme de Chambre* (*The Diary of a Chambermaid*, 1946), which is equally ferocious. The often misused expression "actor's director" here takes on its real significance as Jean-Louis Barrault, who is almost unrecognizable in a role that he practically dances, frenetically attacks passersby in the street.

To bring to life a human being who is pure invention, to make him glide rather than walk, to give him the gestures you have imagined, to load him down with an abstract and mad brutality, that is a filmmaker's dream. *Le Testament du Docteur Cordelier* is this dream realized, just as *Le Déjeuner sur l'Herbe* (made the same year) was born out of the simple but visually powerful idea that it would be amusing to photograph a windstorm in the country, as the wind blows up the women's skirts.

Women are at the center of all Renoir's work. At the risk of simplification, let us cut a path through Renoir's simultaneously benevolent
and cruel jungle. A good but weak and sensual man under the domina-
tion of a beautiful woman—whether or not she is his wife—a woman
of lively temperament, but a difficult disposition, a more or less adora-
ble hussy; you have *Nana, Marquitta, Tire au flanc, La Chienne, La
Nuit du Carrefour, Boudu sauvé des Eaux, Toni, Madame Bovary,
Les Bas-Fonds, La Marseillaise, La Règle du Jeu, The Diary of a
Chambermaid, The Woman on the Beach, Le Carrosse d'Or, French
Cancan, Eléna et les Hommes.*

The "ménage à trois" rarely captured Renoir's interest, but he
was the inventor of the "ménage à quatre." In his world, a woman
loves and is loved by *three* men, or a man loves and is loved by
three women. The films constructed on the first formula are: *Une
Vie sans Joie, La Fille de l'Eau, Nana, La Nuit du Carrefour, Boudu,
Toni, Madame Bovary, Le Crime de Monsieur Lange, La Bête Humaine, La Règle du Jeu, The Diary of a Chambermaid, French Cancan*
and *Le Carrosse d'Or,* which carries the system to perfection with
each man representing one of the three kinds of men a woman meets
during her life. The following films rest on the second principle:
Marquitta, Monsieur Lange, La Bête Humaine (the third woman here
is Louison, the locomotive), *La Règle du Jeu, French Cancan* and
The River, which—analogously to *Le Carrosse*—is a perfect illustration of the system.

Renoir's films draw their animation from real life; we know who
the characters are making love with, a fact that was cruelly absent
in movies before 1960. Renoir hasn't much taste for deaths in films
because they have to be faked: you can harass an actor to get him
to play an agitated character, but if you kill him, you'll have the
Actor's Guild on your back. Nana, Mado, Emma, the pretty Madame
Roubaud and so many others had to be done away with, but when
they died, each time Renoir held up to us what are most alive, songs.
The women whom Renoir kills so regretfully agonize in the everyday
accents of popular songs: Ninon's little heart is so tiny. . . .

Some simpleton attacking Rossellini's *Amore* said that "the actor
must subject himself to the work, rather than the work being subjected
to the actor." Ever since *Une Vie sans Joie,* which is a film in the
form of an engagement ring offered to Catherine Hessling, all of
Jean Renoir's work contradicts this statement. He made films to order
for Jannie Mareze, Valentine Tessier, Nadia Sibirskaia, Sylvia Bataille,

Simone Simon, Nora Gregor, Anne Baxter, Joan Bennett, Paulette Goddard, Anna Magnani, and Ingrid Bergman, subjecting his work to the actresses—and these are among the most beautiful films in the history of moviemaking.

Jean Renoir does not film situations but rather—I ask you to remember the circus attraction of the Hall of Mirrors—characters who are trying to find their way out of the Hall, bumping into the mirrors of reality. Renoir does not film ideas, but men and women who have ideas, and he does not invite us to adopt these ideas or to sort them out no matter how quaint or illusory they may be, but simply to respect them.

When a man makes himself ridiculous by his stubborn insistence on striking a certain pompous pose, whether he is a politician or a megalomaniac artist, we say that he has lost sight of the bawling baby he was in his crib and the groaning wreck he will be on his deathbed. It is clear that the cinematographic work of Jean Renoir never loses sight of this naked man, never loses sight of man himself.

—1967, Introduction of a Renoir Festival at the Maison de La Culture
of Vidauban

THE WHITENESS OF CARL DREYER

When I think of Carl Dreyer, what comes to mind first are those pale white images, the splendid voiceless closeups in *La Passion de Jeanne d'Arc (The Passion of Joan of Arc)* that play back exactly the acerbic dialogue at Rouen between Jeanne and her judges.

Then I think of the whiteness of *Vampyr,* though this time it is accompanied by sounds, the cries and horrible groans of the Doctor (Jean Hieromniko), whose gnarled shadow disappears into the flour bin in the impregnable mill that no one will approach to save him. In the same way that Dreyer's camera is clever in *Jeanne d'Arc,* in *Vampyr* it frees itself and becomes a young man's pen as it follows, darts ahead of, prophesies the vampire's movements along the gray walls.

Unhappily, after the commercial failure of these masterpieces, Dreyer had to wait eleven years, eleven years out of his life, before shouting "Camera! Action!" when at last he made *Vredens Dag (Day of Wrath),* a movie that deals with sorcery and religion, and is a synthesis of the other two films. Here we see the most beautiful image of female nudity in the history of cinema—the least erotic and most carnal nakedness—the white body of Marthe Herloff, the old woman burned as a witch.

Ten years after *Day of Wrath,* at the end of the summer of 1956, *Ordet* overwhelmed the audience at the Lido Biennale. Never in the history of the Venice Festival had a Golden Lion been more justly awarded than to *Ordet,* a drama of faith, more exactly, a metaphysical fable about the aberrations dogmatic rivalries lead to.

The film's hero, Johannes, is a visionary who thinks he is Jesus Christ; but only when he comes to recognize his delusion does he "receive" spiritual power.

Each image in *Ordet* possesses a formal perfection that touches the sublime, but we recognize Dreyer for more than a "cosmetician."

The rhythm is leisurely, the interplay of the actors stylized, but they are utterly controlled. Not a frame escapes Dreyer's vigilance; he is certainly the most demanding director of all since Eisenstein, and his finished films resemble exactly what they were in his mind as he conceived them.

There is no active mimicry from the actors in *Ordet;* they simply set their faces in a particular manner, and from the outset of each scene adopt a static attitude. The important actions take place in the living room of a rich farmer. The sequential shots are highly mobile and seem to have been inspired by Alfred Hitchcock's *The Rope.* (In a number of interviews, Dreyer has mentioned his admiration for the director of *Rear Window.*) And in *Ordet,* white predominates again, this time a milky whiteness, the whiteness of sun-drenched curtains, something we have never seen before or since. The sound is also splendid. Toward the end of the film, the center screen is occupied by a coffin in which the heroine, Inger, is laid out. Johannes, the madman who takes himself for Christ, has promised to raise her from the dead. The silence of the house in mourning is broken only by the sound of the master's steps on the wooden floors, an ordinary sound, the sound of new shoes, Sunday shoes. . . .

Dreyer had a difficult career; he was able to pursue his art only because of the income he had from the Dagmar, the movie theater he managed in Copenhagen. This profoundly religious artist, filled with a passion for the cinema, chased two dreams all his life, both of which eluded him: to make a film on the life of Christ, *Jesus,* and to work in Hollywood like his master, D. W. Griffith.

I only met Carl Dreyer three times, but it pleases me to write these few lines as I sit in the leather-and-wood chair that belonged to him during his working life and was given to me after his death. He was a small man, soft-spoken, terribly stubborn, who gave an impression of severity although he was truly sensitive and warm. His last public act was to gather the eight most important men involved in Danish cinema to write a letter protesting the dismissal of Henri Langlois from the Cinémathèque Française.

Now he is dead; he has joined Griffith, Stroheim, Murnau, Eisenstein, Lubitsch, the kings of the first generation of cinema, the generation that mastered, first, silence, and then sound. We have much to learn from them, and much from Dreyer's images of whiteness.

—1969

LUBITSCH WAS A PRINCE

The startlingly brilliant image of the prewar films is what I love above all else. The characters are small, dark silhouettes on the screen. They emerge onto the set, pushing open doors three times their size. There was no housing crisis at that time and the streets of Paris were Bastille Day all year long. There were "apartment to rent" signs on all the buildings.

The grandiose sets of the films of those days rivaled the stars for top billing; the producers paid a lot of money for them and they had to be noticed. The man who smoked the big cigars wanted his money's worth and I am sure he would have fired a director who dared to shoot his whole film in closeups. At that time, when you didn't know where to put your camera, you put it as far away as possible; now, when in doubt, it's planted smack under the actor's nostrils. We have passed from modest mistakes to pretentious ones.

A nostalgic introduction is not out of place in Lubitsch's case because he firmly believed it was better to laugh in a palace than to weep in the shop around the corner. As André Bazin said, I'm probably not going to have time to be brief.

Like all artists of stylization, Lubitsch, whether consciously or not, was drawn to the great writers of children's stories. In *Angel,* a painful and embarrassing dinner brings together Marlene Dietrich, Herbert Marshall, her husband, and Melvyn Douglas, her lover of a single night she'd thought she'd never see again, but whom her husband has brought home by chance. As so often with Lubitsch, the camera deserts the "stage" side as things are heating up to take us to the "courtyard" side where we can enjoy what's going on even more. We're in the kitchen, for instance. The butler is coming and going from the dining room; he brings in Madame's plate: "Odd, Madame didn't touch her cutlet." Next, he brings in the guest's plate: "Huh, neither did he." (This chop has been cut into innumerable tiny pieces but not touched.) The third plate arrives, empty: "Well, at least

Monsieur seemed to enjoy his chop." We recognize "Goldilocks and the Three Bears": Papa bear's bowl was too hot, Mama bear's too cold, but Baby bear's was just right. Do we know any literature more fundamental than that?

So this is the first trait common to the "Lubitsch touch" and the "Hitchcock touch." The second has to do with their manner of approaching the problem of the script. On the surface, it is simply a matter of telling a story in images; this is what they insist in interviews. But it isn't true. They're not lying for fun or to make fools of us, they're lying to *simplify* matters, because reality is too complicated and it's better to spend one's time working and perfecting oneself. We are dealing with perfectionists.

The truth in their work is that it is a matter of *not* telling the story, even of searching for a way not to tell it. There is, of course, a plot, which can be summed up in a few lines, usually the seduction of a man by a woman who does not want him or vice versa, or an invitation to a night of sin or pleasure—the same themes that Sacha Guitry uses—but the essential consideration here is never to treat the subject *directly*. So, if we are kept outside the closed doors of the bedroom when everything is happening inside, stay at the office when everything is going on in the living room, remain in the salon when the action's on the stairway, or in the telephone booth when it's happening in the wine cellar, it's because Lubitsch has racked his brain during six weeks of writing so that the spectators can work out the plot along with him as they watch the film.

There are two kinds of moviemakers—as there are two kinds of painters and writers—those who would work even if they were stranded on a desert island with no possible public, and those who would give up, wondering "Why bother?" There would be no Lubitsch without an audience—but, watch out—the audience is not something apart from his work; it is *with* him in creating, it is part of the film. On Lubitsch's sound tracks, there are dialogue, sounds, music, and our laughter—this is essential. Otherwise, there would be no film. The prodigious ellipses in his plots work only because our laughter bridges the scenes. In the Lubitsch Swiss cheese, each hole winks.

Though all too often used incorrectly, the expression "mise-en-scène" does boil down to something, in this case a game that can only be played by three parties and only while the film is being projected. And who are the three parties? Lubitsch, the film, and the public.

So, there's nothing in common with a film like *Doctor Zhivago,* for instance. If you said to me, "I have just seen a Lubitsch in which there was one needless shot," I'd call you a liar. His cinema is the opposite of the vague, the imprecise, the unformulated, the incommunicable. There's not a single shot just for decoration; nothing is included just because it looks good. From beginning to end, we are involved only in what's essential.

There is no Lubitsch plot on paper, nor does the movie make any sense after we've seen it. Everything happens *while* we are looking at the film. An hour later, or even if you've just seen it for the sixth time, I defy you to tell me the plot of *To Be or Not to Be*. It's absolutely impossible.

We the viewers are there in the darkness. What is happening on the screen is brilliant. It may have tended to break at a certain point, so, to reassure ourselves, we anticipate the next scene visibly by searching our memories. But Lubitsch, like all geniuses of contradiction, has already examined all the previous solutions so as to offer one that's never been used before—an unthinkable, bizarre, exquisite, and disorienting solution. There are outbursts of laughter as we discover the "Lubitsch solution"—our laughter is uncontainable.

We could use an expression such as "Lubitsch's respect for the public," except that this motto has all too often served as an alibi to justify the worst documentaries and simply incomprehensible stories. Let's forget that and consider another example.

In *Trouble in Paradise*, Edward Everett Horton eyes Herbert Marshall suspiciously during a cocktail party. He tells himself that he's seen this fellow somewhere. *We* know that Marshall is the pickpocket who, at the beginning of the film, had knocked out poor Horton in a palace bedroom in Venice in order to rob him. Clearly, Horton will remember at a certain moment, and with nine out of ten filmmakers—lazy bunch that we are—what do we almost always do? We show the fellow asleep in bed; all of a sudden he wakes up in the middle of the night, slaps his forehead: "That's it! Venice! The dirty bum!" But who's the bum? The one who's contented with such an obvious solution. That was not Lubitsch's way. He worked like a dog, bled himself white, died twenty years too early. Lubitsch shows us Horton smoking a cigarette. Visibly wondering where he could have met Herbert Marshall before, he takes a last draw on his cigarette, crushes it in a silver ashtray shaped like a gondola . . . a shot of the gondola ashtray . . . we return to Horton's face . . . he gazes at the ashtray . . . a gondola . . . Venice. My God! Horton finally understands! Bravo! And the audience rocks with laughter. Perhaps Lubitsch is standing in the shadows at the rear of the theater watching his audience, dreading the slightest delay in their laughter, like Fredric March in *Design for Living,* or glancing toward the prompter who watches Hamlet move toward the ramp and gets ready, if necessary, to whisper, "To be or not to be."

I speak of what can be learned, about talent, about what can be for sale and its eventual price tag. But what cannot be learned or bought is the charm and mischievousness, ah, the mischievous charm of Lubitsch, which truly made him a prince.

—1968

CHARLIE CHAPLIN

The Great Dictator

Has *The Great Dictator*—which Charlie Chaplin made in 1939–1940 and which the European public first saw in 1945—"aged"? The question is almost absurd and can only be answered Yes, of course, naturally. *The Great Dictator* has aged, and that is wonderful. It has aged like a political editorial, like Zola's *J'accuse*, like a press conference. It is an admirable document, a rare piece, a useful object that has now become an art object. Chaplin would be quite correct to reedit it if it would bring him enough money to finance his next film, *Charlie on the Moon*.

What is striking about *The Great Dictator* today, in 1957, is Chaplin's desire to help his fellow men see more clearly. I despise the set mind that rejects ambitious work from someone who's supposed to be a comic. The impulse is good, however, even if it generally begins with snobbism, for it often happens that, as soon as snobs burn what they adore, adoration is justified.

Whenever I hear, "Now that Chaplin is taking himself seriously, his work is finished," I can't help thinking that his work is *beginning*. An artist can create works for himself to "do himself good," or to "do good" for others. Perhaps the greatest artists are those who simultaneously resolve their own problems and those of their public. We have to begin by being born and then by knowing ourselves, and after that comes recognition. The comic artist doesn't wait for us to come to him; he comes to us as clown, mime, buffoon, songster.

To the public whose heart he's made beat to his own rhythm the comic artist owes everything, including his ideas as a man. I hate hearing people say about Chaplin, "He's heard too many times that he was this or that; naturally he ended up believing it." If he has been told that he is a poet or a philosopher, it's because it's true, and he was right to believe what he heard. Without willing it or knowing it, Chaplin helped men live; later, when he became aware of it, would it not have been criminal to stop trying to help them even more?

The extraordinary audience that Chaplin's genius captured bestowed enormous responsibility on him; it wasn't that he believed he had a mission, but that he really was entrusted with one; and, in my opinion, few public men, politicians or pundits, have acquitted themselves of their mission with his integrity and effectiveness.

The Great Dictator was certainly the film that caught the imagination of the greatest number of viewers in most countries in 1940. It was certainly the film of the moment, a scarcely exaggerated nightmare of a world gone mad, of which the film *Nuit et Brouillard (Night and Fog)* was to be the most exact account. Never has a film grown old more nobly, though we can imagine that it will be politely applauded or received coolly by twelve-year-old moviegoers who know nothing of Hitler, Mussolini, Goering and Goebbels.

In one of his most famous articles, André Bazin called *The Great Dictator* Chaplin's settling of accounts with Hitler for having committed the double crime of confiscating Charlie's mustache and of elevating himself to the level of the gods. By forcing Hitler's mustache to reintegrate Charlie's myth, Charlie destroyed the myth of Hitler. In effect, in 1939, Hitler and Chaplin became the two most famous men in the world, the first incarnating the forces of evil, the second those of good. That's why they had to be brought together in the same film to better oppose one another and, seventeen years after *The Pilgrim*, recreate a marvelous pantomime of David and Goliath.

Pierre Leprohon has published an absorbing work, a chronological essay, that tells of Chaplin's refusal, when he was in Venice in 1931, to go to Rome where Mussolini had arranged a reception in his honor. A month earlier, at a gathering at Lady Astor's London home, Chaplin had expounded on the economic crisis: "The world is suffering from government interference in the private sector and from exaggerated expenditures by the State. I would propose a nationalization of the banks and a revision of many laws, like those that govern the Stock Exchange. I would create a governmental office for economic affairs which would control prices, interest rates, and profits. . . . My policy would favor internationalism, worldwide economic cooperation, the abolition of the gold standard and of general inflation. . . ." In 1934, Chaplin had a scenario for a film on Napoleon that had been proposed by a young Italian journalist. In 1935 he announced his definitive decision not to make the Napoleon film and added, "In addition, I shall never again play Charlie, the little tramp."

Chaplin kept his word; he began to write and prepare for *The Great Dictator*. All during 1938 there were any number of attempts to keep him from shooting the film. German diplomatic representatives and several American organizations put pressure on him. The film was finished in the spring of 1940 but was not seen until six months later. Meanwhile, Chaplin was criticized by the Dies Committee, the House Committee on Un-American Activities. As long ago as 1940! This dates the beginning of the American war against Chaplin, which continued relentlessly until 1952.

The Great Dictator is not only a defensive farce but also a very precise essay on the Jewish crisis and the mad racist program of Hitlerism—a little like Jean Renoir's *La Marseillaise*—in which two series of sketches alternate, Hitler's palace and the ghetto. As objectively as possible when one's defending one's own life, Chaplin sets the two worlds in opposition, mocking the first fiercely, smiling tenderly at the second with scrupulous respect for ethnic truths. The sequences in the ghetto glide by, malicious, artful, almost as if choreographed; those in Hitler's palace are jerky, mechanical, frantic to the point of derision. The persecuted are shown with a furious appetite to live, a resourcefulness that skims over cowardice (the scene of drawing lots for the sacrifice); on the part of the persecutors, there is an imbecilic fanaticism.

At the end of the film, in the purest theatrical tradition, the little Jewish barber is brought in to replace the "Great Dictator," whose double he is—without a single remark having been made on the subject—an ellipse of genius. When it comes time to deliver his great discourse, he weeps over primary truths, which I'd be the last to complain about, preferring them to the secondary. The events that wracked our continent not long after the release of this film prove well enough that if Chaplin opened so many doors in this film, they were not open for everybody.

The critics, especially Bazin, have pointed out that the final speech of *The Great Dictator* marks the crucial moment in all of Chaplin's work. It is then that we see the progressive disappearance of Charlie's mask and the substitution of the face of the man Chaplin, without makeup, his hair already graying. He sent the world a message of hope, he cited the words of the Gospel about the oppressed people who waited for happiness in the realization of the Messianic dream.

Chaplin didn't want the film to end focused on his face but on the image of Paulette Goddard, to whom he gave his own mother's name, Hannah (a name spelled the same backward). The device exquisitely sums up the spirit of the film. Hitler is the Jewish barber in reverse. So, he invokes his mother at the end of his speech, as Goddard, looking sublime as she is lying on the ground, raises herself to hear his call: "Lift up your eyes, Hannah. Look toward heaven, Hannah, can you hear me? Listen!"

A King in New York

Okay, Charlie doesn't make us laugh any more. On the other hand, his critics make me laugh. The silliest reviews of *A King in New York* pan it for its plot. You might as well damn the New Testament for lack of suspense. I bring up the New Testament deliberately. King Shadow, recently dethroned, arrives in New York having barely saved his head and the Royal Treasury. But the next day he learns that his prime minister has absconded with the money. The king is ruined. Is the author Charlie Chaplin, or is it Saint Matthew recounting the parable of the talents? A man about to set out on a journey entrusts his fortune to his servants, one of whom plays the same dirty trick on him so that he remonstrates with him: "Wicked and lazy servant! Why didn't you take care of my money?"

There is a dinner party at the home of a famous celebrity hostess and the king is betrayed. A hidden television camera is recording the dinner and the king's clowning. Without realizing how it has happened, Shadow becomes a television star. When he visits a progressive school, the king meets a twelve-year-old boy whose replies astonish and confound the adults. We may call them the "doctors." On a winter evening, as he's going home, Shadow comes upon the boy, who is freezing to death in rags. Ruppert, the boy, tells Shadow that his parents have been arrested for being Communists and have been sentenced because they've refused to denounce their friends. Inside the king's house, Ruppert undresses to take a bath and Shadow goes out to buy him some clothes—another image from the New Testament, the possessed man who was cured. "This man was without clothes at that time to symbolize the fact that we had lost our original faith and justice, which had been like a vestment of light that had covered us in our state of innocence." Shortly, McCarthy's man comes to take the boy away and lead him to Herod, "this hypocrite prince, who concealed the design he had conceived to kill the child he was forced to recognize. For God told the Magi that they should seek the child out, so that they could come and tell the news later."

Shadow is called in turn before the Un-American Activities Committee. The merchants of this temple cannot be driven out, as Jesus had thrown out the buyers and sellers in the Temple, overturning the tables and chairs. Shadow, entangled in a fire hose, lands in front of the wicked judges and floods them with water. The water is purifying, and Shadow is acquitted. Very likely it is God who advises this new Magi-king in a dream to "take a different road to return to his country" to escape the Herod who would confiscate his passport. But the saddest thing that's happened, also the most important, is that the boy has already told the investigators what they wanted to know in order to get his parents freed. The moral isn't as simple as that of Jules Dassin's *Le Christ Recrucifié (He Who Must Die)*. What it's saying is that, if Christ came back today to a land of stool pigeons, he'd end up collaborating with McCarthy.

I'm not saying this interpretation is definitive. But if you can't prove something is beautiful, you have to offer some explanation.

If you stick an arbitrary label on a work, you don't want to have to change it. If Chaplin, at his age, went on playing the clown in those famous cast-offs, it would be a disaster. That's not hard to understand. Anyhow, a man who's made seventy-five films, some of which are among the most famous and admired in the history of movies, doesn't need advice about how to construct a plot.

I don't see any great difference between the first and the second parts of *A King in New York*. I didn't expect to laugh. We all read the newspapers, and I was well aware of Chaplin's misfortunes in America. I knew what his new film was about and I knew how profoundly sad his preceding films were. We could have known that *A King in New York* would be the saddest of all, also the most personal.

The man who made *The Gold Rush* can, if he wants to, make his public laugh or cry at will; he knows all the tricks; he's an ace, that's sure. If we neither cry nor laugh at *A King in New York*, it's because Chaplin made up his mind to touch our heads instead of our hearts. The awful gentleness of this film makes me think of *Nuit et Brouillard*, which also rejected the simplemindedness of the propagandist or the hater.

Take two examples. If Chaplin had wanted to make the audience weep, he could have easily drawn out and dramatized the scene where the boy admits to Shadow that he has denounced his parents' friends; all he had to do was remake a reel of *The Kid*. If Chaplin had wanted us to laugh as he showed the preparations of the investigation committee, he would have dwelt on the moment when the investigator powders his face and makes up for the TV cameras. He could have made him gag three times on the powder puff. That would have gotten a laugh, but would have ruined his film, which is more ambitious. He shows us the scene only once, briefly, in a monitor.

The film doesn't broaden out or force itself on the viewer. There are no scenes that are amusing or ironic or bitter. It is a rapid and dry demonstration of a single point, almost like a documentary. The shots of New York and the two images of airplanes that Chaplin inserts are like a montage of documents. *A King in New York* is not comparable to a novel or a poem; it is more like an article, a few pages from a journal called "Charlie Chaplin comments freely on political reality."

If Chaplin chose to dream up a king, it's because he's lived a king's life. He is received like royalty everywhere and he doesn't need to invent abusive photographers, nosy journalists, and rude receptions. In real life Chaplin is constantly forced to act out a part so he won't spoil the image created by his hosts in Paris, London, or New York. What he seems to be saying is that his acts are funny for everybody but him; he's more like a Hamlet, there to grate on us, not to make us laugh. In the film, someone says, "He's just an ordinary person, but if you warm him up a bit, he can be quite funny." This ironic clarity runs throughout.

At the beginning, in that scene about the money that has disappeared, Chaplin is making fun of himself, his famous stinginess, his paranoia about being robbed. Charlie is sentimental but Chaplin is not. For the first time, he shows us the real relationship between the king and women. No more romance, no more flowers—instead,

Dawn Addams, an American doll so enticing and enflaming that the king jumps on her literally. Everything we know about Chaplin's love life, little girls thrown into his arms by irresponsible mothers who proceed to attack him in court to support themselves for the rest of their lives—it's all summed up in three minutes.

If *A King in New York* is not amusing, it's because Joe McCarthy's America represents a depressing world. It's an autobiographical film and there's no complacency about it. If it's a sadder slice of life than the ones that went before it, it's because Chaplin understands that the most agonizing problem of the time is not poverty or mistakes in the name of progress, but an organized attack on freedom in a world of informants.

"The work of art," Jean Genêt says somewhere, "must resolve the drama, not merely present it." Charlie Chaplin resolves the drama. It's a gift of great lucidity.

1957

Who Is Charlie Chaplin? *

Charles Chaplin is the most famous filmmaker in the world, but his work may be on the point of becoming lost to the history of cinema. As the distribution rights to his films expired, Chaplin forbade them to be shown. He had been cheated from the start of his career by innumerable pirated releases. New generations of moviegoers came along who knew *The Kid, The Circus, City Lights, The Great Dictator, Monsieur Verdoux, Limelight* only by reputation.

Then, in 1970, Chaplin decided to put almost all his work back into circulation, which will make it possible once again—as you'd walk along the railway ties from one station to the next—to follow the development of his thought.

In the years before the talkies were invented, writers and intellectuals the world over were cool to, even disdainful of, cinema which they regarded only as popular entertainment, at best a minor art. They

* This text is a version of the preface to *Charlie Chaplin* (Editions du Cerf), a collection by André Bazin

made one exception: Charlie Chaplin; it is easy to understand how that was offensive to the admirers of Griffith, Stroheim, Keaton. The quarrel may have revolved around whether cinema was an art, but to the public, which never asked such a question, the debate among the intellectuals didn't matter a whit. The enthusiasm of the audiences—it's difficult to imagine its proportions today (we would have to extend the cult of Eva Peron in Argentina to the entire world)—made Chaplin the most popular man in the world in 1920.

If one marvels at this, sixty years after Chaplin's first appearance on the screen, it's because it possesses a telling logic, a logic of great beauty. From its beginnings, cinema has been made by privileged persons, even if in 1920 it was scarcely a matter of practicing an art. Without singing the famous May, 1968, couplet about "cinema/ the art bourgeois," I would point out that there has always been a cultural *and* biographical gap between those who make films and those who watch them.

Charlie Chaplin, abandoned by an alcoholic father, spent his first years in the anguish of seeing his mother taken away to an asylum, and experienced the terror of being picked up by the police. He was a nine-year-old vagrant hugging the walls of Kensington Road, as he wrote in his memoirs, living ". . . on the lowest levels of society." This has often been described and commented on, but I'm returning to it because all the comments may have caused the extreme harshness of his life to be lost sight of, and we really ought to take note of how much explosiveness there is in total misery. In his chase films for Keystone, Chaplin runs faster and farther than his music-hall colleagues because, if he is not the only filmmaker to have described hunger, he is the only one who knew it at first hand. This is what his audiences all over the world felt when his films began to be circulated in 1914.

I am almost of the opinion that Chaplin, whose mother was certifiably mad, came close to complete alienation and that he escaped thanks to his gift of mime, a gift he inherited from her. In recent years there have been serious studies of children who have grown up in isolation, in moral, physical, or material distress. The specialists describe autism as a defense mechanism. But everything that Charlie does is precisely a defense mechanism. When Bazin explains that Charlie is not antisocial but asocial, and that he aspires to enter society, he defines, in almost the same terms as Kanner, the schizophrenic and the autistic child: "While the schizophrenic tries to resolve his problem by quitting a world of which he had been a part, autistic children come progressively to the compromise which consists in having only the most careful contact with a world in which they have been strangers from the beginning."

To take a single example of displacement (the word recurs constantly in Bazin's writing, as it does in Bruno Bettelheim's work about autistic children, *The Empty Fortress*), Bettelheim says: "The autistic child has less fear of things and will perhaps act on them, because it is persons, not things, who seem to threaten his existence. Nevertheless, the use that he makes of things is not that for which they were conceived."

And Bazin: "It seems that objects accept Charlie's help only when they are outside the meaning society has assigned to them. The most beautiful example of such a displacement is the famous dance of the loaves of bread in which the objects' complicity explodes into a free choreography."

In today's terms, Charlie would be the most "marginal" of the marginal. When he became the most famous and richest artist in the world, he felt constrained by age or modesty, or perhaps by logic, to abandon his vagabond character, but he still understood that the roles of "settled" men were forbidden him. He has to change his myth, but he must remain mythic. So, he prepares to do Napoleon, then a life of Christ, and then gives up these projects to shoot *The Great Dictator*, *Monsieur Verdoux*, and *A King in New York*, via the Calvero of *Limelight*, a clown who is so down-and-out that he asks his manager at one point, "What if I continued my career under an assumed name?"

Chaplin dominated and influenced fifty years of cinema to the point that he can be clearly distinguished behind Julien Carette in *La Règle du Jeu;* just as we see Henri Verdoux behind *Archibaldo de la Cruz*, we find the little Jewish barber who watches his house burn in *The Great Dictator* standing twenty-six years later behind the old Pole in Milos Forman's *The Firemen's Ball.*

His work is divided into two parts, the vagabond and the most famous man in the world. The first asks, Do I exist? and the second tries to answer, Who am I? All of Chaplin's work revolves around the major theme of artistic creation, the question of identity.

—1974

GOD BLESS JOHN FORD

John Ford was one of the most celebrated directors in the world, but everything about him, even the way he acted and spoke, gave the impression that he never sought out this celebrity and, indeed, that he never accepted it. Always described as rugged but inwardly tender, Ford was certainly closer to the minor characters in which he cast Victor McLaglen than to the starring roles of John Wayne. Ford was an artist who never said the word "art," a poet who never mentioned "poetry."

What I love in his work is that he always gives priority to characters. For a long time when I was a journalist, I criticized his conceptions of women—I thought they were too nineteenth century—but when I became a director, I realized that because of him a splendid actress like Maureen O'Hara had been able to play some of the best female roles in American cinema between 1941 and 1957.

John Ford might be awarded (the same goes for Howard Hawks) the prize for "invisible direction." The camera work of these two great storytellers is never apparent to the eye. There are very few camera movements, only enough to follow a character, and the majority of shots are fixed and always taken at the same distance. It's a style that creates a suppleness and fluidity that can be compared to Maupassant or Turgenev.

With a kind of royal leisure, John Ford knew how to make the public laugh . . . or cry. The only thing he didn't know how to do was to bore them.

And, since Ford believed in God: God bless John Ford.

—1974

FRITZ LANG IN AMERICA

If you are irritated by the extravagant admiration of younger movie lovers for the American cinema, remember that some of the best Hollywood films have been made by the Englishman Hitchcock, the Greek Kazan, the Dane Sirk, the Hungarian Benedek, the Italian Capra, the Russian Milestone, and the Viennese directors Preminger, Ulmer, Zinnemann, Wilder, Sternberg *and* Fritz Lang.

Like the French *Quai des Brumes,* and a lot of prewar films, *You Only Live Once,* which was shot in 1936, is about destiny and fate. At the start of the action, we find Henry Fonda just out of prison after two or three small-time crimes such as car theft, determined to follow the straight-and-narrow. He marries his lawyer's secretary, who has gotten him a job as a truck driver.

You Only Live Once is about interlocking forces: everything may seem to be going well, but the truth is, everything is going badly. If, against his will, Fonda "goes back to his old game," "falls" again, it isn't because "once a thief, always a thief" *(qui vole un oeuf, vole un boeuf),* but because society *dictates* once a thief, always a thief. In short, since the law-abiding people are determined to see Fonda as a former convict, they have to send him back to prison, first by driving him out of his hotel, then by chasing him from his job. He is falsely accused of a holdup and condemned to the electric chair, but he escapes at the very moment that his innocence is about to be established. He kills the priest who tries to stop him, and he and his wife flee into the woods where they are both killed by the police.

The film is both polemical and broad-minded; it is organized around the principle that law-abiding people are villains. The artist must first prove that there is a sort of beauty in what has been considered ugly, and vice versa. Throughout *You Only Live Once,* Fritz Lang accentuates the low character of ordinary citizens and the nobility of the asocial couple. Since they have no money, Eddie and Joan get their gas tank filled at the point of a revolver. As soon as they drive away, the station attendant calls the police and reports they have taken the cashbox too. As the car breaks through the first police roadblock, a bullet that should certainly have hit Joan instead hits a can of condensed milk. Milk—purity; their purity protects our heroes for a moment.

In the woods, Joan gives birth to a child. They don't name the infant: "We'll call him baby." Civil status is an invention of society.

There's no lack of romanticism here, but if the broad outlines of *You Only Live Once* have aged some, the film itself is unwrinkled because of some unusual insights, a certain directness, which holds up, and a straightforward violence which is still surprising.

Fritz Lang seems to be constantly settling his accounts with society. His main characters are always outsiders, marginal people. The hero of *M* was portrayed as a victim. In 1933, Lang had to get out of Germany quickly in the face of Nazism. From then on, all of his work, even the Westerns and the thrillers, will reflect this violent break and very soon afterward we see the theme of revenge grafted on to the experiences of persecution. Several of Lang's Hollywood films are painted on this canvas: a man becomes involved in a struggle that is larger than any one person; perhaps he is a policeman, a scientist, a soldier, a resister. Then someone close to him, a woman or a child he loves, dies and the conflict becomes his individual fight, he is personally affected; the larger cause moves into the background and what takes its place is personal vengeance: *Man Hunt, Cloak and Dagger, Rancho Notorious, The Big Heat. . . .*

Lang is obsessed with lynching, gun-to-the-head justice, and good conscience. His pessimism seems to grow with each film, and in recent years his work has become the bitterest in the history of film. That's why his latest films have failed commercially. First there was the hero-victim, subsequently the hero-avenger. Now there is only the man who is marked by sin. There are no longer any likable characters in his recent movies such as *While the City Sleeps* or *Beyond a Reasonable Doubt*. They are all schemers, opportunists, evil. Life is like a ride on a roller coaster.

In *Beyond a Reasonable Doubt*, Lang seems to be pleading for keeping the death penalty. Dana Andrews, a newspaper reporter, allows himself to be accused of a crime just to provide a dramatic climax to his campaign against capital punishment. On the eve of his execution, his innocence is established and he's freed, but he betrays himself to his fiancée and she realizes that, in fact, he actually did kill a chorus girl. The whole idea of staging a journalistic investigation was a way to cover his tracks and get away with his crime. His fiancée denounces him without hesitation.

The critics were outraged by the plot, but it should not have been surprising from a man whom the world, Nazism, war, deportation, McCarthyism, etc., confirmed as a rebel. His rebellion had turned to disgust.

Lang takes larger-than-life stories and improves on them, not by making them psychologically subtle, or more believable, but by bending them to his own obsessions. Lang expresses himself with great freedom. I know more about Lang, what he is and how he thinks, after seeing *While the City Sleeps*, a film he made to order, than I know about René Clément after watching *Gervaise*, in which, although it is a successful and high-quality film, the designer, the writers, and the star are as important as the director.

While the City Sleeps shows us the actions of about ten people whose lives revolve around a large newspaper. The publisher has died suddenly and his son, a degenerate and incompetent snob, offers the job to the one among the three candidates who can track down a strangler of young girls who is at large in the city. This time Lang rejects the mystery film's technique. Even before the credits, he's shown us the criminal in action. The most overwhelming thing in this movie is the way Lang looks at his characters with unrelieved harshness; they are all damned. Nothing could be less soft or sentimental, really more cruel, than a love scene Lang directs. In the film, Dana Andrews is the journalist of integrity, the only candidate who refuses to go along with the cynical competition, but does that do him any good, does it make him any better than the other characters? Not at all. Look at his relationship with his virginal fiancée, Sally Forrest, who is anxious to find a suitable husband with a good job. Andrews fits the bill, but he'd rather have her as a mistress than a wife; his behavior becomes a kind of implicit sexual blackmail. His caresses go a little farther each time. Sally lets him feel her legs because, after all, he mustn't be completely discouraged, but anything more will have to wait until they're married. Finally, Andrews gives in, after an enthusiastic flirtation with Ida Lupino, the newspaper's gossip columnist, a "free" woman who wants only to get ahead. The wife of the newspaper's owner pretends she's visiting her mother when she goes to her lover's home. There's a scene in a massage room when she lies to her husband so blatantly that she has to put on dark glasses to carry it off.

Lang makes ferocious remarks about all his characters, not with satire or parody in mind, but out of simple pessimism. Of all the German filmmakers who fled Nazism in 1932, he's the one who has never recovered—and added on is the fact that America, which made him welcome, seems to repel him.

Lang did not doubt that man is born wicked, and the terrible sadness of his last films reminds us of Alain Resnais' *Nuit et Brouillard:* "It is all you can do to imagine that night torn by screams, interrupted by delousings, a night that sets the teeth chattering. You have to sleep quickly. They wake you up with a club, you scramble, looking for belongings that have been stolen. . . ." In that remarkable film, Resnais continues: "They even got to the point of organizing themselves politically; they would argue over the inner control of the camp on the basis of common law."

Jean Genêt, probably France's greatest writer, certainly our only moralist, has succeeded better than any in explaining this turning of the honest man to the "common law," in a prohibited radio talk called "The Criminal Child": "The papers still show us photographs of corpses overflowing from barns or strewn across fields, caught on barbed wire in the extermination camps; they show torn-out fingernails, tattooed skins tanned and made into lampshades. These are Hitler's crimes. But no one calls our attention to the fact that in French prisons there have always been torturers who have victimized both men and children. According to the standards of a justice that is humane, or even better than that, it isn't important to decide who's guilty or innocent. To the Germans, the French were guilty. . . . The good folk applauded when we were handcuffed and the cops beat us in the ribs with their clubs." This is exactly the idea—that no one can judge anyone, that everyone is both criminal and victim—that Lang illustrates with such stubborn genius in his work. *You Only Live Once* is a pivotal film in this regard.

There is only one word to describe Lang's style: inexorable. Each shot, each maneuver of the camera, each frame, each movement of an actor is a decision and is inimitable. I'll give you an example: There's a prison scene in *You Only Live Once* where Fonda asks his wife, who's on the other side of the grate, to get him a revolver. As he whispers "Get me a gun," exaggerating the words with his mouth, we only hear the consonants—just the guttural sounds of the two *g*'s and the *t*, which are pronounced with a look of chilling intensity.

You Only Live Once should be seen often, and Lang's later films should be thought about in light of it. The man was not only a genius, he was also the most isolated and the least understood of contemporary filmmakers.

—1958

FRANK CAPRA, THE HEALER

After he'd directed the marvelous silent films of Harry Langdon, Frank Capra found fame with *It Happened One Night,* a movie that has been imitated a hundred times since. Capra's work is, unfortunately, not well known in France because of poor distribution, but I need only recall *Mr. Deeds Goes to Town, You Can't Take It With You, Mr. Smith Goes to Washington* (Watergate thirty-five years ahead of its time), *Meet John Doe,* and *It's a Wonderful Life* to realize how great an influence this marvelous filmmaker has had throughout the world. His influence can be found in the youthful work of the English "boy" director, Alfred Hitchcock (before 1940) and in the young Swede, Ingmar Bergman, in his period of conjugal comedies before 1955.

Capra is the last survivor of that great quartet of American comedy: Leo McCarey, Ernst Lubitsch, and Preston Sturges. An Italian, born in Palermo, he brought to Hollywood the secrets of the *commedia dell'arte.* He was a navigator who knew how to steer his characters into the deepest dimensions of desperate human situations (I have often wept during the tragic moments of Capra's comedies) before he reestablished a balance and brought off the miracle that let us leave the theater with a renewed confidence in life.

The growing harshness of social life after the war, the spread of egoism, the obstinate conviction of the rich that they could "take it with them" made his miracles even more improbable. But, in the face of human anguish, doubt, unrest, and the struggle just to manage daily life, Capra was a kind of healer, that is, the enemy of "official" medicine. This good doctor was also a great director.

—1974

HOWARD HAWKS

Scarface

Although *Scarface* is recognized and holds a place of honor in the history of cinema, Howard Hawks, its maker, has nonetheless been the most underestimated of Hollywood filmmakers. *Scarface* was no mere stroke of luck, and its obvious beauties shouldn't make us forget the more subtle beauties of *The Big Sleep, Red River* or *Big Sky.* Made in 1930, *Scarface,* based on the romanticized life of Al Capone and his cronies, abounds in lovely discoveries.

It's important to remember that Howard Hawks is a moralist. Far from sympathizing with his characters, he treats them with utter disdain. To him, Tony Camonte is a brute and a degenerate. He deliberately directed Paul Muni to make him look like a monkey, his arms hanging loosely and slightly curved, his face caught in a perpetual grimace. All through *Scarface* you will notice the motif of the cross—it's on walls, doors, patterns of light—a visual obsession which "orchestrates," as a musical theme would, Tony's scar and evokes the idea of death. The most striking scene in the movie is unquestionably Boris Karloff's death. He squats down to throw a ball in a game of ninepins and doesn't get up; a rifle shot prostrates him. The camera follows the ball he's thrown as it knocks down all the pins except one that keeps spinning until it finally falls over, the exact symbol of Karloff himself, the last survivor of a rival gang that's been wiped out by Muni. This isn't literature. It may be dance or poetry. It is certainly cinema.

—1954

Gentlemen Prefer Blondes

Is Howard Hawks's technicolor movie, *Gentlemen Prefer Blondes,* a work of intellect or is it entirely superficial?

Let me refresh your memories with some of the cornerstone films by this prestigious filmmaker (Howard Hawks was the only director William Faulkner would agree to work with): *Scarface, Only Angels Have Wings, Sergeant York, Bringing Up Baby, I Was a Male War Bride, Red River, The Big Sky, Monkey Business.* His films are divided into adventures and comedies. The former are a tribute to man, they celebrate his intelligence and his physical and moral greatness. The latter are directed at his degeneration and the emptiness in modern society. Hawks is a moralist in his own way, and *Gentlemen Prefer Blondes,* far from being a cynical entertainment made for pleasure, is mean and strict, an intelligent and pitiless film.

The outwardly thin story is familiar: Lorelei, the blonde (Marilyn Monroe), and Dorothy, the brunette (Jane Russell), are moving along in life, leaving behind them a trail of devoted millionaires. Lorelei loves diamonds more than anything else, while Dorothy dotes on male muscles. After wandering all over Europe, they both get married aboard ship on their way back to America. Lorelei chooses a dull millionaire and Dorothy a virile but penniless lawyer. There are almost no laughs in this movie, and it's not that the plot or production are weak—quite to the contrary, it's that the laughs get caught in our throats. This is where the judgment that this is an "intellectual film" comes near to winning out. On principle, Howard Hawks always pushes things as far as possible, and scenes which may seem merely affected to start with become monstrous as they reach extreme but logical conclusions.

Lorelei and Dorothy cease to be merely extravagant personalities and become essences; they are more than symbols: they are *the* blonde and *the* brunette, greed and lust, frigidity and nymphomania. The real intentions of the authors (Charles Lederer, Hawks's usual scenarist, and Hawks himself) become clear in two central scenes of such a level of madness and abstraction that two whole ballets and two songs can't do justice to their sense of unreality. First a long sequence in the ship's swimming pool shows Jane Russell singing, surrounded by about twenty athletes in briefs who are calling her attention to their muscles, showing off their physiques by posing and flexing their arms. The second scene features Marilyn Monroe singing "Diamonds Are a Girl's Best Friend," surrounded by five young men in dinner jackets. Each holds a long diamond necklace in his right hand, and a revolver in his left with which each in turn shoots himself in the head after Marilyn has slapped him with her diamond-studded fan. During this same scene the red lighting fades suddenly, leaving a single projector that diffuses a kind of dim church light; and immediately the twenty men fall on their knees in an ecstatic gesture. Another scene I think is significant shows Lorelei, having just been given a diamond tiara, hiding it behind her back. She holds it absolutely, perfectly horizontally, as if she were simultaneously crowning the "object" of her efforts, or the tool of her work.

This explosive mixture of styles, used by many artists, though by none better than Hawks in films, doesn't often succeed. Another example is a burlesque sketch, adapted from the O. Henry story "The Ransom of Red Chief," which Twentieth Century-Fox actually withdrew from circulation because it didn't make anybody laugh. In that story kidnappers have taken a small boy who is so obnoxious that they vainly offer his parents money to take him back. Hawks had found the story singularly rich, filled with themes he likes—the child-monster and the infantile adult.

Hawks's comedies, whatever label you put on them, are bright and original, derived more from a nice sense of the absurd than from a sense of commercialism. Whether you laugh or grit your teeth, you won't be bored.

—1954

Land of the Pharaohs

The story takes place almost three millennia before Christ, under the Sixth Dynasty, when Cheops, the great Pharaoh, has undertaken the construction of the pyramid that will be his tomb. The film follows this work to which several generations of workers dedicated their lives and where "on-the-job accidents" were common.

If *Land of the Pharaohs* is not Hawks's best film, it is nevertheless the first one on such a subject and on such a grand scale and such epic dimensions that did not succumb to the more ridiculous forms of Hollywood's Egyptomania.

The production credits contain the prestigious name of William Faulkner, who worked on the script and the dialogue. The script's strong point is that all the themes and everything that happens relate one way or another to the actual building of the pyramid, thus avoiding the double trap of diffuseness and sloppy pictorial showiness. There are no poisoned cups, orgies, or fake elegance. The architect, Valsthar, has invented a way of placing the stone blocks of the pyramid so that when Cheops dies and is enclosed in the center of the pyramid with his slaves, it will only be necessary to break two clay pots to cause a stream of sand to start flowing, which will eventually settle the entire building. This is clearly Faulknerian—the work of twenty years finished in a few seconds with a wave of sand. The idea will show you clearly that you're not dealing with a variation of *The Egyptian* or *The Ten Commandments*.

The Warnercolor process doesn't work very well here but the Cinemascope is once again overwhelming, if only because it allows us during the great crowd scenes to see a little of the famous frescoes showing the workers carving the stones with careful blows of their hammers.

In a genre of films that is often and justly decried, *Land of the Pharaohs* offers originality and intelligence.

—1955

JOSEPH VON STERNBERG

Jet Pilot

Jet Pilot is an anti-Soviet propaganda film made in 1950 by Joseph von Sternberg, the eminent director of *The Blue Angel, Underworld, Shanghai Gesture, The Saga of Anatahan.*

It is a classic American comedy along the lines of the theme of *Ninotchka:* an idyll between an American aviator and a Soviet aviatrix, and her conversion to the joy of the capitalist world. It isn't a likable film and it isn't inspired by any ideology. It only seeks to demonstrate that American aviation is the best, and that life in Russia is a nightmare. So much for the anti-Soviet sentiment; what is worse is that it caters to the stock portfolios of café society. This was a film made "on order" by the austere and fastidious von Sternberg. He now denies any responsibility for it, since the editing was done without him and against his wishes several years after he'd shot it. Howard Hughes, the producer, is an avid flier and was the most capricious and tyrannical of its backers. Still, amazingly enough, it is a successful, even a beautiful film.

For Hughes, it was simply a matter of satisfying his three passions of the moment: aviation, Janet Leigh, and anti-Communism. We could say that his three wishes were granted beyond his hopes. *Jet Pilot* is one of the best aviation films of the period, Janet Leigh is magnificent, and the anti-Communism is of rare wickedness.

Leigh, a great Soviet aviatrix, lands on American soil, supposedly having defected in pursuit of freedom. John Wayne, a famous American pilot, is ordered to play up to her to extract military information from her. Second act: Leigh is discovered to have been a spy, and the authorities are ready to deport her from the United States. Wayne, who's really fallen in love, marries her and defects to the Soviet Union. Third act: Life there is little better than hell. Wayne, who refuses to give any information about U. S. aviation, is subjected to brainwashing such as we've read about in the newspapers. Before it's too late, Janet and John flee to America, pursued by the entire Soviet air force. The last scene is reassuring. We see them very much in love, eating hamburgers in Palm Springs.

What makes *Jet Pilot* a good film in spite of itself? The scenes between Wayne and Leigh are directed with an art, inventiveness, and an intelligence that marks each image. And the eroticism is as insidious, subtle, effective, and refined as it is possible to be. I shall never forget the scene where Wayne has to frisk Leigh, who's wearing a wool-lined flying suit with slanted pockets at her breast and abdomen; or the moment when she kicks her panties through the narrow opening of the door, with the tip of her foot thrust out for inspection. I shall not forget Leigh in her nightgown, in the airplane, in Russia, in good form in every scene. We already knew that it's women Von Sternberg was interested in; because he *also* had to film airplanes for half the movie, he was somehow able to "humanize" them with breathtaking skill. When the machine piloted by Janet Leigh appears in the sky, flying beside Wayne's, and we hear their love talk over the radio, we are in the realm of pure emotion, poetically expressed. The inventiveness and beauty catches in our throats. To be sure, the film's intention is stupid propaganda, but Sternberg constantly turns it aside so that tears come to our eyes in the face of such beauty, as when the male plane and the female plane seek each other out, find one another, fly one on top of the other, struggle, calm themselves, and finally fly side by side. The airplanes make love.

—1958

P.S. The next year (1951) Howard Hughes again wanted Von Sternberg, this time to direct *Macao* with the actress Jane Russell, whom the producer-flier had discovered, directed, and launched in *The Outlaw*. He was unhappy with the first rushes and Von Sternberg was dismissed, to be replaced by Nicholas Ray. Paraphrasing Guillaume Apollinaire without realizing it ("Your breasts are the only shells I love"), Hughes demonstrates in the following memo (reprinted by Noah Dietrich in his book, *Howard, The Amazing Mr. Hughes*) that an actress's brassiere demands the same design precision as an airplane.

I think that Jane Russell's outfits, as they appear in the tests, are damned awful. They are totally unbecoming, and hide everything. There is only one word for them: horrible.

There is one exception: the dress made of metallic fabric . . . really great. It has to be used.

But it doesn't work on her breasts, and it might lead people to think— God help us—that they are padded or false. The reason is simple; the line is not natural. You'd think she was wearing a stiff brassiere that didn't mold with her figure. Especially around the nipples, it gives the impression that a piece of stiff fabric has been inserted under the dress; the contour is not natural.

I am not recommending doing without a brassiere, because I know Russell needs one. But I think that a half-brassiere, or a very light one made of very light material which would let the form of her breast come through the dress would be much more effective.

On the other hand, it would be helpful to put into the brassiere or the dress at the place where the nipples are something a bit pointed since I know that they don't show naturally with Russell. Since her breasts are completely rounded, an artifice would be desirable, so long as it can be incorporated without destroying the natural line of her breasts. The trouble with what you've got now is that at the presumed location of the nipples, there appear to be several, which is not at all natural. Likewise, the silhouette of the breast, from the point to the body, is too conical; it looks like a mechanically manufactured object.

It is difficult to explain, but I am sure you will see what I mean when you watch the film.

These particular observations refer to the dress made of metallic fabric. But they apply to all her costumes in this film and I want them observed in her entire wardrobe. Nevertheless, I want all the other costumes to be cut as low as the law allows so that the customers who pay to see this part of Russell can look at it without its being covered with material, metallic or not.

ALFRED HITCHCOCK

Rear Window

There are two kinds of directors: those who have the public in mind when they conceive and make their films and those who don't consider the public at all. For the former, cinema is an art of spectacle; for the latter, it is an individual adventure. There is nothing intrinsically better about one or the other; it's simply a matter of different approaches. For Hitchcock as for Renoir, as for that matter almost all American directors, a film has not succeeded unless it is a success, that is, unless it touches the public that one has had in mind right from the moment of choosing the subject matter to the end of production. While Bresson, Tati, Rossellini, Ray make films their own way and then invite the public to join the "game," Renoir, Clouzot, Hitchcock and Hawks make movies for the public, and ask themselves all the questions they think will interest their audience.

Alfred Hitchcock, who is a remarkably intelligent man, formed the habit early—right from the start of his career in England—of predicting each aspect of his films. All his life he has worked to make his own tastes coincide with the public's, emphasizing humor in his English period and suspense in his American period. This dosage of humor and suspense has made Hitchcock one of the most commercial directors in the world (his films regularly bring in four times what they cost). It is the strict demands he makes on himself and on his art that have made him a great director.

Summing up the intrigue in *Rear Window* will not by any means convey its inventiveness, which is too complicated simply to recap. Confined to his armchair because of a broken leg, reporter/photographer Jeffrey (James Stewart) watches his neighbors through his rear window. As he watches, he becomes convinced that one of them has killed his bad-tempered, complaining, ill wife. The investigation, as he carries it out, even though he's immobilized by his cast, is part of the movie's plot. Now we have to add a bright young woman who would like to marry Jeffrey (Grace Kelly), and then, one by one, his neighbors across the courtyard. There is the childless household devastated by the death of a little dog they believe has been "poisoned"; a slightly exhibitionist young lady; a lonely woman and a failed composer who will in the end join together against their mutual temptations to suicide and maybe establish a home; the young newlyweds who make love all day; and finally the killer and his victim.

I see when I sum it up in this way that the plot seems more slick than profound, and yet I am convinced that this film is one of the most important of all the seventeen Hitchcock has made in Hollywood, one of those rare films without imperfection or weakness, which concedes nothing. For example, it is clear that the entire film revolves around the idea of marriage. When Kelly goes into the suspect's apartment, the proof she is looking for is the murdered woman's wedding ring; Kelly puts it on her own finger as Stewart follows her movements through his binoculars from the other side of the courtyard. But there is nothing at the end that indicates that they will marry. *Rear Window* goes beyond pessimism; it is really a cruel film. Stewart fixes his glasses on his neighbors only to catch them in moments of failure, in ridiculous postures, when they appear grotesque or even hateful.

The film's construction is very like a musical composition: several themes are intermingled and are in perfect counterpoint to each other—marriage, suicide, degradation, and death—and they are all bathed in a refined eroticism (the sound recording of lovemaking is extraordinarily precise and realistic). Hitchcock's impassiveness and "objectivity" are more apparent than real. In the plot treatment, the direction, sets, acting, details, and especially an unusual tone that includes realism, poetry, macabre humor and pure fairy tale, there is a vision of the world that verges on misanthropy.

Rear Window is a film about indiscretion, about intimacy violated and taken by surprise at its most wretched moments; a film about the impossibility of happiness, about dirty linen that gets washed in the courtyard; a film about moral solitude, an extraordinary symphony of daily life and ruined dreams.

There has been a lot of talk about Hitchcock's sadism. I think the truth is more complex, and that *Rear Window* is the first film in which he has given himself away to such a degree. For the hero of *Shadow of a Doubt*, the world was a pigsty. But in *Rear Window* I think it is Hitchcock who is expressing himself through his character. I ought not to be accused of reading things into it, since the honest subjectivity of *Rear Window* breaks through each shot, and all the more so because the tone (always serious in Hitchcock's films) is geared as usual to its interest as a spectacle, that is, its commercial appeal. It's really a matter of the moral attitude of a director who looks at the world with the exaggerated severity of a sensual puritan.

Hitchcock has acquired such expertise at cinematographic recital that he has, in thirty years, become much more than a good storyteller. As he loves his craft passionately, never stops making movies, and has long since resolved any production problems, he must invent difficulties and create new disciplines for himself to avoid boredom and repetition. His recent films are filled with fascinating constraints that he always overcomes brilliantly.

In this case, the challenge was to shoot a whole film in one single place, and solely from Stewart's point of view. We see only what he sees, and from his vantage point, at the exact moment he sees it. What could have been a dry and academic gamble, an exercise in cold virtuosity, turns out to be a fascinating spectacle because of a sustained inventiveness which nails us to our seats as firmly as James Stewart is immobilized by his plaster cast.

In the face of such a film, so odd and so novel, we are liable to forget somewhat the stunning virtuosity; each scene by itself is a gamble that has been won. The effort to achieve freshness and novelty affects the camera's movements, the special effects, decor, color. (Recall the murderer's gold-framed eyeglasses lit in the dark only by the intermittent glow of a cigarette!)

Anyone who has perfectly understood *Rear Window* (which is not possible in one viewing) can, if he so wishes, dislike it and refuse to be involved in a game where blackness of character is the rule. But it is so rare to find such a precise idea of the world in a film that one must bow to its success, which is unarguable.

To clarify *Rear Window*, I'd suggest this parable: The courtyard is the world, the reporter/photographer is the filmmaker, the binoculars stand for the camera and its lenses. And Hitchcock? He is the man we love to be hated by.

—1954

To Catch a Thief

John Robie (Cary Grant), an American thief who had worked in France before the war, had such a personal technique that each of his crimes bore his stamp, and he had been dubbed "the Cat." Eventually caught and imprisoned, Robie, when the prison was accidentally bombed, took advantage of the situation. He escaped, joined the underground and eventually became a Resistance hero.

The film finds Robie some years later, when he has completely retired to a villa in Saint-Paul-de-Vence to live in considerable comfort on the profits of his earlier career. His tranquility is soon spoiled by a series of jewel thefts in the great mansions and hotels of the French Riviera, thefts committed by someone as expert as he and in his style.

He falls under suspicion and his retirement and daily routine are disrupted. So the ex-Cat decides that the only way to get back his peace and quiet is to unmask the plagiarist burglar who has baffled the police. To track down his imitator he employs a dialectic Arsène Lupin would not disavow: "To unmask the new Cat, I must catch him in the act during his next theft; to figure out who his next victim will be (since "he" reasons by imagining himself in "my" place) all I have to do is imagine what I would once have done, or what I would do now if I were in his place; *that is, in the final analysis, in my own place.*" Naturally, Robie succeeds.

I have bothered to tell you the story line of *To Catch a Thief* in such detail to demonstrate that, in spite of appearances, once more Hitchcock remains absolutely faithful to his perennial themes: interchangeability, the reversed crime, moral and almost physical identification between two human beings.

Without wanting to reveal the outcome of *To Catch a Thief*, I am sure that it is no accident that Brigitte Auber resembles Grant and wears an identical striped jersey: blue-and-white for Grant, red-and-white for Auber. Grant's hair is parted on the right, Auber's on the left. They are look-alikes and opposites at the same time, so that there is a perfect symmetry throughout the work, a symmetry that carries over to the smallest details in the intrigue.

To Catch a Thief is not a black film, nor is there a lot of suspense in it. The framework is different from *I Confess* or *Strangers on a Train*, but the basics remain the same and the same relationships bind the characters to each other.

I mentioned Arsène Lupin before because this new film of Hitchcock's is elegant, humorous, sentimental almost to the point of bitterness, somewhat in the manner of *813* or *L'Aiguille Creuse*. It is, of course, a crime story that is designed to make us laugh, but nonetheless Hitchcock's basic idea led him to Jacques Becker's formula in *Touchez pas au Grisbi:* the thieves are burned out. The protagonist, admirably portrayed by Cary Grant, is disillusioned, finished. This last job, which forces him to use all his skill as a burglar for the ends of a policeman, fills him with nostalgia for action. You may be surprised that I consider *To Catch a Thief* a pessimistic film, but you have only to listen to Georgie Auld's and Lyn Murray's melancholy music and watch Grant's unusual performance.

As in *Dial M for Murder* and *Rear Window,* Hitchcock's use of Grace Kelly is critical: here she embodies the character of a superb Yankee Marie-Chantal, and she's the one who finally catches Grant by getting him to marry her.

I have read that *To Catch a Thief* has been criticized for its lack of realism. But André Bazin has pointed out the nature of Hitchcock's relationship to realism:

Hitchcock does not cheat the spectator; whether it is a case of simple dramatic interest or of profound anguish, our curiosity is not compelled by a vagueness about what the threats are. It isn't a question of mysterious "atmosphere" out of which all sorts of perils might emerge as from a shadow, but of an unbalance: a great mass of iron begins to slip on a smooth slope, and we can calculate quite easily how it will accelerate. The direction then becomes the art of showing reality only at those moments when the suspended perpendicular of the dramatic center of gravity is about to break away from its supporting polygon. Such direction disdains both initial shock and the final crash. For my part, I would certainly see the key to Hitchcock's style—a style that's so personal that we recognize it at first glance in even his most ordinary shots—in the wonderfully determinant quality of this unbalance.

To keep up this imbalance, which creates a nervous tension throughout a film, Hitchcock must obviously sacrifice all those scenes that would be indispensable in a psychological film (connections, exposition, climax), the more since it would obviously bore him to death to shoot them. He is inclined to neglect verisimilitude in his mysteries, and even to despise plausibility, especially since a whole generation of misguided viewers credits only plots that are "historically . . . sociologically . . . psychologically" plausible.

Alfred Hitchcock has in common with Renoir, Rossellini, Orson Welles and a few other great filmmakers the fact that psychology is the least of his worries. Where the master of suspense achieves realism is in the fidelity to the exactitude and the correctness of the effects within the most improbable scenes. In *To Catch a Thief*, three or four basic implausibilities leap out at the viewer, but never has there been such precision within each image.

Here is an entry from the record: After Hitchcock had returned to Hollywood to direct the studio scenes for *To Catch a Thief*, his assistants remained in France to film the "transparencies" on the Riviera. Here is the text of a telegram he sent from Hollywood to his assistant in Nice to have him redo a scene which would last two, or perhaps three, seconds at the most on screen:

DEAR HERBY: Have watched scene where auto avoids oncoming bus. Afraid it doesn't work for following reasons: as we-the-camera take the curve the bus appears so suddenly that it is already past before the danger is realized. Two corrections: first: move along the long straight road with the curve at the end so that we are warned about the curve before we get there. When we reach the curve, we should be shocked to find autobus appearing and coming straight at us, because since the curve is narrow the bus should be on the left but we-the-camera should never take the curve straight. Second: in the projected shot, only half the autobus appears on the screen. I realize that this is due to the fact that you are swerving. This error can be corrected by keeping camera trained on the left so that at the same time as the auto takes the curve the camera can pan from left to right. All the rest of the shooting is breathtakingly beautiful. Regards to the whole crew. HITCH.

While it may be a minor film in the career of a man who knows better than all the others what he wants and how to get it, *To Catch a Thief* completely satisfies all his fans—the snobbiest and the most ordinary—and still manages to be one of the most cynical films Hitchcock has ever made. The last scene between Grant and Kelly is classic. It is a curious film that both renews Hitchcock and leaves him unchanged, an amusing, interesting film, very wicked about French police and American tourists.

—1955

The Wrong Man

Two and a half years ago, my friend Claude Chabrol and I met Alfred Hitchcock when we both fell into an icy pond at the Studio Saint-Maurice under the gaze, at first mocking and then compassionate, of the master of anguish. Because we were soaked, it was several hours before we were able to seek him out again with a new tape recorder. The first one had literally drowned; it was ruined.

It was an extremely concise interview. We wanted to persuade Hitchcock that his recent American films were much better than his earlier English ones. It wasn't very hard: "In London, certain journalists want me to say that everything that comes from America is bad. They are very anti-American in London; I don't know why, but it's a fact." Hitchcock spoke to us about an ideal film one would make for one's own pleasure that could be projected on one's living-room wall the same way one might hang a beautiful painting. We "worked" on this film together.

"Would this ideal film be closer to *I Confess* or to *The Lady Vanishes?*"

"Oh, to *I Confess!*"

"*I Confess?*"

"Yes, by all means. For example, right now I'm thinking over an idea for a film that attracts me very much. Two years ago, a musician from the Stork Club in New York, returning home after work at about two in the morning, was accosted by two men at his door who dragged him to a number of different places, including several bars. In each place they asked, 'Is this the man? Is this the man?' He was then arrested for several robberies. Although he was completely innocent, he had to go through a trial, and by its end his wife had lost her mind. She had to be institutionalized and is to this day. During the trial, one of the jurors, who was convinced of the defendant's guilt, interrupted the defense lawyer as he was questioning one of the prosecution witnesses; the juror raised his hand and asked the judge, 'Your honor, do we have to listen to all this?' It was a small infringement of the ritual, but it caused a mistrial. As preparations were being made for a new trial, the real culprit was arrested and he confessed. I think this would make an interesting movie, if we showed everything from the point of view of the innocent man, what he has to go through, how his head is on the block for another man's crimes. All the while, everybody is being very friendly, very gentle with him. He insists, 'I'm innocent,' and everybody answers, 'Of course you are, sure you are.' Completely horrible. I think I'd like to make a film from this news item. It would be very interesting. You see, in this movie, the innocent man would be in prison all the time, and a reporter or a detective would work to get him out. They never make films from the point of view of the accused man. I would like to do that."

A year ago, we learned from the American newspapers that Hitchcock was in the process of making a film called *The Wrong Man*. One didn't have to be a mind reader to figure out that it was based on the event we'd discussed.

Hitchcock has never been more himself than in this film, which nevertheless runs the risk of disappointing lovers of suspense and of English humor. There is very little suspense in it and almost no humor, English or otherwise. *The Wrong Man* is Hitchcock's most stripped-down film since *Lifeboat;* it is the roast without the gravy, the news event served up raw and, as Bresson would say, "without adornment." Hitchcock is no fool. If *The Wrong Man,* his first black-and-white film since *I Confess,* is shot inexpensively in the street, subway, the places where the action really occurred, it's because he knew he was making a difficult and relatively less commercial film than he usually does. When it was finished, Hitchcock was undoubtedly worried, for he renounced his usual cameo in the course of the film, and instead showed us his silhouette before the title appeared to warn us that what he was offering this time was something different, a drama based on fact.

There cannot fail to be comparisons made between *The Wrong Man* and Robert Bresson's *Un Condamné à Mort s'est échappé (A Man Escaped)*. It would be foolish to assume that this would work to the detriment of Hitchcock's film, which is sufficiently impressive right from the start not to have to beg for pride of place. The comparison is no less fascinating when pushed to its utmost, to where the divergences between the two movies cast a mutual light on each other.

The point of departure is identical: the scrupulous reconstruction of an actual event, its faithful rendering limited solely to the facts. For Bresson's film is as far from the account of Commandant Devigny as Hitchcock's is from the event reported in *Life* magazine. The reality, for both Hitchcock and for Bresson, was simply a pretext, a springboard for a second reality that is the *only* thing that interests them.

Since we are discussing the elements they have in common, we should point out that, faced with an identical problem, although they were seeking different solutions, Bresson and Hitchcock coincided on more than one point. For example, the acting. Just like Leterrier in Bresson's film, Henry Fonda is impassive, expressionless, almost immobile. Fonda is only a look. If his attitude is more crushed and more humble than Bresson's man who is condemned to death, it is because he is not a political prisoner who knows he has won to his cause half the world who thinks as he does, but an ordinary prisoner in criminal court, with all appearances against him and, as the film goes on, less and less chance of proving his innocence. Never was Fonda so fine, so grand and noble as in this film where he has only to present his honest man's face, just barely lit with a sad, an almost transparent, expression.

Another point in common—indeed the most striking—is that Hitchcock has almost made it impossible for the spectator to identify with the drama's hero; we are limited to the role of witnesses. We are at Fonda's side throughout, in his cell, in his home, in the car, on the street, but we are never in his place. That is an innovation in Hitchcock's work, since the suspense of his earlier films was based precisely on identification.

Hitchcock, the director who is most concerned about innovation, this time wants the public to experience a different kind of emotional shock, something clearly rarer than the famous shiver. One final common point: Hitchcock and Bresson have both built their films on one of those coincidences that make scrupulous screenwriters scream. Lieutenant Fontaine escapes miraculously; the stupid intervention of a hostile juror saves Henry Fonda. To this authentic miracle Hitchcock added another of his own making, and it will doubtless shock my colleagues. Fonda (in the film, he is of Italian descent and is named Balestrero) is lost. Waiting for his second trial, he cannot find any proof of his innocence. His wife is in a mental institution and his mother tells him, "You should pray."

So Fonda kneels before a statue of Jesus Christ and prays—"My

God, only a miracle can save me." There is a closeup of Christ, a dissolve, and then a shot in the street that shows a man who somewhat resembles Fonda walking toward the camera until the frame catches him in a closeup with his face and Fonda's superimposed. This is certainly the most beautiful shot in Hitchcock's work and it summarizes all of it. It is the transfer of culpability, the theme of the double, already present in his first English movies, and still present in all his later ones, improved, enriched, and deepened from film to film. With this affirmation of belief in Providence—in Hitchcock's work, too, the wind blows where it will—the similarities culminate and cease.

With Bresson there is a dialogue between the soul and objects, the relationship of the one to others. Hitchcock is more human, obsessed as always by innocence and guilt, and truly agonized by judicial error. As a motto to *The Wrong Man* he could have used this *pensée* of Pascal's: "Truth and justice are two such subtle points that our instruments are too dull to reach them exactly. If they do reach them, they conceal the point and bear down all around, more on what is false than on what is true."

Hitchcock offers a film about the role of the accused man, an accused man and the fragility of human testimony and justice. It has nothing in common with documentaries except its appearance; in its pessimism and skepticism, I believe it is closer to *Nuit et Brouillard* than to André Cayatte's films. In any case, it is probably his best film, the one that goes farthest in the direction he chose so long ago.

—1957

The Birds

In *8½* someone tries to waylay Guido to propose a script that opposes nuclear arms. Like Fellini, I think that the "noble" film is the trap of traps, the sneakiest swindle in the industry. For a real filmmaker, nothing could be more boring to make than a *Bridge on the River Kwai:* scenes set inside offices alternating with discussions between old fogies and some action scenes usually filmed by another crew. Rubbish, traps for fools, Oscar machines.

Hitchcock has never won an Oscar, although he is the only living filmmaker whose films, when they are reissued twenty years after their first appearance, are as strong at the box office as new films. His last film, *The Birds*, is admittedly not perfect. Rod Taylor and Tippi Hedren are imperfectly matched, and the sentimental story (as almost always, husband hunting) suffers from it. But what an injustice there is in the generally bad reception. I am so disappointed that no critic admired the basic premise of the film: "Birds attack people." I am convinced that cinema was invented so that such a film could be made. Everyday birds—sparrows, seagulls, crows—take to attacking ordinary people, the inhabitants of a seacoast village. This is an artist's dream; to carry it off requires a lot of art, and you need to be the greatest technician in the world.

Alfred Hitchcock and his collaborator, Evan Hunter *(Asphalt Jungle)*, kept only the idea of Daphne du Maurier's short story: seaside birds take to attacking humans, first in the countryside, then in the town, at the exits of schools, and even in their homes.

No film of Hitchcock's has ever shown a more deliberate progression: as the action unfolds, the birds become blacker and blacker, more and more numerous, increasingly evil. When they attack people, they prefer to go for their eyes. Basically fed up with being captured and put in cages—if not eaten—the birds behave as if they had decided to reverse the roles.

Hitchcock thinks that *The Birds* is his most important film. I think so too in a certain way—although I'm not sure. Starting with such a powerful mold, Hitch realized that he had to be extremely careful with the plot so that it would be more than a pretext to connect scenes of bravura or suspense. He created a very successful character, a young San Francisco woman, sophisticated and snobbish, who, in enduring all these bloody experiences, discovers simplicity and naturalness.

The Birds can be considered a special-effects film, indeed, but the special effects are realistic. In fact, Hitchcock's mastery of the art grows greater with each film and he constantly needs to invent new difficulties for himself. He has become the ultimate athlete of cinema.

In actual fact, Hitchcock is never forgiven for making us afraid, deliberately making us afraid. I believe, however, that fear is a "noble emotion" and that it can also be "noble" to cause fear. It is "noble" to admit that one has been afraid and has taken pleasure in it. One day, only children will possess this nobility.

—1963

Frenzy

In contemporary London, a sex maniac strangles women with a necktie. Fifteen minutes after the film begins, Hitchcock reveals the assassin's identity (we had met him in the second scene). Another man, the focus of the story, is accused of the murders. He will be watched, pursued, arrested, and condemned. We will watch him for an hour and a half as he struggles to survive, like a fly caught in a spider's web.

Frenzy is a combination of two kinds of movies: those where Hitchcock invites us to follow the assassin's course: *Shadow of a Doubt, Stage Fright, Dial M for Murder, Psycho* . . . and those in which he describes the torments of an innocent person who is being persecuted: *The Thirty-nine Steps, I Confess, The Wrong Man, North by Northwest. Frenzy* is a kind of nightmare in which everyone recognizes himself: the murderer, the innocent man, the victims, the witnesses; a world in which every conversation, whether in a shop or a café, bears on the murders—a world made up of coincidences so rigorously ordered that they crisscross horizontally and vertically. *Frenzy* is like the design of crossword puzzle squares imposed on the theme of murder.

Hitchcock, who is six months older than Luis Buñuel (both are seventy-two), began his career in London, where he was born and where he made the first half of his films. In the forties he became an American citizen and a Hollywood filmmaker. For a long time, critical opinion has been divided between those who admire his American films—*Rebecca, Notorious, The Rope, Strangers on a Train, Rear Window, The Birds*—and those who prefer his English films: *The Thirty-nine Steps, The Lady Vanishes, Jamaica Inn.* Hitchcock's fifty-second film, *Frenzy,* was a triumph at the Cannes Festival and reconciled both schools of critics, who acclaimed it unanimously, perhaps because it is the first film he's made in Great Britain in twenty years. Hitchcock often says, "Some directors film slices of life, but I film slices of cake." *Frenzy* indeed looks like a cake, a "homemade" cake by the septuagenarian gastronome who is still the "boy director" of his London beginnings.

Everybody praised the performances of Jon Finch as the innocent man and of Barry Foster as the strangler. I'd rather emphasize the high quality of the female acting. In *Frenzy,* for the first time Hitchcock turned away from glamorous and sophisticated heroines (of whom Grace Kelly remains the best example) toward everyday women. They are well chosen: Barbara Leigh-Hunt, Anna Massey, Vivien Merchant, and Billie Whitelaw, and they bring a new realism to Hitchcock's work. The formidable ovation given *Frenzy* at the Cannes Festival redeems the contempt that greeted the presentations there of *Notorious* (1946), *The Man Who Knew Too Much* (1957) and *The Birds* (1963). Hitchcock's triumph is one of style in *recitative;* here it has found its definitive form in a dizzying and poignant narration that never comes to rest, a breathless recitation in which the images follow one another as imperiously and harmoniously as the swift notes of the imperturbable musical score.

Hitchcock has long been judged by the flowers he places in the vase. Now we have at least realized that the flowers are always the same, and that his efforts are directed at the shape of the vase and its beauty. We come out of *Frenzy* saying to ourselves, "I can't wait for Hitchcock's fifty-third movie."

—1973

II

THE GENERATION OF THE TALKIES: THE AMERICANS

ROBERT ALDRICH

Kiss Me Deadly

The scene is a highway, at night. A girl, naked under her raincoat, is trying to stop a passing car. In despair, she finally throws herself in front of an oncoming Jaguar, which goes into a skid to avoid hitting her. "Get in!" Then, in the road in front of the car, the opening credits roll *in reverse*, the most original opening in years, punctuated by the girl's heavy breathing.

It is pointless to try to sum up the plot of *Kiss Me Deadly*. You have to see it a few times before you realize it is very solidly constructed, and that it tells an ultimately quite logical story.

The pretty young hitchhiker is murdered. Mike Hammer, the private detective who owns the Jaguar, investigates the murder. About three-quarters of the way through the film, he is shot dead and then three minutes later he *revives*. If *Kiss Me Deadly* is the most original American film since Orson Welles' *The Lady from Shanghai*, it still does not possess the latter's multiple resonances, and it scarcely merits our attention on the level of intrigue.

The Mickey Spillane novel on which the film is based is apparently also mediocre. Ten people kill each other over several million dollars that are locked away in a white iron box. The film's authors were shrewd enough to use all the book's conventionally precise details to show off the abstract, almost fairy-tale aspect of the story. Thus, in the film, the box contains not bank notes, but a kind of fireball that gives off radiation and burns anyone who comes into contact with it. When the hero, opening the box, finds his wrist burned like the skin of a Hiroshima survivor, a policeman, looking at it, makes a remark that turns the whole story suddenly very serious: "Listen to me, Mike, mark my words. I'm going to say a few neutral words . . . but try to figure out what they mean: Manhattan Project . . . Los Alamos . . . Trinity." This is Aldrich's subterfuge to avoid using the word "atomic" even once during a film which will end in a cataclysm: The Pandora's box is opened by an overanxious, too-curious girl, the "sun" burns everything around it. As the hero and his mistress take refuge under the sea, "The End" appears on the screen.

To appreciate *Kiss Me Deadly*, you have to love movies passionately and to have a vivid memory of those evenings when you saw *Scarface, Under Capricorn, Le Sang d'un poète (Blood of a Poet), Les Dames du Bois de Boulogne,* and *The Lady from Shanghai.* We have loved films that had only one idea, or twenty, or even fifty. In Aldrich's films, it is not unusual to encounter a new idea with each shot. In this movie the inventiveness is so rich that we don't know what to look at—the images are almost too full, too fertile. Watching a film like this is such an intense experience that we want it to last for hours. It is easy to picture its author as a man overflowing with vitality, as much at ease behind a camera as Henry Miller facing a blank page. This is the film of a young director who is not yet worrying about restraint. He works with a freedom and gaiety that remind us of Jean Renoir at the same age, shooting *Tire au flanc* in the forest of Fontainebleau.

There can be no doubt that the revelation of Robert Aldrich will be the cinema event of 1955. When the year began, we didn't even know his name. Then came *World for Ransom,* a witty little film shot under conditions that resemble those of home movies; *Bronco Apache,* poetic and delicate; *Vera Cruz,* a violent farce; *The Big Knife,* which has just set off a strong reaction at the Venice festival; and finally *Kiss Me Deadly,* which despite its adapted screenplay, combines all the qualities of his earlier works.

You must see *Kiss Me Deadly.* If you know the conditions under which films are made today, you can only admire the extraordinary freedom of this movie, which, surprisingly enough, may be compared in some ways to Jean Cocteau's *Le Sang d'un poète,* a favorite classic of the ciné-clubs.

—1955

Vera Cruz

Vera Cruz is above all a dazzling lesson in story construction. I shall try to sum up the screenplay in the clearest possible way.

1. Mexico, 1866. Gary Cooper, alone in the middle of the desert, finds himself without a horse.

2. He meets Burt Lancaster, who sells him one.

3. When the Emperor Maximilian's soldiers appear, Lancaster takes off posthaste. Cooper, who has nothing to hide, stays put.

4. A soldier fires at him.

5. Cooper now flees and rejoins Lancaster, who says only, "You're still on your horse."

6. Cooper is lying on the ground, grazed by a bullet from the Imperial soldiers. Thinking he's dead, Lancaster steals his wallet. But Cooper revives, takes Lancaster's horse, leaves him the stolen one, and takes off. "Where I'm from, in Louisiana, we hang horse thieves."

7. Cooper arrives in the town and is captured by bandits, who work for Lancaster: "If that's your horse, you must have killed him; and, if you killed him, it must be because he turned his back." A broken bottle is about to dispatch Cooper to the paradise of adventurers when . . .

8. Lancaster arrives on the scene and fires a single shot that shatters the broken bottle. Ernest Borgnine: "I didn't know he was a friend of yours . . ." "I don't have any friends, idiot . . . except you."

9. The town square. The Marquis de Labordère (Cesar Romero) has just proposed that Lancaster and his men fight for the Emperor against Juarez. Negotiations follow. A general of the Juarez forces arrives and suggests the opposite arrangement: "We are not as rich as the Emperor but our cause is better." There is hesitation. "In any case," the general goes on, "you have no choice, because

you are all my prisoners, including the Marquis and his men." The camera pans over the ramparts to show the plaza surrounded by Juarez' soldiers, their guns at the ready. The population has fled indoors . . .

10. . . . except for a group of children who remain on the square. Cooper suggests they bring the children inside. Delighted, Lancaster signals two of his men to bring the children inside through a stable door.

11. The children are now hostages of the Emperor's men. If the general orders his forces to fire, the youngsters will be killed. The general gives in: "We'll meet again."

12. Cooper and Lancaster and his men are at the Emperor's court. A conversation between the Emperor and the Marquis shows Maximilian's treachery. He will agree to all the bandits' financial demands, but on the day of payment he will have them slaughtered if the rebels haven't already taken care of them.

13. The mercenaries' task is to escort the Countess Marie Duvarre (Denise Darcel) to Vera Cruz.

14. As they proceed, the deep tracks the coach is making indicate to Cooper and Lancaster that the Countess' protection is merely a pretext and that they have a load of gold on their hands.

15. A visit to the coach in the dead of night confirms their suspicions. They agree to split the treasure between the two of them. The Countess discovers them and proposes a deal: she will split it three ways when they arrive in Vera Cruz.

16. Vera Cruz. The Marquis de Labordère is aware that the Countess will betray him there.

17. The Countess is planning to get rid of her two "partners."

18. Lancaster, who can read her like a book, slaps her around and "persuades" her to get rid of Cooper and split the gold two ways.

19. Meanwhile the Marquis has had the gold transferred from the carriage to a cattle car and has the carriage take off as a diversionary tactic. Cooper, Lancaster and his men follow in hot pursuit and find it in a ditch.

20. The bandits now hold Lancaster and Cooper at gunpoint: "You seem awfully attached to this stagecoach; if we find gold in it, that means you were ready to betray us." Obviously, the stagecoach is empty.

21. Lancaster, Cooper, and the bandits are surrounded by

the Juarez forces, who want the gold they still believe is in the stage-coach. To avenge themselves on the Marquis, and to recover the gold, they all decide to form an alliance.

    22. The final pitched battle is won by the Juaristas. As Lancaster is preparing to betray the Countess, Cooper, and the Juaristas, and to make off with the booty, Cooper kills him and turns the gold over to the Juaristas. He will now fight on their side.

    I have deliberately stripped the screenplay to its bare bones to bring out its ingenuity. I've even left out some important points. But what is clear is that each scene would justify a film all by itself; each has its own dramatic structure and is turned inside out, as Sartre would say, like a glove.

    Vera Cruz is built on the repetition of themes: two encirclements by the Juaristas; two thefts of the same loot; Cooper saves Lancaster's life and Lancaster Cooper's. I have left out the role of Nina, which is perfect: a) she is caught by a bandit's lasso; b) Cooper frees her by catching the fool with *his* lasso; c) Nina thanks Cooper with a kiss on the mouth d) during which she steals his wallet; e) as he starts to leave, she offers him an apple; f) he starts to reach for his wallet to pay for it, and g) she tells him "Don't bother; it's free"; h) later, they meet and Cooper scolds her for stealing his wallet. "Have you looked carefully for it?" He finds it in his pocket. It's Nina who brings Cooper to the Juaristas. In the next-to-last scene we see them walking toward each other. We don't see them in the last scene.

    But this Borden Chase story, adapted by Roland Kibbee and James R. Webb and directed by Robert Aldrich, is more than a painstakingly constructed mechanism of weights and balances like a Swiss watchworks. One example: At the end of the first part, Lancaster tells the story of his life to Cooper. His father had been killed in a card game by Ace Hannah, who afterward adopted the orphaned child. This single moment of weakness, the only one he had ever given in to in his lifetime, turned out to be his downfall. Lancaster, grown up, killed him in turn. Ace Hannah had been a philosopher: "Never do anything unless you get something out of it." And Lancaster's whole behavior pattern reflects this brand of morality. He admires Cooper only because Cooper also follows it sometimes, although unwittingly. Their conversations are full of: "Ace Hannah would have liked that," or "If Ace Hannah were here, he'd be proud of us." And when they are angry at each other Lancaster says, "Ace Hannah would never have been a friend of yours," and Cooper replies, "Who says I'd want him for a friend?" Lancaster believes he, not Cooper, is the spiritual heir of Ace Hannah. Hannah, however, is probably a combination of Lancaster's trickiness and Cooper's intelligence. All the characters in *Vera Cruz*, from the Countess to the Emperor, are defined in Hannah's terms, even when they couldn't know he had ever existed. Everybody betrays everybody else; everybody lies, and all know how to read the truth in others' faces. The Countess introduces Lancaster to a ship's captain, who then walks out leaving them alone. Lancaster slaps her hard across the face: "That guy looked at me the way you look at someone who's going to die; are you trying to get rid of me?"

Is *Vera Cruz* an intellectual Western? Yes, in a way, though it is far removed from the others—the facetious *High Noon,* and the outright phoniness of *Shane* or *Treasure of the Sierra Madre. Vera Cruz* made me realize that you cannot criticize John Huston's movies on principle. They fail because of a lack of style and weak direction. *Vera Cruz* is precisely a "Huston" movie that succeeds.

Aldrich's direction is a little showy and full of effects. Some are excellent and others superfluous, but they all serve the story.

It is a shame that many of my colleagues have completely missed the point about *Vera Cruz.* Some of them, understanding nothing at all about it, denounced it as pompous and childish. It was Victor Hugo who asked, "Who are all these children, not one of whom knows how to laugh?"

—1955

The Big Knife

The Big Knife is adapted from a play by Clifford Odets which had some success on Broadway, and which Jean Renoir plans to bring to the Paris stage.

The action is set in contemporary Hollywood, in the home of a star, Charlie Castle (Jack Palance), whose wife (Ida Lupino) is about to leave him. A few months earlier, Charlie's studio had rescued him from scandal. Driving with a starlet, Charlie had run over a child and fled the scene. The studio's publicity director had done a few months in jail in Charlie's place, and the starlet's salary had gone up tenfold.

A suspicious gossip columnist wants to expose the affair, and she could raise a considerable ruckus.

In addition, it seems Charlie could win his wife back if he'd give up everything and leave with her. But the studio head has no intention of allowing that to happen. If his star doesn't renew his contract for another seven years, the very people who had hushed up the scandal will turn on him.

At the moment when everything seems settled and the reconciled couple are getting ready to leave Hollywood, Charlie kills himself to escape a world whose laws he can no longer live with, and to escape his own ignominy.

We may well wonder if it is interesting to make films out of plays, especially, as in this case, if the director doesn't allow himself to adapt them freely. I believe it's natural for a filmmaker, fascinated by the technique of his own art as well as possessing experience in the theater, to be tempted to stamp and embellish a play with a certain literary quality, shaping it by using the endless possibilities of cinematic editing.

Robert Aldrich has not merely filmed a play; he has indeed directed a theater production cinematically; he has "edited" and filmed an arch-theatrical production. All the pounding on tables, the arms raised to heaven, the about-faces with the whole body clearly come from the stage. But Aldrich imposes his rhythm on them, a tempo that is all his own. Even his least accomplished movies are fascinating.

With his lyricism, his modernity, his contempt for the slightest vulgarity, his desire to universalize and stylize the subjects he treats, Aldrich's effects remind us constantly of Jean Cocteau and Orson Welles, whose films he cannot have missed seeing.

The action of *The Big Knife* is moved forward not by the interplay of emotions or of actions, but only—and this is both rarer and more beautiful—through exploration of the moral construction of the characters. As the film progresses, the producer becomes more and more the producer, the starlet more and more the starlet, until the moment of shock and explosion at the end.

Films of this kind need exceptional acting, and in this case we are more than satisfied by Jack Palance, Ida Lupino, Shelley Winters, and especially Rod Steiger, who plays the producer magnificently. He is a patriot, a democrat, both fierce and sentimental, completely mad.

Aside from presenting a very exact picture of Hollywood, *The Big Knife* is the most refined and intelligent American film we have seen for a number of months.

—1955

WILLIAM BEAUDINE

The Feathered Serpent

An open letter to Mr. Chan, Chinese detective, Beverly Hills, California:

DEAR MR. CHAN:

Please begin an investigation, with the assistance of honorable number one son and honorable number two son, into the reasons why the Charlie Chan series keeps getting worse. Warner Oland much talent, Sidney Toler little talent, Roland Winters no talent at all. Norman Foster honorable director, William Beaudine not honorable; work always bungled. On tablet of jade is written: "Folly is the sister of genius," but Charlie Chan series of films less folly every day than day before. Send explanation immediately. Payment in Chinese dollars. May Confucius be with you.

—1953

BUDD BOETTICHER

The Killer Is Loose

Leon Pool (Wendell Corey) is a weekend gangster, an amateur. He gets involved in a holdup at the bank where he works as a teller. As the police close in, he barricades himself in his house with his pretty wife, who knows nothing about his activities. Police lieutenant Joseph Cotten aims carelessly and kills the timid gangster's wife. The widower is sentenced to ten years at hard labor, but because he is so well behaved, he is kept under light security. He shoots a guard on the prison farm where he works, and he escapes. He returns to the city where the holdup happened with only one idea: to kill the wife of the cop who killed his wife. Just as he is about to succeed, he is caught. Disguised as a woman to throw the police off his trail, he is betrayed, a few seconds before he can fire, by his carelessly rolled-up trousers which fall down from under his skirt.

It's an amusing plot. Fritz Lang would have refused to direct it unless he could have reversed the end to show the vengeance of the just man, his favorite theme. But in this case, the enterprise limps from the very beginning, precisely because the plot is so offbeat. In a slick film every touch of boldness is a pleasant surprise, but in a daring film even the slightest compromise is exasperating.

The killer, created by John and Kard Hawkins in a short story, and by Harold Medford, who wrote the screenplay, is likable from the start. He is fearful and timid; he suffers from an inferiority complex which his admiring wife, the only one who never makes fun of him, is gradually curing. During the war in the Pacific, Leon Pool hardly killed any "Japs" because he was too gentle a soldier, timorous and clumsy. His buddies nicknamed him "fog." His teller's salary is inadequate and he gets involved in the holdup to raise his standard of living. When Joseph Cotten kills his wife, Pool's one idea is to kill Cotten, a notion that would occur to a simple, uncomplicated man, unburdened by logic and the constrictions of traditional morality. Unfortunately, the screenwriters begin to make concessions at this point. Pool has to kill the prison guard so the audience will turn against him and his desire for revenge will appear unjustified. The logic of the character falls apart; the good guy becomes a killer, the corpses pile up to no purpose, and the film loses interest except for a few moments of madness when slightly ridiculous but beautiful ideas surface, as when Pool, with the innocent air of a frightened duck, appears in the street disguised as a woman.

But Boetticher is a likable filmmaker, whose earlier work for Universal we must now forget, since his contract there forced him to spend from 1948 to 1955 making inane (if sometimes very handsome) Westerns.

—1956

GEORGE CUKOR

It Should Happen to You

Cinema was born with well-defined genres: Westerns, thrillers, sophisticated comedies. It was born American and remains so. I am just as certain that each genre is heroic. For all that its sanctity amuses us, the so-called American comedy has adopted sanctity as one of its favorite themes: Capra's Mr. Deeds and Irene Girard in *Europe 51* climb similar calvaries. The greatest filmmakers of the world have always worked in all genres and still do. And they also know the art of moving and amusing within the same scene *(True Heart Susie, Sergeant York).* The greatest actors—those who emerge triumphant without direction—are also capable of this art: Grant, Cooper, Stewart, Fonda, Bogart.

Capra, a controversial genius but a genius all the same, *improvised* the essentials: echoes *(Deeds);* a tuba, the walls of Jericho, hitchhiking *(It Happened One Night).* You couldn't fail to shed tears watching Stewart weep in the telephone booth in *It's a Wonderful Life,* biting his lips, tearing his handkerchief, pulling it around his neck, twisting the telephone wire. Another comedy with sanctity as its subject was *Good Sam* by the great Leo McCarey.

Some of Hawks's venerable films, like *I Was a Male War Bride,* or *A Song Is Born* pushed comedy forward; but Cukor still gives us movies like the earlier ones, and we shall not reproach him with it, because he is who he is and everything he does is fine. I'm aware that these observations may seem disjointed, but what am I to do? "You like Cukor, you like *It Should Happen to You;* write a review." I said, "OK." But the trouble is that Cukor isn't the kind of director you write about; he's someone to talk about with friends on the street or sitting in a café.

Garson Kanin, who has talent to burn (but who is no fool and is saving it for winter) has dreamed up the idea that a young woman named Gladys Glover (not an opportunist by any means, she simply wants to be known, for no particular reason) spends her last penny to rent a gigantic billboard on which she has her name inscribed in giant letters. This is not the place to explain how the billboard proliferates; the point is that Gladys becomes a celebrity, absurdly enough, for no reason. It is as gratuitous as the crimes that fascinated André Gide. But, if gratuitous crime doesn't pay, that is by no means true of unjustified celebrity. In the eyes of her mother, America, Gladys becomes the symbol of the average American girl, a kind of Miss Person of 1953.

The theme of *It Should Happen to You* is marvelous. It is much more than a tasteful diversion. If you look carefully you see the whole mechanism of celebrity against a background of the absurd. The moral of the story is that it is easier to find glory than to justify it, and that such glory has little meaning since it is acquired within a society that is unconscious of its absurdity.

Cukor, the director, and Garson Kanin, the writer, have invented a curious, eccentric, even absurd, character for the actress. If we laugh at her countless blunders, she inspires enough sympathy to keep us going during the "dead" times that are necessary to set up Kanin's gags.

Comedy is a noble genre and, since all Hollywood genres are heroic, its comedy is heroic too. Everyone knows it's harder to make people laugh than to make them cry—everyone knows it but no one believes it. You explain to someone that it was more difficult, and more authentic, to make *It Should Happen to You* than some particular war film. They get their backs up, they accuse you of having gotten your values backward. To understand, it suffices to imagine two typewriters. Sitting at one, a fellow is writing a mighty epic of Pearl Harbor; at the other, someone is writing *It Should Happen to You*. The first fellow is putting in a few hours' work; in the second case, there has to be genius. In the first case, you can get by with a well-tried formula: war is monstrous but exalting. In the second there must be: a) an idea from which to start; b) an idea to arrive at; c) gags; d) recoveries. Some comedies have only two characters, but if you give the couple one or two children as you go along, it'll take another two weeks or a month of work to *create* the children, to find ideas for them, to compose their dialogue. This is why we can say in all seriousness that *It Should Happen to You* is a masterpiece. To keep up the rhythm for ninety minutes with no letup, to keep the smiles constant even between laughs, to direct people that way . . . that takes a *master*.

—1954

SAMUEL FULLER

Verboten

Bom . . . bom . . . bom . . . *bomm.* Bom . . . bom . . . bom . . . *bomm.* To the strains of Beethoven's Fifth Symphony, four or five American soldiers liberate a German village with nothing but hand weapons. Ludwig von Fuller, who doesn't fool around when he's making movies, gives us the illusion that we're watching the entire American army. A wounded GI is cared for by a young German girl, Helga—an idyllic touch, love, Wagner takes over for Beethoven. Samuel Fuller, who handles his camera with great style, takes his forbidden lovers on a honeymoon on the Rhine that is straight out of Guillaume Apollinaire.

But Helga has a younger brother fascinated by Hitler, whose corpse is still smoking. To make him understand the horrible truth of Nazism, Helga takes him to the Nuremberg trials.

In the courtroom we see closeup shots of Helga and the brother watching . . . watching what? Reverse shots from newsreels: Nazi torturers attempting to justify themselves before the tribunal. It's a mark of Fuller's cleverness that from this point on, one out of every two shots was filmed by him (shot) and the other (a reverse shot) is from the archives. But Fuller, who keeps his eye on the ball and has more than one trick in his bag, goes one step further with his effective ruses: he brings a 16 mm. projector into the courtroom which will show those who are attending the trial (and, of course, the audience of *Verboten*) those atrocious images that were filmed when the camps were liberated and which have become famous—all that dark material to which Resnais gave definitive form in *Nuit et Brouillard.*

The Paris press has generally looked down on *Verboten* and made fun of it, and I have just described it in a similar tone, but now I'd like to say why I liked it and why I admire Samuel Fuller.

To make a completely successful film means imbuing it with qualities that are varied and almost contradictory, a difficult and rare achievement. It's often said that a film is "cinema" or "not cinema" without saying precisely why. For me, a *filmmaker* must know how to make or show something better than the others do. That chap, for example, is not a good storyteller but he directs actors better than someone else; another one spoils scenes, but every shot is perfect; a third piles up three hundred prosaic shots that add up to a powerful movie; a fourth has wonderful camera work; a fifth allows things to get confused but he knows how to create real characters, etcetera, etcetera. In short, no film is a total success, and it's awfully easy to criticize what it's not. It's our job to try to discover what it is.

As I watched *Verboten*, I realized all that I still have to learn to dominate a film perfectly, to give it rhythm and style, to bring out the beauty in each scene without taking refuge in extrinsic effects, to bring out the poetry as simply as possible without ever forcing it.

Samuel Fuller is not a beginner, he is a primitive; his mind is not rudimentary, it is rude; his films are not simplistic, they are simple, and it is this simplicity that I most admire. We can't learn anything from an Eisenstein or an Orson Welles, because their genius makes them inimitable, and we only make ourselves ridiculous when we try to imitate them by placing the camera on the floor or on the ceiling. On the other hand, we have everything to learn from those talented American directors like Samuel Fuller who place their cameras at "the height of the human eye" (Howard Hawks), who "don't look, they find" (Picasso). It's impossible to say to yourself, faced with a Samuel Fuller film, "It should have been done differently, faster, this way or that." Things are what they are, they are filmed as they must be; this is direct cinema, uncriticizable, irreproachable, "given" cinema, rather than assimilated, digested, or reflected upon. Fuller doesn't take time to think; it is clear that he is in his glory when he is shooting.

That a committed filmmaker, overwhelmed by the strength and power of the documents from the Nuremburg trials on the horrors of Nazism and the camps, should have imagined a fictitious story around them so as to insert them into life, to remove them from cruel objectivity in order to draw a moral lesson, is a powerful and beautiful idea for cinema. Especially so when you think that the American distributors never wanted to buy the rights to *Nuit et Brouillard.* That this filmmaker's work manages to match the strength, crudity, and truth of those famous documents, as did Balzac's the Civil War, is what I find fabulous about *Verboten.*

I shall go to see this film again because I always come away from Samuel Fuller films both admiring and jealous. I like to take lessons in filmmaking.

—1960

ELIA KAZAN

Baby Doll

There are a number of ways to tell the story of *Baby Doll*, but I think the plot, as imagined by Tennessee Williams and filmed by Elia Kazan, was only a pretext for the former to delineate a woman's portrait, and the latter to direct an actress.

Nonetheless there is something quite new on the screen here, which harmonizes well with the sort of experimentation that is being pursued by some directors who have interested us this year. Carroll Baker, the heroine of *Baby Doll*, takes her place in the sun beside Marilyn Monroe in *Bus Stop*, Brigitte Bardot in *Et Dieu créa la Femme*, and Ingrid Bergman in *Eléna et les Hommes*.

What is new here, and fairly daring, is that sex is the only focus of attention. The feelings that are portrayed, basically Karl Malden's jealousy, are merely the occasion of deliberate and fierce derision.

The love-doll, almost twenty, married already but still a virgin as may still be possible only along the banks of the Mississippi, is a baby-woman, a thumb-sucker, but clearheaded and without illusions to the point of cynicism. She is the maiden wife of a baker who kneads bread as his only fantasy. Now arrives on the scene another baker, a Sicilian, a maker of bastards, an injured flier whose hangar has been burned down by an arsonist. He has headed home to find the culprit and get revenge.

The authors (worse luck for them) don't want the audience to know whether the Sicilian wants only to avenge himself on the old husband (the arsonist and cuckold-to-be) or whether, in the middle of his quest for vengeance, his attention will be utterly distracted by the possibility of ravishing an available maidenhead. Right in the midst of their love duet, between the seduction scene and when they go to sleep in the nursery, the camera wanders away for five minutes searching for Malden. It finds him.

If we consider that a lot of French and American directors never manage to illustrate their text, we must take off our hats to Kazan who throughout *Baby Doll* succeeds intentionally in filming action that bears no relation at all to the dialogue. The characters think one thing, say another, and convey yet a third.

Kazan is no storyteller; his talent is for description rather than narrative. He never succeeds in making a unified film, just a certain number of scenes. His cinematic unit is neither the shot nor the film itself, but the scene. If *Baby Doll*, from one viewpoint, is stronger than *East of Eden* (if not more successful, at least more daring), it is because essentially it consists of two great scenes, one of which is as long, detailed, and powerful as the second third of *Queen Kelly*. (The comparison between these two films seems foolish only at first sight.)

Baby Doll is almost two hours long. The first thirty minutes are exposition. Precisely at the thirtieth minute, Karl Malden introduces Eli Wallach, the Sicilian, to his young wife and leaves. The first scene between these two perfectly matched partners lasts exactly a half-hour; their conversation begins on the front steps, continues behind the house, then in the old car, again in front of the house, and finally on the swing.

There, after Wallach's sly questioning, really a cross-examination, he becomes certain that Malden is the arsonist; the camera draws closer and closer to their faces, which move gradually toward each other; the scene ends with this suggestion of inevitable contact.

At the sixtieth minute, Carroll Baker breaks away abruptly and, followed by a grinning Wallach, rejoins Malden as the loving wife. Malden, coarser than ever, slaps her. (How many cuckolds owe their misfortune to an undeserved slap?)

The second hour of the film is also made up of two long, even scenes: the first takes place between Wallach and Carroll Baker outdoors and then in the house; the second shows us the household *à trois* in confrontation. The third half-hour of the film: They return to the house, Baker describes her marriage, there is a promise of lemonade for two, a great number by Wallach concerning evil geniuses, Baby Doll's fears, diabolism, a paper denouncing Malden signed by the girl, laughs, intimacy in the nursery, and cut to . . .

Malden is coming back like an idiot from the town. Final half-hour scene; Malden's jealousy, his horrible suspicions, the transformation of Baby Doll (a woman now), a tense dinner, a tragicomic after-dinner drink, and a fantastic chase in the night, ending with Wallach's takeoff in a fishtail. Will he, the most interesting character in the film, return tomorrow?

The handsome Sicilian belongs to an ancient race; he wears a little flat cap at a rakish angle, a black shirt with thin white stripes open at the chest; he carries a stick in his fist and uses it to emphasize his sarcastic remarks. With his barrel chest and opera singer's carriage, his is an impressive presence. Above all, there is his clear, animal glance which gleams out of two small eyes that are filled with insatiable lust, and not least, there is the fox's body ready to slip between the sheets to eat his neighbor's chicken, in this case, Baby Doll. All this is a constant ingredient of this film which is held together by the desirability of a woman.

All great filmmakers aspire to be free from the constraints of drama; they dream of making a film without progression, without psychology, in which the spectators' interest would be aroused by means other than changes of place and time, the cleverness of the dialogue, or the characters' comings and goings. *Un Condamné à Mort s'est échappé (A Man Escaped)*, *Lola Montès*, *Woman on the Beach*, and *Rear Window* all achieve a considerable amount in this tricky game, each one in its own way.

In *Baby Doll*, Kazan has succeeded almost completely, by means of a style of direction that is unique, in making this sort of film, while simultaneously mocking the emotions that are portrayed and analyzed in conventional films.

What bothers Kazan, what he cannot seem to manage, are the transition scenes involving several characters. In *Baby Doll* he succeeds in dodging them except at the beginning of the film, and from the moment the Sicilian starts to court the woman-child, we are watching a film in which each gesture and glance is made to count, so perfect is its precision. It is a film masterfully dominated by one man.

Kazan's talent, which is essentially of a decorative nature, is more effective with subjects of this type (those that come from Broadway, we could say quite simply) than those laborious social theses which are necessarily dishonest.

We know now that Elia Kazan has nothing more to say to us

than what his screenplay writers have written for him, and at the same time that he is the man who knows best of all how to reveal actors to themselves.

The second time we see *Baby Doll*, we discover a second film which is still richer. Whether it is a work of genius or mere talent, whether decadent or generous, profound or brilliant, *Baby Doll* is fascinating.

—1957

A Face in the Crowd

A Face in the Crowd, which I believe to be a great and beautiful work whose importance transcends the dimensions of a cinema review, was a vivid disappointment to the American public and to the French public as well—almost surely because it is the exact opposite of *On the Waterfront* and because one must attack today whomever one flattered yesterday.

Does that mean that Budd Schulberg and Elia Kazan have changed their colors? No. But *On the Waterfront*, a screenplay that passed from hand to hand for five years, was so emasculated by the end that all that remained of its anti-fascist intentions was an unconsciously but nonetheless basically demagogic movie.

This time out, Schulberg and Kazan were their own producers, and thus have been able to bring us a film that conforms entirely to their initial intentions. The result is sensational.

Demagoguery, because it contains a certain euphoria, a good-guy aspect, is pre-eminently American. It is slowly but surely gaining a foothold in France in journalism, radio, and television by dint of the fact that the media are more and more inspired by American methods every day.

In the film it all begins when a pretty girl, the niece of the owner of a small radio station, has an idea for a program to be called "A Face in the Crowd." The program will let the man in the street speak or sing into a mike.

As she develops the program, she unearths a bearded brute in a prison in a scene that is the most important moment of the film. It is the trigger that will catapult this man, Rhodes, out from the underbelly of society. She asks his name, and he answers, "Rhodes." "Rhodes what? . . . I see, just Rhodes." She takes the microphone and says, "His name is Rhodes but his last name is Lonesome." The spirit of the film is contained in that sentence. A small journalistic trick starts the whole machinery. The girl is honest and sensitive; nevertheless, all the fraudulence of the journalistic world is fully expressed in that little trick: "His last name is Lonesome." We await his reaction. He may become angry and stalk off. What happens is that he looks at the girl (Patricia Neal), is silent for a moment, hesitates, and then breaks into laughter. From this point on, whatever may happen, whatever his crimes and however innocent she may be, we are unable to pity the good girl; she represents corruption, he is the corrupted. It's he who has a right to complain right up to the end.

How will Rhodes act in front of a mike? He stutters, but he doesn't let it throw him. He offers improvised, offbeat little songs and familiar chatter, which his female listeners eat up; he talks to them about his mother, about laundry soaps that roughen their hands, about the dishes that have to be done again and again; he seduces, astonishes, wheedles, and little by little he has America safely in his pocket.

He moves from radio to television, his destiny lifts him higher and higher each day, though his natural spontaneity doesn't follow suit. He is frank; he puts his foot in his mouth; he invites a black woman on camera; he puts down the brand of mattress that is advertised on the show. In America, politics always overlaps show business, as show business overlaps advertising. As a result, Lonesome soon finds his support solicited by candidates for the presidency. The scene in which he educates an old politician-general is absolutely great; he tries to teach him how to be popular: Don't keep your lips closed, learn how to make fun of yourself, come on camera with a pet—a dog or cat—in your arms.

And, on every landing of this staircase to glory, there is a carnival atmosphere, valets, unmade beds, empty and hysterical frenzy. Girls sleep beneath his photograph. The more he is loved by the public, the more he is detested behind the scenes by all those who are living off his powerful personality. Neal, who is clearly his mistress, though deceived several times a day, hangs onto him with all her strength, and each time she manages to get him alone for five minutes, he becomes once again her fragile baby.

The end, which is of necessity somewhat contrived, as Rhodes is publicly unmasked, comes through as truly and authentically as the rest because it is verifiable that these inflated human sausages explode in short order, as the capricious career of Senator Joseph McCarthy (whom the authors had in mind) proves.

That *A Face in the Crowd* was directed by Elia Kazan says in itself that it is a film acted to perfection. Andy Griffith's interpretation is indeed a performance—but it belongs to Kazan; never has an actor been so completely carried by a director.

There's no denying that the film lacks consistency, but to hell with consistency! What's important is not its structure but its unassailable spirit, its power, and what I dare call its necessity. The usual fault with "honest" films is their softness, timidity and anesthetic neutrality. This film is passionate, exalted, fierce, as inexorable as a "Mythology" of Roland Barthes—and, like it, a pleasure for the mind.

—1957

STANLEY KUBRICK

Paths of Glory

I have just seen *Paths of Glory*, an independently produced American film that was shot in Belgium after the French authorities refused to allow it to be made in France. The filmmakers, I believe, have no intention of even submitting their work to the censorship commission.

Paths of Glory is adapted from a novel of the same title which is based on a true event—an event that, because the truth has been kept fairly quiet, mars the usual heroic history of World War I.

As the film opens, we are present at a conversation between two French generals portrayed by George Macready, with his scarred face, and the Hollywood actor of French descent, Adolphe Menjou (not his first role as turncoat, since it appears that, despite "public opinion," * he denounced his old friend Charlie Chaplin to the House Committee on Un-American Activities). Menjou, speaking for general headquarters, asks Macready to capture a trench network considered impregnable, whatever the cost. The real purpose is to quiet down the criticisms of the press. At first Macready refuses to sacrifice his men to no purpose, but then gives in when Menjou promises him personal advancement. As a result, the general deliberately sends an entire company of brave men to their death, led gallantly by their colonel, Kirk Douglas.

The trenches are, in truth, impregnable, and the attack scene be-

---

* *L'Opinion publique* is the French title of *A Woman of Paris* (1923), Charlie Chaplin's only dramatic film, which established Adolphe Menjou as the prototypical European seducer in Hollywood films.

comes a frightful, bloody slaughterhouse. This desperate advance is the best segment of the film. At the height of his madness, the general orders an artillery barrage on his own troops as they are pinned down by the enemy; the artillery officers refuse to carry out the order. When the few survivors return, the general orders three of them, chosen by lot, to be shot as examples of cowardice. The film ends with the scene of the execution; one of the three, mortally wounded in a prison fight in which he had attacked the chaplain, is tied down to a stretcher. Kirk Douglas, in a rage, decides to get the general; he muses aloud on the remark of Samuel Johnson: "Patriotism is the last refuge of scoundrels."

This film, which was withdrawn from a Brussels movie house at the demand of Belgian veterans, will never be released in France, not as long as there are soldiers around, in any case. It's a shame, because it is very beautiful from a number of points of view. It is admirably directed, even better than *The Killing*, with many very fluid long shots. The splendid camera work captures the plastic style of that epoch—we think of the war as it was pictured in the photographs of *L'Illustration*.

The film's weakness—what keeps it from being an irrefutable indictment—is a certain lack of psychological credibility in the "villains'" behavior. There were, certainly, during World War I, a number of similar "war crimes," barrages aimed at our own troops out of error and ignorance and confusion rather than from personal ambition. Cowardice is one thing, cynicism another. This general, who is both cowardly and cynical, is not very believable. The screenplay would have been strengthened if one officer, a coward, had panicked and ordered a barrage on his own troops, and another officer had had the three survivors shot as an example.

Similarly, Robert Aldrich in *Attack*, irritates us with psychological error when he has the frightened captain push over with his foot the revolver that had fallen to the ground, the gun the lieutenant whom he had betrayed was going to use to kill him. It's easier to forgive Kubrick a technical error, which is nevertheless obvious; Colonel Kirk Douglas several times salutes his superiors bareheaded!

I would have thought that Stanley Kubrick, who from the start had decided not to try to distribute his film in France, could have found better examples of military abuses in more recent wars. They abound: pillaging by French officers; the Indochina war with all the scandals we know so well; the Algerian war, with which, after Henri

Alleg's experience, the director could have posed his "question" more effectively.

In any case, despite its psychological oversimplification and its theatricality, *Paths of Glory* is an important film that establishes the talent and energy of a new American director, Stanley Kubrick.

—1958

CHARLES LAUGHTON

The Night of the Hunter

There are two things about *The Night of the Hunter* that make it an important event: it's the first time the American actor Charles Laughton (whose performances in *Mutiny on the Bounty, The Private Life of Henry VIII,* and *The Paradine Case* are quite rightly famous) has directed a film; and it marks the return to the screen of Lillian Gish, the greatest actress from the silent movies.

The subject matter disconcerts: a father is paid ten thousand dollars to commit a murder; he hides the money away in a rag doll, and makes his two small children swear to keep it absolutely secret until they are grown up and can use the money. Soon after, he is arrested, sentenced to death, and executed.

His former cellmate (Robert Mitchum), a preacher who is in jail for theft, is now released. To achieve his life's ambition to build a chapel, he determines to get hold of the ten thousand dollars. He only knows of its existence, not where it is hidden. He marries his cellmate's widow (Shelley Winters), refuses to sleep with her, and then kills her when she discovers him grilling her children to find out where the money is. The children, a boy and girl, terrified of their stepfather, flee with the doll in their arms. An old lady (Lillian Gish) takes them in and turns in Mitchum. The boy, reliving his father's arrest, rips the doll open and offers the money to the unlucky preacher-murderer right under the eyes of the police.

I should hasten to add that the preacher has "love" tattooed on the fingers of his right hand, and "hate" on the left, so you'll know that this is no ordinary film. *The Night of the Hunter* is a bizarre adventure; it must be regarded as cruel farce, or better still as a parable about the relativity of good and evil. All the characters are good, even the apparently evil preacher.

Screenplays such as this are not the way to launch your career as a Hollywood director. The film runs counter to the rules of commercialism; it will probably be Laughton's single experience as a director. It's a pity, for despite failures of style, *The Night of the Hunter* is immensely inventive. It's like a horrifying news item retold by small children. In spite of Stanley Cortez's gorgeous photography—Cortez is the man who shot *The Magnificent Ambersons* in such exquisite light—the production flounders between the Scandinavian and the German styles, touching expressionism but forgetting to keep on Griffith's track. Still, Laughton isn't afraid to knock over a few red lights and some traffic cops in his unusual film. It makes us fall in love again with an experimental cinema that truly *experiments,* and a cinema of discovery that, in fact, *discovers.*

—1956

MERVYN LeROY

The Bad Seed

The original source of this film is a novel by William March on which Maxwell Anderson based a play. John Lee Mahin's screenplay is taken, I believe, from the play rather than the novel. Mervyn LeRoy directed the film. Why has there been so much working over of a single property? Probably because there's a pretty successful idea here: an eight-year-old girl who skips happily through life to the tune of *Au clair de la lune* is actually a precocious criminal, the murderer of an old woman, a little boy, another old woman, and finally a derelict named, like the director, LeRoy.

If censorship were ever justified, it would be by prohibiting films like this where exhibitionism competes with vulgarity. This is an overblown and empty vehicle, a natural to make a lot of money for a handful of backers who rack their brains year in and year out to find a "good story," as if the heart of the seventh lively art were the lucky discovery or the clever idea, whereas the most beautiful and fascinating film of the year is the one with the fewest events, *Un Condamné à Mort s'est échappé.*

The Bad Seed is a useless movie, like many others, all the more scandalous because it hides its futility behind a situation of extreme seriousness, and childhood is made to pay the price. Despite its baseness, it's perfectly designed to please the snobs: "Go see *The Bad Seed,* darling, it's terrific."

To launch the film, the press was invited to a luncheon on the occasion of Mervyn LeRoy's arrival in Paris. I recall that I ate very well, but that's hardly the issue. I'd prefer never to have met Mervyn

LeRoy, since now I have no desire to see anything he'll ever make again.

LeRoy is a pioneer, an artisan who came to films at a time when directing was manual labor, a physical performance. He is one of those filmmakers who are always available. Having no preferences, no themes, no obsessions, no style and very little temperament, they never know what films to make. They make comedies, war films, Westerns, melodramas, musical comedies, and occasionally direct a screenplay that pretends to insight, like *The Bad Seed*, which will attract the critics' attention.

The Bad Seed is clumsily directed but well enough acted. The actors had played their roles during a long theater run and had grown into them. The little girl is quite good. But the movie is to be avoided, all the more so since the adaptation is careless. The ending, which follows neither the novel nor the play, is quite simply ridiculous.

—1957

ANATOLE LITVAK

Anastasia

As devoted as they are to liberty, equality and fraternity, the French are also devoted to ceremony. The coronation of a Queen of England increases the sale of television sets ten times. I'll never forget the sighs of pleasure that ran through the five thousand spectators in the Gaumont-Palace movie theater one day in 1948 when, in an American film directed by Otto Preminger, Charles II says to Linda Darnell: "Amber, you don't love me and you never have."

Of the fifty-two covers a year on *Paris Match*, how many do not show a princess, queen, empress, or someone of the sort? But this is 1957, when it is our governments that would cheerfully declare, "The State is us." Which brings me to *Anastasia*, a most mediocre film which has for its theme an historical enigma, one of the stupidest and emptiest subjects in a category that never fails to fill the theaters.

Docile slave that he is, Anatole Litvak directed *Anastasia* with laziness, lack of imagination and bad taste that even his advanced age cannot excuse. He was chosen to direct Ingrid Bergman, recently returned to Hollywood, because Vivien Leigh whom he directed badly in *The Deep Blue Sea* received an acting award at the Venice Festival (another proof that the jurors are charged with responsibility beyond their competence).

I have seen the best Ingrid Bergman films, those directed by Hitchcock, Rossellini, and Renoir, five and six times each. Those directors knew how to push her to her limit, each of them in a different direction. Elegant and agonized with Hitchcock, nervous and without makeup with Rossellini, a voluptuous Venus descended to earth with Renoir, in this film she is badly photographed and awkwardly costumed. It is the worst role she's ever had.

Anastasia pretends to draw us into the world of "if you were there." Don't go to see this cynical and mediocre film. Anatole Litvak despises you; despise him back.

—1957

JOSHUA LOGAN

Picnic

On a beautiful day, in the early afternoon, William Holden, a little the worse for wear, but sunburned and carefree, turns up in a small Kansas town. In exchange for a square meal, he agrees to dispose of an old woman's garbage and she offers to wash his shirt for him. So he is bare-chested when he meets a pretty girl (Kim Novak) and her younger sister (Susan Strasberg). Once the shirt is laundered he goes on his way to see Cliff Robertson, an old college chum, grown prosperous and now engaged to Novak.

The next day the annual day-long town picnic takes place, a genuine country fair. Holden shines. He's a marvelous dancer and the life of the party. In no time he has to resist the advances of a schoolteacher, Rosalind Russell, who's had too much to drink. As he begins to give in, she lashes out at him, he's disgusted with himself and retreats, only to be rescued by Kim Novak, in whose arms he spends the night. Then he gets into a fight with Robertson *and* the police as well and hops a freight train, begging Kim Novak to meet him in Tulsa. In spite of her mother's tearful pleas, she gets on a bus and follows him. The last scene—we see it from a helicopter—shows the freight train meeting the bus.

I don't know whether William Inge's play *Picnic* (he also wrote *Come Back, Little Sheba* and *Bus Stop*) is a work of genius, but Daniel Taradash's screenplay, directed by Joshua Logan (who also directed the Broadway production), comes close.

With this slice of life, Logan paints an unmalicious portrait of America almost without sentimentality. The starkness is slightly cruel, a bit like Jean Renoir. But if one has to see *Eléna et les hommes* a few times to uncover all its beauties, there is nothing in *Picnic* that is not clear from the first. This may be why *Picnic* is more seductive than Renoir's film. To push the comparison further, the films are also alike because they transcend simple stories told in images; they offer a view of love more authentic than we usually get to see on the screen—love that is carnal and, in the end, disenchanted.

Joshua Logan lets us take our pick of emotions in *Picnic:* you can laugh or cry at his characters' oddities; each notion carries both heads and tails, pathos and humor. If Logan were younger, *Picnic* would be a crueler film, but also more open and naïve. As he is forty-eight years old, robust, voluble, and in vigorous health, he wanted to dominate his subject and still treat it from a certain distance. I think it was all to the good.

In Logan we are introduced to a new and very great director. Jacques Rivette called him an "Elia Kazan multiplied by Robert Aldrich." And it's true: *Picnic* makes you think of *East of Eden* in its delicacy of detail and of *Vera Cruz* because of its brilliance. After seeing *Picnic*, which was his first film, and then *Bus Stop*, I find Logan such a gifted filmmaker (in terms of directing actors, camera work, screenplay amelioration, clarity) that I think the only way he could spoil a film would be on purpose. He is a pure director, a man we know will not be walked on. (He left Hollywood about 1935 when *History Is Made Tonight* was being shot. It would have been his first director's job.)

Picnic, which I prefer to *Bus Stop*, is always inventive; every image is filled with energy. Logan wills us to laugh during a sad scene and, conversely, to feel saddened during a funny one. He leads us by the nose and the audiences that fill the theaters can only marvel at it.

—1955

SIDNEY LUMET

Twelve Angry Men

There's the screenplay. Let's talk about it. It's clever, in the best sense of the word, and we at the *Cahiers* don't have much use for movies constructed on good ideas, on astuteness, ingenuity. Still, the script of *Twelve Angry Men* discourages criticism: 1) we are present at a deliberation with a strict continuity of time, place, and action, and experience intensely the feeling, not of something done, but of something being done. It's a triumph of the television style; 2) the stereotyping of the jurors is so nuanced that instead of twelve "specimens," we have only six, each represented twice: two intellectuals, two laborers, two bigots, two smokers, two scrupulous types, two who are absolutely "proper." Each character trades details with an almost identical counterpart, rather than displaying the broad and somewhat strained strokes that are usual in this sort of "conflict cinema."

Many films (some of the best) are boring and make you feel as if you might want to leave to get a drink or look for an available woman. This movie makes it increasingly more difficult to leave as the story unfolds; a man's life is at stake, and only a unanimous verdict can save him from death. One by one the jurors relent under the urgent pleading of Henry Fonda, until only the most obdurate remains unmoved. You're surprised to find yourself rooting for him in the darkness. The last three jurors give in together. What a fantastic idea it was—the most hesitant one changes his mind, becoming a lever on the other two, thus making a verdict of "not guilty" possible.

It's a screenwriter's film, and what an author! Justice is done; it is proven that we are all murderers. Lumet, in his first film, shows himself a director of more than ordinary gifts. The movie must have started as a sort of exercise, but the exercise turned into a courageous, powerful, intelligent, and idealistic film, both generous and moving. We must take this director seriously.

—1957

JOSEPH MANKIEWICZ

The Barefoot Contessa

I recently saw *A Letter to Three Wives* for the second time and I realize that I can never ignore Joseph Mankiewicz again. Its story is brilliant, intelligent and elegant, tasteful and refined, packaged with an almost eerie precision, style, and professionalism. The actors are directed with an extravagant theatricalism. Mankiewicz has a sure instinct for extending his shots and using special effects in a way we don't expect anymore except with Cukor. This is Mankiewicz' art. He's in control of his genre—dramatic comedy—and we shall leave aside its limitations for now, especially since its good qualities are too often ignored.

The Barefoot Contessa is perplexing. We leave it, uncertain that we have understood everything, but unsure that there was, in fact, more to understand. We don't know what the author was up to. But what is beyond doubt is its total sincerity, novelty, daring, and fascination. Mankiewicz has been reproached as the favorite director of the snobs, but it's the fashionable viewers (the very ones who made *All About Eve* a success) who gleefully hiss each evening at the Countess, while the housewives on the Place Blanche explain it to their husbands: "That one, yes, the Count. Well, he's impotent. . . ." And the husbands answer, "Oh, I see."

After the failure of his novel *Armance*, whose theme was impotence, Stendhal remarked, "Lack of style caused the vulgar not to appreciate my novel. Too bad for them." He could have been responding to Sainte-Beuve: "This basically enigmatic novel which lacks truth in every detail demonstrates neither invention nor genius."

The one sure thing about Mankiewicz's film is that he is cursing the cliques of Hollywood, of the idle, of the Riviera. It's not an indulgent satire like his earlier films. This time he portrays a furious hatred of vulgarity. All right as far as that goes, but what about the Countess?

Three American movie executives discover an extraordinary and marvelous Spanish dancer, Maria Vargas (Ava Gardner). They bring her to Hollywood and "launch" her as a star. The producer, Kirk (Warren Stevens), a dictator, a sexist, and a bigot, courts her futilely. She despises him and finds her lovers among truck drivers, gypsies, guitarists, and handsome young men.

At a certain point, to humiliate Kirk, Maria agrees to go for a cruise along the Riviera with Bravano, a South American multimillionaire. Bravano (Marius Goering) won't have any more luck than Kirk, but he comforts himself with the thought that everybody will think he's Maria's lover. Bravano turns out to be a weird imbecile and Maria leaves him for Count Vincenzo Torlato-Favrini (Rossano Brazzi) whom she falls in love with and who is in love with her. They marry. Then the Count tells his bride that he cannot "love her with all his heart," since he has been mutilated in the war. Maria makes a daring resolution: the most beautiful gift she can offer her husband is a child. She is about to accomplish her purpose when her husband surprises her and kills her, along with her dupe.

The pivotal scene occurs in the cemetery in the rain, as the great star is buried. The story line is related by a number of the characters, among them the director Harry Dawes (Humphrey Bogart), who was Maria's sole friend and confidant. He has arrived on the scene too late to make things right though he had anticipated how it would all end.

It would be off the mark to reproach Mankiewicz for opening up a number of themes without grappling with any of them since his idea was not so much to make a satire about Hollywood (although it is the most vicious one ever made), or a film about impotence (which is, of course, symbolic), or a guide to the Riviera and its denizens as to paint one of the most beautiful portraits of woman ever filmed, in the person of Ava Gardner, Hollywood's most exquisitely beautiful actress.

Mankiewicz places his heroine—wild, natural, enigmatic—in four spots, in different life situations, faced with contradictory personalities, in order to watch her reactions and to visualize the separate moralities a famous star creates around her.

Maria Vargas is not, as some reviews have said, a nymphomaniac. It's not perversion that pushes her into the arms of lower-class men, but profound disgust, really a physical repulsion, for the princes of her world, the producers, the millionaires, the displaced and idle kings. In her eyes they are the "sick" ones. Their infirmity is made concrete in the impotence of Vincenzo, the last count of an illustrious line. (It is no accident that his sister, Valentina Cortese, is also sterile.) Since it is his fate to find first love with this "child of nature," it is reasonable that Vargas, to assure Vincenzo's happiness, will react with an extravagance that matches his extravagant personality.

This is not a film to be picked apart; either one rejects it or accepts it whole. I myself accept and value it for its freshness, intelligence, and beauty. The opening credits announce a production of "Figaro Incorporated," printed over a reproduction of "L'Indifférent," with a few bars of *The Marriage of Figaro* in the background. Mankiewicz' taste for the eighteenth century evidently moved him to place this film he wrote, directed, and produced, under the triple patronage of Beaumarchais, Watteau and Mozart. (Obviously, *The Barefoot Contessa*, because of its originality of plot and the fierceness of its attack on Hollywood, could never have been produced by a Zanuck or a Hughes.) It is a daring, novel, and most satisfying venture, and Mankiewicz uses it to settle scores with the Hollywood which condemned him to polishing furniture when he had dreamed of breaking down walls.

Thanks to the success of his psychological comedies, Mankiewicz had assured himself a privileged place in Hollywood, which makes it all the more praiseworthy to have risked such originality. *The Barefoot Contessa*, we can be sure, is hardly going to be welcomed by the same people who sang the praises of his earlier pleasant, intelligent, but more accessible films: *All About Eve, A Letter to Three Wives, Five Fingers*. When the moviegoers on the Champs-Elysées snicker as a man admits physical impotence to a woman, it says a great deal about the public's responsibility for the banality and vulgarity of the average screenplay. It's one more proof that the time has not come for adapting Stendhal's *Armance*. In *The Red and the Black*, Claude Autant-Lara did not dare film Mathilde holding the severed head of Julien Sorel on her lap. Mankiewicz is more Stendhalian. The Countess' last try—to have a baby by the chauffeur so that she can offer it to her husband—would be in character for Mathilde de la Môle.

It was wrong to bill *Barefoot Contessa* as a film *à clef*. It's easy to recognize the two producers who are the models for the demagoguery, bigotry, and lewdness of the producer in the film, but Maria Vargas is no more Rita Hayworth than Bravano is Ali Khan. What is more likely is that Mankiewicz depicts himself in the personality of the director, played so well by Humphrey Bogart.

A subtle and intelligent film, beautifully directed and acted, it is the best thing around right now.

—1955

ANTHONY MANN

Men in War

War movies are a Hollywood specialty. The commercial success of this kind of film is more certain than any other; as a result, you don't have to make too many concessions. And if the screenplay isn't too subversive, it's possible to obtain the cooperation of the Armed Forces to borrow men, materiel, munitions, horses, airplanes, etcetera. After *The Big Knife* failed commercially, Robert Aldrich refloated his production company with *Attack*. If it is well conceived, a war movie can be made for peanuts: a few men in the sun in the underbrush, a small patrol, a few bayonets, a dozen helmets, fake rifles, and, if you don't need the Army's help, you can make an antimilitarist, or at least an antiwar, film.

All this is pertinent to *Men in War*, Anthony Mann's latest film—and his favorite one, he said recently. It also marks the debut of a young actor, Aldo Ray, who will soon give us his view on war with *Bitter Victory*.

I rate *Men in War* very highly, higher than *Attack*. (We have to keep seeing certain films and revising our judgments.) With the same methods at his disposal as Aldrich, Anthony Mann takes them further, employs purer, less theatrical approaches. There is no sadism, nothing gratuitous, just a strong, solid, strict, implacable story.

A small patrol in Korea is commanded by a lieutenant, Robert Ryan, humane, intelligent, courageous, a good officer. A jeep driven by a rough, cynical sergeant arrives. Next to him, in utter silence, sits a colonel, who appears to be completely wiped out, and whom the sergeant appears to idolize, lighting his cigarettes, keeping him neat, whispering to him, watching over him like a baby or an old grandmother.

The colonel remains in that state, and the film revolves around the lieutenant and the sergeant, two distinct types of fighters—the intelligent, poised, logical lieutenant (Ryan), and the sergeant (Ray), who acts on instinct but is stronger, probably because he knows the terrain better. If a blade of grass moves, he fires without a second thought. There is no question of taking prisoners. A character alternately fascinating and repugnant, he is magnificently played by Ray.

The ending resembles *Bandera*, but is even more sober: there are only two survivors, the two main characters, surrounded by corpses.

Unless I am mistaken, it has been a long while since Anthony Mann has shot in black and white, but Ernest Haller's magnificent photography removes any need for regret. At this moment Mann is the American director who is most sensitive to nature. In *Men in War*, each blade of grass, each bush, every branch of a tree, every ray of sunlight is given the same emotional weight as a rumbling tank. Besides, there are no tanks in *Men in War*—just a handful of men walking the trails.

Morally, the story is very fine, noble, irreproachable, concerned simply with man, his fears and sweat, his shoes and cigarettes. To the obvious virtues of this beautiful work we must add that there is the quality of what it is not—the absence of certain clichés which are usually considered essential to this kind of film: the stereotypes, the soldier who makes his buddies laugh with dumb remarks, the one who spends all his time reading his wife's letters.

It should be pointed out that the screenplay is signed by Philip Yordan, the author of *Johnny Guitar*, one of the most gifted writers in Hollywood.

—1957

ROBERT MULLIGAN

Fear Strikes Out

Shown as a "filler" before the holidays, one of the best American films of this year is about to disappear without notice. This is *Fear Strikes Out*, the first film of a young American filmmaker, Robert Mulligan. Like Sidney Lumet, he comes to movies from television, but you'd have to be told that to know it. *Fear Strikes Out*, as distinct from *Twelve Angry Men*, is utterly cinematic. Its realism, the truth of its setting and its facts, and the stylization of the acting put it in the "New York school," the style imposed by Elia Kazan in his most recent films, a deliberately anti-Hollywood manner.

Fear Strikes Out is the story of a young boy through whom his father acts out all his dreams of being a baseball player. He trains his son, overworks him, forces him into precociousness until he becomes a "pro." He never compliments the boy; indeed, he's always finding something to carp at. He is the perfectionist ever thirsting after the unattainable. Predictably the young champion's nerves give out, and one day he breaks down. The film ends with his first session of psychoanalysis, which is described at length and in detail on screen, precise and lifelike, remarkably exact and well directed.

It is rare to see a first film so free of faults and bombast. Everything is in proportion; no one scene is less good than another in this serene, calm, frank film, whose high quality would suggest long and solid experience.

The undertaking rests squarely on the broad shoulders of Karl Malden, the father, and on the considerably frailer shoulders of the young actor Anthony Perkins, who combines the simplicity of the young stars of an older generation, Jimmy Stewart and Gary Cooper, with the physical modernity of the Brandos and James Deans, without ever resorting to trickiness or exhibitionism.

Fear Strikes Out is a bitter and disillusioned film that doesn't make you want to live in America. But if there were French directors as lucid and talented as Mulligan, as capable of telling something more than anecdotes, the image of our country on the screen would be a bit less oversimplified.

—1958

OTTO PREMINGER

Bonjour Tristesse

I can spare the reader the usual speech about faithful or unfaithful adaptation, since I haven't read Françoise Sagan's *Bonjour Tristesse,* or her two other novels. Each of her published interviews is more remarkable than the previous one; rich in ideas, they show a lucidity, tact, and cool intelligence that belong more to the essayist than to the novelist.

In short, what Sagan thinks interests me more than what she invents, and what she is more than what she does. A solemn Mademoiselle Teste * slumbers within her, and her efforts to kill the marionette make Sagan infinitely more likeable than her fellow novelists who pretend to be the dupes of their laborious tales.

Otto Preminger, on the other hand, seems to me more valuable for what he does rather than for what he is. To the interviewer who loves films he offers nothing beyond commonplaces about Catholic censorship, the profitability of films, the box-office draw of certain stars. A famous and envied businessman and former actor, this fifty-year-old Viennese is also an artist, the kind that is often called, with a slightly pejorative meaning, a formalist. This director, and he is nothing if not that—he can bring order into any piece of confusion—is as little interested as a blood donor in knowing who is the beneficiary of the transfusion.

So, if Françoise Sagan is "of her age," the twentieth century and

* A reference to Valéry's *La Soirée avec Monsieur Teste;* T. is "the monster of the intellect who 'ne connait que deux valeurs . . . le possible et l'impossible.' . . ."— *Oxford Companion to French Literature.* Trans.

its thinkers, Otto Preminger is a man of a hundred years ago, a man of instinct, an inspired artist whose work defies scientific exegesis.

Let the fervent admirers of the novel *Bonjour Tristesse* howl at its betrayal by the film. That is their right. Just as it is mine to prefer a work by Preminger alone to one of those collective enterprises that end by being anonymous, like one I shall not name,* which we don't know whether to attribute to Pierre Boulle, David Lean, Alec Guinness, or Sam Spiegel.

Have you noticed that the inherent sterility of their function leads critics always to pay more attention to the character than to the actor who plays him? It is certainly also a pretentious sterility that leads them to prefer the screenplay to the film itself, to the intentions rather than the result, the idea to the deed, in short, the abstract to the concrete. Yet, a director must work with what military strategists call the "human matériel." A novelist talking about "his" characters has often struck me as ridiculous, but a filmmaker talking about his actors, never. This is probably why I prefer cinema to literature.

Cinema is an art of the woman, that is, of the actress. The director's work consists in getting pretty women to do pretty things. For me, the great moments of cinema are when the director's gifts mesh with the gifts of an actress: Griffith and Lillian Gish, Sternberg and Marlene Dietrich, Fritz Lang and Joan Bennett, Renoir and Simone Simon, Hitchcock and Joan Fontaine, Rossellini and Anna Magnani, Ophuls and Danielle Darrieux, Fellini and Giulietta Masina, Vadim and Brigitte Bardot. Now we can add Preminger and Jean Seberg to the list.

When he organized the *"Bonjour Tristesse* Competition," Preminger was not looking for Cecile, he was looking for Jean Seberg. And, when he had found her, it wasn't a question of whether she was worthy of Cecile, but whether Cecile was worthy of being made real by Jean Seberg. So, faithful or not, Arthur Laurents' adaptation consists of leaning toward what I shall call, in the best sense of the word, the "exhibition" of Jean Seberg, or if you prefer, bringing out her strong points, setting her in motion, placing her in her setting.

The automobile racers of Le Mans obviously don't risk their necks for the people who come to see them, and yet, do they not put on quite a show? Preminger is like them: he offers us a show, but it stays his secret, the show concerns only him.

Preminger is not a very commercial filmmaker, probably because

* *The Bridge on the River Kwai*—Ed.

he devotes himself to a search for a bit of truth that is particularly well hidden, almost imperceptible, the truth that is hidden in looks, gestures, attitudes. If he is happy working in the realm of scandal (recall his films: *Forever Amber, The Moon Is Blue, Carmen Jones, The Man with the Golden Arm*), it is because he can safeguard his purity better that way. With this loving painter of small unstriking detail, the magnificence of the frame accents the deliberate insignificance of the design. Preminger's pretentious openings are deliberate jokes. In this case, the combination of the names of Sagan, Juliette Greco (who sings "Bonjour Tristesse"!!) and Georges Auric is a cynical gag. If Preminger were making *Bonjour Tristesse* today, he'd probably have Yves Saint-Laurent do the costumes and Bernard Buffet the decor.

Another gag: David Niven, sitting on the beach, opens a copy of *Elle*. This is an amiable greeting to Pierre Lazareff, whose sumptuous villa is, after Seberg, the star of the film. But that isn't all: on the cover of *Elle* is a photograph of Christine Carrère, chosen by Fox to star in *A Certain Smile*, a film based on another Sagan novel, which will certainly be massacred by that obtuse drone, Jean Negulesco. The mischievous Otto is signaling Fox: "Sorry about that, old boy, but I know my film will be out before yours."

When I read the early notices of Sagan's first novel, I was struck by the resemblances to and analogies with an American film, *Angel Face*. In this film, like *Bonjour Tristesse* also produced and directed by Preminger, the exquisite Jean Simmons is living a boring life in a luxurious mansion with a father whom she adores and a killjoy stepmother. She intends to get Robert Mitchum, whom she has hired as chauffeur and lover, to murder her stepmother. In the end, unknown to Mitchum, she herself causes a fatal car accident in which not only the hated stepmother but also the adored father die. The lovers are both accused, and they get married in prison on the advice of their lawyer, who sees this as their only hope for acquittal.

Without going so far as to suggest that Sagan's first novel was inspired by *Angel Face*, it is clear that *Bonjour Tristesse* immediately interested Preminger, who bought the film rights three months later from Ray Ventura, an inspired college student who pocketed in passing a goodly sum as payment for having a good nose for that sort of thing. This is why it's stupid to write that Preminger was not the man to make *Bonjour Tristesse*. The film is only a remake, a pretext to embroider on his favorite theme: the child-woman and her sadness at approaching age. I would even suggest that *Saint Joan* and *Bonjour Tristesse* complement each other perfectly. In the first, the English land in France, and Joan is burned; in the second, the same character, one year later, doesn't give herself to the first Bishop Cauchon who comes along, but defends herself, attacks the Englishwoman Deborah Kerr, and kicks her out of France.

I haven't really analyzed the film. Is it my fault if it is obscure in mysterious ways? It would seem that Preminger, who has proved himself an admirable storyteller ten times over, doesn't want to tell us anything this time, only wants to show, almost without imposing any order, things that interest him just as they are. He does nothing to make us believe in this frail, simple, and basically incredible tale. Worse, he cuts it up, taking us from a colored past to bathe us in a black-and-white present. Does his Riviera with its Provençal folk dancers strike you as ridiculous? Don't forget that two years ago, when Preminger was named to the Cannes Festival jury, he had to watch the beach promenade of a "War of the Flowers" that was ten times more ridiculous. His vision of Saint-Tropez is not overly severe. *Bonjour Tristesse* is not France naïvely seen by an American, but France shown to Americans as they like to see it by a sharp and disdainful observer.

The acting, which is uneven, is nonetheless the essential point of the film. In any case, when Jean Seberg is on the screen, which is all the time, you can't look at anything else. Her every movement is graceful, each glance is precise. The shape of her head, her silhouette, her walk, everything is perfect; this kind of sex appeal hasn't been seen on the screen. It is designed, controlled, directed to the nth degree by her director, who is, they say, her fiancé. I wouldn't be surprised, given the kind of love one needs to obtain such perfection. In the blue shorts slit on the side, in pirate pantaloons, in a skirt, an evening gown, a bathing suit, a man's shirt with the shirttails out, or tied in front over her stomach, or wearing a corsage and behaving herself (but not for long), Jean Seberg, short blond hair on a pharaoh's skull, wide-open blue eyes with a glint of boyish malice, carries the entire weight of this film on her tiny shoulders. It is Otto Preminger's love poem to her.

—1958

NICHOLAS RAY

Johnny Guitar

We discovered Nicholas Ray about seven or eight years ago with *Knock on Any Door*. Then, at the film festival, "Rendezvous de Biarritz," there was the dazzling confirmation of *They Live By Night*, which is still his best film. Then followed, though unnoticed in Paris, *In a Lonely Place, On Dangerous Ground, The Lusty Men*, and now, *Johnny Guitar*.

A young American filmmaker—of the generation of Robert Wise, Jules Dassin, Joseph Losey—Nicholas Raymond Kienzle is an *auteur* in the best sense of the word. All his films tell the same story: the violent man who wants to renounce violence and his relationship with a morally stronger woman. Ray's constant hero, the bully, is a weak man-child, when he is not simply a child. He is wrapped in moral solitude, always hunted, sometimes lynched. Those who have seen the films I have just mentioned can multiply and enrich these connections for themselves; the others will simply have to take my word for it.

Johnny Guitar is not far from being its author's best film. Ray's films usually bore the public because of their leisurely pace, their seriousness, their realism—the realism of words and poetic insights, much like Cocteau. This film is a string of preciosity, truer than the truth. The cowboys in *Johnny Guitar*, ridiculously, call each other "monsieur" in the dubbed French version, which is superior for once to the subtitled version because it lets us see the film's theatricality better. We already have learned that this Western was shockingly extravagant. *Johnny Guitar* is a phony Western, but not an "intellectual" one. It is dreamed, a fairy tale, a hallucinatory Western. It was only a step from the dream to Freud, which our Anglo-Saxon colleagues took up when they began talking about "psychoanalytic Westerns." But the qualities of Ray's film are something different, not very visible perhaps to those who have never looked through a camera's viewer. We are going to try, as opposed to a different form of criticism, to trace the sources of this cinematic creation. Contrary to André Bazin, I believe it is important for a director to be able to recognize himself in the portrait of him and his films that one draws.

Insofar as we can divide filmmakers into two groups, the cerebral and the instinctual, I would certainly classify Ray in the second, the school of sincerity and sensitivity. And yet, we sense in him an intellectual who can abstract everything that does not come from the heart. He is not a particularly great technician, but what is clear is that his aim is less to achieve the traditional, universal success of his films than to give each shot a certain emotional quality. *Johnny Guitar* was "made" rather hastily, out of very long scenes that were cut up into ten segments. The editing is jerky, but what interests us is something else: for example, an extraordinarily beautiful placement of individuals in a certain setting. (The members of the patrol at Vienna's, for example, arrange themselves in the *V* of migratory birds.)

There are two films in *Johnny Guitar:* Ray's recurring theme—the relationships among the two men and two women, the violence and bitterness—and an extravagant catch-all done in Joseph von Sternberg style, a style which is absolutely foreign to Ray's work, but which in this case is no less interesting. For instance, we watch Joan Crawford, in a white dress, playing the piano in a cavernous saloon, with a candlestick and a pistol beside her. *Johnny Guitar* is the *Beauty and the Beast* of Westerns, a Western dream. The cowboys vanish and die with the grace of ballerinas. The bold, violent color (by Trucolor) contributes to the sense of strangeness; the hues are vivid, sometimes very beautiful, always unexpected.

The public on the Champs-Elysées wasn't mistaken to snicker at *Johnny Guitar.* In five years they'll be crowding into the Cinéma d'Essai to applaud it (as they did the *Les Dames du Bois de Boulogne*). The audience in Montmartre received the dubbed version very well. For the Champs-Elysées crowd, it lacks Huston's wink.

Johnny Guitar was made to order for Joan Crawford, as *Rancho Notorious* was made by Fritz Lang for Marlene Dietrich. Crawford used to be one of the most beautiful women in Hollywood. Now she is beyond considerations of beauty. She has become unreal, a phantom of herself. Whiteness has invaded her eyes, muscles have taken over her face, a will of iron behind a face of steel. She is a phenomenon. She is becoming more manly as she grows older. Her clipped, tense acting, pushed almost to paroxysm by Ray, is in itself a strange and fascinating spectacle.

Ray is a kind of Hollywood Rossellini. Like Rossellini, he never explains, never underscores his meaning. He makes outlines rather than films. Another point they have in common is that Ray is horrified by the death of children. Nicholas Ray lovingly fashions pretty little objects out of holly wood. Down with the amateur! There are no Ray films that do not have a scene at the close of day; he is the poet of nightfall, and of course everything is permitted in Hollywood except poetry. So, in Hollywood, a Howard Hawks arrives on the scene and takes his time, flirts with tradition in order to flout it, and always triumphs. Ray is incapable of getting along with the devil, and when he tries to make a pact for profit, he is defeated before the fight even begins.

Hawks and Ray are opposites, a little bit as Castellani and Rossellini are. In Hawks we see the triumph of the mind; in Nick Ray, the triumph of the heart. One can argue against Hawks and for Ray— or the other way around; one can condemn *Big Sky* in the name of *Johnny Guitar* or accept them both. But anyone who rejects either should never go to the movies again, never see any more films. Such people will never recognize inspiration, poetic intuition, or a framed picture, a shot, an idea, a good film, or even cinema itself.

—1955

Bigger Than Life

If the film he prefers is *Rebel Without a Cause*, which is all his, Nicholas Ray seems satisfied enough with *Bigger Than Life*, whose screenplay, attributed to Cyril Hume and Richard Maibaum in the opening credits, was almost entirely rewritten by Clifford Odets, Gavin Lambert and himself.

The enormous freedom Ray enjoyed in making *Bigger Than Life* was undoubtedly due to the fact that the producer, James Mason, was also the star of the film. He bought the rights to the story, which had appeared in *The New Yorker,* and which is based on a true incident: a teacher suffering from an arterial inflammation was being treated with cortisone, a new medicine still in the experimental stage but already being hailed as a "miracle drug." Despite the fact that he was scrupulous about the dosage, he gradually succumbed to megalomania. He became harsh, excitable, paranoid, manic; he threw himself feverishly into utopian projects to reform education; he became a domestic tyrant, terrorizing all around him until he was taken off to a hospital and given a new treatment.

In their first screenplay, Hume and Maibaum made the hero a cousin of Jekyll and Hyde. During the day he was perfectly balanced; at night he was a terrifying brute who struck out at everything. Ray preferred to go back to the true story and push it as far as possible dramatically.

An underpaid teacher, Ed Avery (James Mason), works several nights a week as a switchboard operator in a taxi garage unknown to his wife and son. As a result of overwork, he falls ill with an inflammation of the arteries and is treated with cortisone. Under pressure from the medical associations, which are very powerful in the United States and were extremely hostile to the film, Ray had to change one detail. In the film, Avery increases the prescribed dosage in order to attain the euphoric state the cortisone brings him. Soon he begins using it as a narcotic.

His behavior changes; he develops a self-assured and self-satisfied manner that he had never shown before. One day, in a high-fashion salon, he makes his wife buy two dresses he hasn't got the money to pay for. He becomes critical of everybody and everything, arrogant, and extremely irritable.

Soon, as in the real story, he claims to have discovered his mission: he must reform education. He will write a series of important articles. He tries out his new principles of education on his young son; he is going to make him a genius. A veritable nightmare for the mother and son begins. The family scenes become increasingly violent. One day, Avery discovers his son trying to throw out the vials of cortisone. Shortly after that, upon hearing a sermon in church on Abraham, he decides he is a theologian and makes up his mind to imitate the deed of the Father of faith with his own son. His wife tries to prevent him: "God didn't want Abraham to sacrifice his son." Avery responds exaltedly, "God was wrong." But, at the moment when he sets out to sacrifice his son, a scissors in his hand, he is seized with a fainting spell. God has intervened, and Avery sees a spinning ball of fire, as in Genesis: "When the sun set and the darkness came, a fire passed between the parted animals." When Avery comes to, he is restrained by one of the neighbors, and a little later we see his wife and son visit him at a hospital from which he will emerge cured.

This is the screenplay which a number of my colleagues judged unconvincing after its presentation at the Venice festival. They argued that you cannot construct a tragedy out of as ordinary an incident as a man taking an overdose of cortisone. In fact, Ray did not want to make a tragedy, or even tell a believable psychological story. He conceived his film as a fable. He filmed an idea, a process of reasoning, a supposition. It could have been alcohol instead of cortisone. The prime consideration is not the pretext but the way it is worked out.

Ray wanted to show the public that it is wrong to believe in medical miracles and "miracle drugs," since any one of them, just like the atom, can both save and destroy. Science has its limits and it is unwise to put blind faith in it. The only thing he couldn't show openly was his own antipathy for doctors. Nonetheless, he filmed the doctors in groups of three, and framed them like gangsters in crime films. He had them speak arrogantly in a pedantic and detached manner. Had he wished to make his unusual message more easily acceptable, Ray could have enclosed the entire film in a dream: the teacher would awaken having dreamed the adventure, including his wish to kill his son. The public would have received the film more warmly, but he would have given in to the worst possible film convention, and the critics would still have sneered.

The screenplay of *Bigger Than Life* is intelligent, subtle, and completely logical. The cortisone wasn't responsible for Avery's megalomania; it simply revealed it. From the outset, the authors offer hints: travel posters cover the walls of the Avery house; before his first giddy spell he says to his wife, "We're dull, you know."

Even when he feels lucid, he really is dull, and yet, just as a drunkard sometimes does, he still states a number of truths. The marvelous thing is that he is never completely wrong or right. This is best illustrated in a meeting with the parents of the pupils. Avery gets up to explain to the parents that the children they are so proud of are at the evolutionary stage of chimpanzees. An offended woman stalks from the room in fury. Avery takes a puff of his cigarette, smiles with satisfaction, and goes on with his talk, which slowly takes on fascist overtones. "The truth is that we need a leader." With that, a great bear of a man with a mustache comes up to Avery, his eyes on fire. "That's what I like to hear. Bravo!" Truths, countertruths, that's what the whole film is about. It is sprinkled throughout with touches of a rather restrained black humor.

In his first films Ray treated violence and the moral solitude of the violent with a certain approval. Gradually he has set out to demonstrate the vanity of violence and the importance of clearheadedness. Now, he gives us again the portrait of a man whose intransigence leads him to moral solitude, but, although he shows him as wrong, he nevertheless, while demonstrating the emptiness of violence, also offers proof that lucidity is not an end in itself; his hero is an escapee from the hell of logic.

Although the essence of the film belongs in the category of fable rather than psychology, it is extraordinarily accurate to the last detail. Rather than inventing crises, the authors preferred to portray the evolution of Avery's illness by showing us how he reacted to everyday occurrences. One morning Avery takes the milkman aside and accuses him of deliberately rattling the milk bottles in the metal case to bother him, to keep him from working, probably out of jealousy.

The character of Avery is close to Francesco in Buñuel's *El*, and the two films bear other bonds of kinship as well. The scene in which Avery gazes with satisfaction into the bathroom mirror while his wife brings up hot water for his bath, kettle by kettle, could be out of the Buñuel film.

Mason's acting has extraordinary precision. Under Ray's masterful direction, he is given three or four of the most beautiful face closeups I have had the chance to see since the advent of CinemaScope. The trenchant direction imposes a terrific pace. Short scenes sweep across the screen, all concerned with Ed Avery's deterioration. *Bigger Than Life* is the very opposite of a decorative film, but the slightest detail— clothing, an accessory, a stance—has an overwhelming beauty.

There is another aspect of Ray's film that rings profoundly true. Even if one refused to follow the author in the upheavals of his screenplay (and why refuse?), we still have to admire one thing: this is the first time the relationship of an intellectual with his simpler wife has been depicted on the screen with an almost shocking clarity and frankness. For the first time we see the intellectual at home, confident of the superiority of his vocabulary, knowing that his understanding of dialectics works in his favor vis-à-vis his wife, who *feels* things but has given up trying to express them, since she cannot handle the language. She is, like many women, intuitive, governed above all by love and sensitivity. All sorts of variations on this theme make *Bigger Than Life*, even aside from its exceptional story, an excellent portrait of marriage.

A film of implacable logic and sanity, *Bigger Than Life* uses those very qualities as targets, and scores a bull's-eye in every frame.

If *Bigger Than Life* throws some people off, it's because Ray's films resemble each other too much for the newest one to display its meaning immediately. But isn't the critic's duty to serve as intermediary between the authors of such a film and the audience it's aimed at?

—1957

DOUGLAS SIRK

Written on the Wind

Publishers of "true romance" wring hearts like so many sponges. "Heart" . . . "Dreams" . . . "Secrets" . . . "The Two of Us" . . . "Intimate." For a dollar and a half, young lady, you can have six hours of reading while luxuriating in your tears. The little orphan who has been taken in by her godfather, a simple Breton fisherman living on a rock whipped by the fierce waves of the Channel, has been noticed by Norbert de la Globule, the son of the manor, called Monsieur Norbert around here. A sweet idyl.

There is a certain style and tone in these famous "true romance" magazines that I regret not to find more often in minor movies. A good melodrama, filmed by a director who is not afraid of emotional upheavals, would be closer to Balzac than Charles Spaak's *Crime and Punishment* is to Dostoevsky.

All of which brings me to *Written on the Wind*, the best work that has been done in this direction; both visually and intellectually, it is an exact equivalent of a very good "photo-novel" in color.

Robert Stack, who plays the alcoholic son of a wealthy oilman, and his boyhood friend, Rock Hudson, his father's trusted adviser, meet Lauren Bacall, a secretary. Stack marries Bacall and she cures him both of his inferiority complex and his drinking. Stack's sister, Dorothy Malone, a nymphomaniac, is hopelessly in love with the upright Rock Hudson, who is, of course, in love with Lauren Bacall, his best friend's wife.

Stack, his body poisoned by alcohol, learns from his doctor that he is partially impotent, more exactly, intermittently sterile. So, when

Lauren Bacall tells him one evening that she is pregnant, he thinks he has been betrayed by his friend. He is encouraged in this belief by his malevolent sister who becomes more and more disturbed as the movie progresses. There are fistfights, pistol shots, breathtaking chases in the night, bottles emptied and then broken. In the end, Stack kills himself by accident, the old trick of confusion working in favor of disarmament. The beautiful Dorothy redeems her ten years of debauchery by telling the truth in court, so that Rock Hudson and Lauren Bacall, a beautiful widow indeed, can satisfy their perfect love.

At the end, Douglas Sirk, who is a villain, shows us Dorothy Malone, the nymphomaniac, dressed in a skin-tight suit, sitting beside her father's fireplace, caressing a minature gold oil derrick, the symbol of her new preoccupation: the black gold may flow instead of sperm, but Oedipus will always be there!

Sirk is no newcomer. A Dane, born at the turn of the century in Skagen, he was a theater director in Berlin and he made films in Germany, Spain, and Australia before reaching Hollywood, where he matured with excellent little films, which Parisian film lovers know well: *Summer Storm; Lured; Sleep, My Love; Shockproof; Thunder on the Hill; Mystery Submarine;* and *Captain Lightfoot.* All these movies, none of which achieved the virtuosity of his latest, had the same precision and the same fantasy. This is moviemaking unashamed of what it is, with no complexes, no hesitations, simply good workmanship.

But it is in visual terms that *Written on the Wind* merits our attention. In the old days critics used to say, "There will be good color films when painters get involved." Nonsense! The quality of movie color has nothing to do with the painter's taste, nor even, for that matter, with good taste. We watch Stack in the half-shadow of a *blue* bedroom, watch him dash into a *red* corridor and jump into a *yellow* taxi which lets him out in front of a *steel-gray* airplane. All these hues are vivid and frank, varnished and lacquered to such a degree that a painter would scream. But they are the colors of the twentieth century, the colors of America, the colors of the luxury civilization, the industrial colors that remind us that we live in the age of plastics.

I would not recommend *Written on the Wind* to the film lover who only goes to see the fifteen or twenty undoubted masterpieces of each year, because its naïveté, deliberate or not, and its absurdity would offend him. But the real movie nut, the guy who forgives Hollywood a lot because its films are so alive, will come out ecstatic, dazzled, satisfied for one evening—at least until the next good marital comedy comes along.

—1957

FRANK TASHLIN

The Girl Can't Help It

I'll make my praise brief. *The Girl Can't Help It* is more than a good film, more than a funny film, more than an excellent parody; it is a kind of masterpiece of the genre.

After *The Lieutenant Wore Skirts* and *Artists and Models,* I wrote (and I ask your pardon for quoting myself, since I do so in order to contradict myself): "Since he cannot delude or fascinate us, Frank Tashlin intrigues us." This time, there can be no doubt about it: Tashlin fascinates us.

We are dealing with a variation—or, if you will, variations—on the Pygmalion theme. In this case, the sculptor falls in love with a model he refuses to carve. He's more like the happy playboy of *The Seven Year Itch,* an impresario lost in alcoholic daydreams because of unrequited love, making a star out of a bleached-blond doll who's kept by an ex-gangster. But the doll in question is the exact opposite of *Baby Doll.* Her dream is to prepare delicious meals for a loving husband who will give her a pack of kids. She either can't (or won't) sing. When she moves up the scale even to "re," the electric bulbs break. Still, everything turns out in the best possible way, thank heavens, for Tashlin is so effective that an unhappy ending to one of his films would probably cause suicides.

The story is put together out of 347 gags—Tashlin counted them himself—with seven or eight musical numbers that are remarkably well directed and elevate rock and roll even as they satirize it.

This is a crucial point. Parody in movies is a minor genre. It brings us only a small moment of spiteful pleasure, like a good cabaret number.

Parody is full of surprises and invitations to share the joke but almost always disappoints on a second look, since it depends on caricature, an unsightly exaggeration. If Frank Tashlin is a great filmmaker, it's because he has solved the problem of satirical comedy and even criticism. Rather than mock a subject with caricature, he exaggerates the very excesses of what he parodies—in the present film, rock and roll. The numbers he chooses are the epitome of stupidity, howling hysteria, perverted taste. He clothes them in even more garish colors, tightens the rhythms, and syncopates them. He literally hammers them out and gives them a power, even a purity they previously lacked. In *The Girl Can't Help It*, rock and roll is refined and becomes, in its own way, rather grand.

This is an even more radical version of Howard Hawks's lesson in *Gentlemen Prefer Blondes*. I'm using the word "lesson" intentionally. It's not a question of making fun of the original by going it one better with the same instruments. In this case, you want rock and roll; OK, here it is! And it's very beautiful.

His work with the screenplay and the characters is all of a piece. Tashlin exaggerates Jayne Mansfield's statuesque figure with false breasts and all the rest of it, but instead of ridiculing her, he makes her a likable and moving personality, like Marilyn Monroe in *Bus Stop*.

The Girl Can't Help It is funny all the way through, and beautiful all the way through as well. The picnic on the beach, when Jayne Mansfield sits by the sea in a bathing suit and talks, is a wonderful example.

I had a chance to see *The Girl Can't Help It* three times before I finished these notes. Like all great films, it's more beautiful and more successful each time you see it. You laugh less, but you love it more each time, and you feel increased emotion.

—1957

Hollywood or Bust

Dean Martin, a gambler down on his luck, is counting on winning a luxurious convertible in a lottery; not to rely on mere luck, he has a suitcase full of phony tickets. At the same time, Jerry Lewis has bought up an enormous number of legitimate tickets so as to arrive in Hollywood at the wheel of a stunning convertible and to meet and seduce Anita Ekberg, whom he dreams about.

The upshot is that they are declared co-winners, and they drive off to Los Angeles together. In between songs Dean Martin tries unsuccessfully to shake down Lewis, who is protected by Mister Bascom, a huge Great Dane who can drive a car and applaud just like his elder brothers, the humans.

Frank Tashlin's film (which was made before *The Girl Can't Help It*) is the story of their trip, filled with incidents one funnier than the next—a nutty ride in a laugh-house Cadillac.

In the Paramount studios, when we at last get to Hollywood, there's a wonderful satire of moviemaking, parodying *War and Peace*. Anita Ekberg in a nightgown is lying on a bed, listening to the director's instructions: "Napoleon is about to return from Elba and you are waiting for him impatiently. He's your husband and there you are trembling and sighing. . . ."

I am very much afraid that this film will not meet with the approval of those who love "good taste." But we should understand that the lens does not register simple reality, that good taste in cinema bears no relation to pictorial good taste. Splashes of vivid color on the screen, the roof of a taxi, a suspension bridge, a field of alfalfa, a swimming pool, a bathing suit are chosen and organized to create a whole by the director, in this case, Frank Tashlin, the maker of comedies today who best knows how to refine his material.

It's not enough just to be funny. To give the gags some meaning, one must avoid vulgarity, elevate the humor, create beauty, establish harmony of forms and colors; only if satire is positive can it really destroy the mediocrity it mocks. And here is a lesson in good cinema that takes a slap at Hollywood's mediocrities.

The title *Hollywood or Bust* has a double meaning: Hollywood or Die in the Attempt . . . and Hollywood or (Anita Ekberg's) Bust. In comparison with this intelligent American innovation, *Un Vrai Cinglé de Cinéma* seems like typical French foolishness. But it is also true that Paramount, which in the age of VistaVision still offers black-and-white animated cartoons as program fillers, hasn't found a good title since *War and Peace!*

Dean Martin, the habitual fall guy of the twosome, is handled very well here by Tashlin. He's been able to transform what is usually a trial—listening to his songs—into sensitive poetic sequences. Jerry

Lewis is more and more delightful with every picture. He is a nightclub artist who has been worked into cinema very cleverly as Robert Hirsh, Jacques Jouanneau, Poiret, Serrault and many others in France could be, if some of our better filmmakers would interest themselves in musical comedy.

Go see *Hollywood or Bust* and go see *The Girl Can't Help It* again, and applaud Frank Tashlin, who doubtless has lots more surprises in store for us.

—1957

EDGAR ULMER

The Naked Dawn

The Naked Dawn is one of those small American films with so little advance publicity that you might easily miss them. Universal sabotaged this film instead of distributing it, as if they wanted to keep it away from the critics. But we won't give in to the merchandisers. *The Naked Dawn,* a low-budget film, is poetic and violent, tender and droll, moving and subtle, joyously energetic and wholesome.

The opening credits unfold during a train holdup on the Mexican border. One of the two bandits dies in the arms of his accomplice, Santiago (Arthur Kennedy), who wanders around all night until he meets a young farmer, Manuel (Eugene Iglesias), and his charming wife, Maria (Betta St. John). The film tells the story of Santiago and Manuel's trip to the city to sell the watches Santiago has stolen, their stopover in a cabaret on the way home, and an explosive and unexpected finale.

What counts are the delicate and ambiguous relationships among the three, the stuff of a good novel. One of the most beautiful modern novels I know is *Jules et Jim* by Henri-Pierre Roché, which shows how, over a lifetime, two friends and the woman companion they share love one another with tenderness and almost no harshness, thanks to an esthetic morality constantly reconsidered. *The Naked Dawn* is the first film that has made me think that *Jules et Jim* could be done as a film.

Edgar Ulmer is undoubtedly the least-known American filmmaker. Few of my colleagues are able to boast of having seen the few films of his that have made it to France, all of which are surprisingly fresh, sincere, and inventive: *The Strange Woman* (Mauriac crossed with Julian Green), *Babes in Baghdad* (a Voltairean tease), and *Ruthless* (Balzac). This Viennese, born with the century, first an assistant of Max Reinhardt's and then of the great Murnau, hasn't had much luck in Hollywood, probably because he doesn't know how to fit into the system. His carefree humor and pleasant manner, his tenderness toward the characters he depicts remind us inevitably of Jean Renoir and Max Ophuls. Nevertheless, the public on the Champs-Elysées took to this film, as they did a few months ago to Robert Aldrich's *Kiss Me Deadly.*

Talking about *The Naked Dawn* is equivalent to drawing the portrait of its author, because we see him behind every image and feel we know him intimately when the lights go back on. Wise and indulgent, playful and serene, vital and clear, in short, a good man like the ones I've compared him to.

The Naked Dawn is one of those movies we know was made with joy; every shot shows a love of cinema, and pleasure in working in it. It is also a pleasure to see it again and to talk to friends about it. A small gift from Hollywood.

—1956

CHARLES VIDOR

Love Me or Leave Me

As I left the theater after watching *Love Me or Leave Me*, a psychological American musical, or if you prefer, a dramatic comedy with singing, I thought how apt Jean Renoir's remark was: "There is no realism in American films. No realism, but something much better, great truth."

Indeed, it often happens that searing flashes of truth, nuances whose sincerity is beyond doubt, creative and sublime mimicry of all sorts are injected into the most conventional Hollywood sequences. It sometimes seems that the element of truth is all the more powerful as the framework, ambience, or genre of the film are all the more phony and artificial.

When, in a psychological film based on a serious novel, a couple is breaking up, it is sad, of course, but such is life. The same scene in *An American in Paris*, or *Singin' in the Rain*, or *Love Me or Leave Me* takes on more cruelty and gives off a more tragic, more disturbing resonance; it sounds more exact.

Love Me or Leave Me is filmed biography. The truth of its literary base may be what makes it superior to many others of the type. It is a personal drama, repeated many times over between a singer, Doris Day, who has great erotic presence, and her protector, who is first her friend, then her fiancé, then her husband, and finally her dependent. The man is James Cagney, magnificent in his spirit, his gaiety, and his naïve and crafty conviction. What an actor!

Ruth Etting (Doris Day) is a taxi-dance girl who longs for romance. Snyder (James Cagney) an obnoxious small-time gangster, takes her in hand, becomes her manager, and, with his fists, gets her jobs in a few nightclubs. The only thing wrong is that Ruth is a really gifted singer, and offers are soon flowing in. She no longer needs Snyder.

From that point on, they are at each other constantly. Snyder more or less forces Ruth to marry him. They leave for Hollywood. A gentle musician silently adores the pretty singer. There is a three-way scene with a revolver, and finally, Snyder sacrifices his own desires and lets his wife gather some of life's less thorny roses.

It isn't necessary any longer to continue to praise the American musical film, in which realism emerges all the more beneath a light cover. If we had to list the most shattering and moving scenes in movies, we would have to cite many of these Hollywood "singing comedies": after a few refrains and a few dances, there is a sentimental rupture, and tears are all the more serious.

Love Me or Leave Me, a very pretty CinemaScope musical by Charles Vidor, is no exception. It is an extremely believable and intelligent picture of the married life of a singer and her manager, a story of rare finesse and authority.

The action takes place in 1930, which means the clothes, songs, and cars have added charm. Doris Day is a very attractive actress, and James Cagney, patiently limping, presents an enjoyable, sour portrait.

Less exotic and serious than the memorable *Gilda* that first brought us the name of Charles Vidor after the war, *Love Me or Leave Me* constitutes an entirely sympathetic work. You should see it.

—1956

BILLY WILDER

The Seven Year Itch

The metaphor is exaggerated. It doesn't take seven minutes to realize that *The Seven Year Itch* is beyond smut and licentiousness and that it takes us past the limits of evil to a kind of worn-down regret, good humor, and kindness.

An "average" American (Tom Ewell) accompanies his wife and son to the train as they go off on vacation. He returns home alone, determined on conjugal morality, and determined also to follow the advice of his doctor not to drink, and maybe that of his minister.

But a girl—the likes of which you've never known (in the biblical sense) except in dreams—has just moved into the apartment upstairs, and she sows troubled thoughts in his mind, already disoriented by temporary celibacy.

The most important character in the play, the focus of all attention, is the man who is deliberately ordinary, somewhat less than average both physically and intellectually, so as to ensure the identification of the male audience and the greater enjoyment—sadistic, "superior," maybe envious—of the women. In the film, the center of interest shifts to the heroine, for the excellent reason that when she is on screen there is nowhere to look but at her body, from head to toe, with a thousand stops along the way. Her body draws us up from our seats to the screen as a magnet attracts a scrap of metal.

On screen, there is no chance to reflect. Hips, nape, knees, ears, elbows, lips, palms of the hand, profiles win out over tracking shots, framing, sustained panoramas, dissolves. All this, it must be admitted, doesn't happen without a deliberate, measured, finally very effective vulgarity. Billy Wilder, the libidinous old fox, moves along with such incessant suggestiveness that, ten minutes into the film, we aren't sure what are the original or literal meanings of faucet, Frigidaire, under, above, soap, perfume, panties, breeze, and Rachmaninoff.

If we admire, rather than grow annoyed, it is because the film's verve and inventiveness, its cavalier vigor and naughtiness demand complicity.

The film is sincere, really much better than that. The bawdyness lies not in you or me but in Wilder, who has pushed daring to the point of directing a few purely pornographic shots with great precision (although because they are stylized they will elude 98 percent of the audience). Take, for example, the milk bottle between Tom Ewell's legs as he squats on the floor in front of a half-open door.

Another interesting thing about the film is that, maybe for the first time, we are given a filmed critique of films. Jacques Rivette says, and I agree with him pretty much, that the first scene in *Scarface*, when a nightclub employee angrily throws out confetti, streamers, and a forgotten brassiere, *signifies* in Hawks's mind that the film bears no relation to the exoticism of *Underworld*, made the year before by Joseph von Sternberg, also with a script by Ben Hecht. In both cases, in *Underworld* and in *Seven Year Itch*, we have a polemical cinema that is also something more.

We may also recall in *Stalag 17* a happy prisoner doing a series of imitations, including a pretty good one of Cary Grant. In *The Seven Year Itch*, for the first time we are given deliberate citations from other directors, with the same frames, angles, and positions of the actors. Elia Kazan, Fred Zinnemann, Frank Borzage and others are more or less directly cited. But the film Wilder constantly refers to, so that each scene becomes a vengeful slap, is David Lean's *Brief Encounter* with its streams of tears and its amorously awkward couple—the least sensual and most sentimental film ever wept over. Some people even weep thinking about it—inexhaustible tears from English crocodiles. "Rachmaninoff! His second concerto for piano and orchestra never loses its effect," Tom Ewell declares, just because he's seen *Brief Encounter* and he has figured out that Rachmaninoff is infallible in affairs of the heart and body.

If *The Seven Year Itch* were only a weapon aimed at the English cinema it would already be estimable for its attempt at demystification.

I have not mentioned the name of the actress. I have loved her since *Niagara* and even before. She is a person of grace, somewhere

between Chaplin and James Dean. How could anyone resist a film
that has Marilyn Monroe in it?

—1956

Stalag 17

Before he became a director, Billy Wilder was a marvelous
screenwriter of American comedies. We are indebted to him for the
scripts of *Bluebeard's Eighth Wife*, *Ball of Fire*, and others. As a
director he has made only three comedies—the wonderful *The Major
and the Minor*, the worthy *A Foreign Affair*, and *The Emperor Waltz*—
and four or five films inspired by French "psychological realism," in
a style that wavers between German expressionism and purest
Americanism.

Stalag 17, which I admire, is both a psychological and a comic
film, but the comedy is far weaker than that "psychology" I've just
disparaged. The latter is so unusual and subtle that I think it makes
this Wilder's best film.

Taking note that *Stalag 17* is, in Wilder's fantastic work, the exception that proves the rule, let us provide a quick plot summary, which
in this case is necessary.

An evil spell seems to have been cast on Barracks 4 of an American
prisoner of war camp somewhere in Austria. (Barracks 4 is distinguished from the other barracks in that a number of well-known
Paramount actors are billeted there, while the others are inhabited
by extras.) Whenever the occupants of this particular barracks break
the rules—trying to escape, assassination attempts, sabotage, listening
to clandestine radios—they are immediately caught by the guards,
in spite of the fact that the guards aren't very sharp. Among the
prisoners is Sefton (William Holden), who behaves oddly, keeping
to himself, never taking part in the dubious jokes or puerile tricks
of his simpleminded companions. Sefton is not vulgar, and that seems
fishy; he's intelligent, and that makes him unusual; he's a loner, and
that's disturbing.

Two prisoners (who have not seen *Grand Illusion*) are digging a tunnel for reasons that are obviously forbidden. Sefton is the only one who does not encourage them, and as soon as they disappear into the tunnel, he bets that they'll fail. Shamed by Sefton, the others all take the bet, putting on the table their entire ration of Red Cross cigarettes. A few minutes go by and there is the sound of gunfire; the men look at each other, stunned. Without a word, Sefton puts the cigarettes in his pockets and goes to bed.

One day, some Soviet women prisoner-soldiers are billeted nearby. Using what materials are at hand, Sefton constructs a makeshift telescope and rents it out for a small sum to spy on the women as they take their showers.

An American lieutenant who was captured alone is brought in. He tells his fellow prisoners how he blew up a German train. That fact immediately becomes known to the authorities. The lieutenant is "invited" to the camp commandant's office, where he isn't tortured but simply told that as soon as he chooses to talk, he'll be allowed to sit down and even go to sleep.

Obviously there is an informer in Barracks 4. When idiots conduct an investigation, it's dangerous to be intelligent. Sefton is immediately suspect, Sefton the racketeer, Sefton who makes money off his buddies every Sunday by organizing races using white mice, Sefton who is always swapping and selling for profit, who collaborates with the enemy, Sefton the haughty skeptic.

One day, Sefton suddenly disappears. They talk about him in his absence: "It's got to be him, he must be the stool pigeon." He returns, and when his companions learn that, with the guards' blessing, he has spent two hours with the Russian women, they are even more certain he is guilty. They gang up on him, twenty to one, and beat him up.

Meanwhile the exhausted lieutenant has admitted his sabotage and will be executed unless he is helped to escape. The barracks' trusted leader volunteers to direct the escape, but Sefton, who has already figured out that the leader is the guilty party, publicly accuses him of it, and decides that he himself will help the lieutenant escape. Everybody learns that Sefton was innocent. They ask his pardon.

Sefton and the lieutenant get away. But before he goes, Sefton turns to his companions, who are wishing him luck, and says, "If I get away and we meet some day after the war, don't try to shake hands with me; it'd be better if you crossed the street." *Stalag 17* is a harsh and uncompromising film.

And who is Sefton? On the outside, he is an egoist, a hustler. His disdain for his companions makes him seem "pretentious" and "above them," so they turn against him. He maintains friendly relations with the German guards and does "business" with them. He is a sort of collaborator. For these simpleminded men, whom imprisonment has robbed of whatever small mental abilities they had possessed, this man has to be the informer. But when they gang up on him and bloody his face, twenty to one, it is jealousy (he has just returned from two hours with the Russian women) rather than any certitude that he is the guilty party that moves them to this particular justice. Isn't this a symbol of those so-called summary executions that leave us with a clear conscience?

Sefton is intelligent; that's why he acts as he does. For the first time in films the philosophy of the solitary man is elaborated; this film is an apologia for individualism. (Certainly, the solitary man has been a theme in films, as with Charlie Chaplin and many other comedians. But he has usually been an inept person whose only desire was to fit into society.) *Sefton is alone because he wants to be alone.* He has the qualities of leadership, and everything would tend to establish him as the barracks' trusted leader. After the deception has been uncovered by Sefton himself, and the leader the men trusted has been unmasked and convicted, we may wonder if Sefton escapes in order to avoid being named to take his place, knowing his fellow prisoners would do exactly that, both to exonerate themselves and because they finally recognize him as their only possible leader.

What's sure is that Sefton escapes to get away from the companions whom he despises rather than from a regime he has come to terms with and guards he's been able to bend to his needs.

Sefton needs those whom he despises to despise him in turn. If he remains, he will be a hero—a role he rejects no matter what the cost. Having lost his moral solitude, he hastens to regain it by becoming an escapee, with all the risk that entails.

The baseness of the crowd has frequently been portrayed in films in stories of lynchings in which, nine times out of ten, the victim is guilty and the respectable folk, led by contemptible leaders, become executioners. What can be more dreadful than good folk who take justice into their own hands? What is worse than this moral superiority born of a clear conscience and a certainty of total innocence? Here— better than with civilians, soldiers, or fighters—the authors have chosen prisoners to show that groups, majorities, or simply ten good men together are always wrong, even when they are right—especially when they are right. Prisoners always attract our sympathy, since they are wrong in the eyes of their captors; they are men whose very state elicits compassion. This is a supremely clever idea. With a single blow, the sophistry that shared misfortune brings out the best in us and creates closeness is exploded.

The depravity of the group versus the individual's moral solitude, is this not a large theme? Are we not right to salute a movie that dares to depart from the exigencies of life that make the beggar an accomplice of the very order that he denounces, and shows us that the answers are in us and only in us? So, I would put *Stalag 17* with *Europe 51* and *I Confess,* after excusing myself for giving in to the taste of the day, which is not cinematographic.

—1954

ROBERT WISE

So Big

Selena (Jane Wyman), a young orphan whose ruined father has killed himself, leaves school in 1898 and becomes a teacher in a hamlet in New Zealand. She has based her entire life on the love of beauty. When she arrives in the hamlet, looks at the immense stretch of the fields, and cries out, "How beautiful the cabbages are," we see the sympathetic amusement she arouses. Selena has inherited a rather odd theory from her father, actually an ethical theory. According to Selena, the world is divided into two types: the first is wheat, the second diamonds. Those belonging to the first, bent over the soil to extract its material goods from it, nourish their fellows; they are wheat, or rather, blades of wheat. The second are the artists who create harmony and beauty; they are diamonds.

Selena teaches the young son of a farming family (Walter Coy— Roef) to play the piano, and he shows such great aptitude that she is sure she can make him a pure diamond. Meanwhile, she marries a blade of wheat, a young farmer (Sterling Hayden), who gives her a son, Dirck (Steve Forrest). When she is left a widow, and Roef has gone off to "live his own life," Selena dedicates herself to the education of her son, whom she intends to make into a diamond also.

The years pass. Dirck receives his architectural degree with great honors—he will be a builder, a blade of wheat and a diamond at the same time. Unfortunately he falls into the hands of a worldly young woman and becomes engaged to her. Paula (Martha Hyer) is vain, superficial, flighty, and fiercely ambitious. The only thing on her mind is that Dirck should make as much money as possible; she turns him into a businessman. Roef has become a great musician and is in love with a painter, Dallas (Nancy Olson), who returns his love. Dirck also loves Dallas but realizes that he does not deserve her. Selena finds the words to console her son, who eventually renounces Paula, abandons his materialistic ambitions, and goes to work to become the pure diamond his mother had always wanted to make him.

The movie belongs to a category that could be called the "portrait" film, a typical genre of American films. It follows a person from birth or adolescence to death. We can compare *So Big* to others of the type: *Mrs. Parkington*, directed by Tay Garnett, *The Keys of the Kingdom* by John Stahl, *The President's Lady* by Henry Levin. These are the most successful, and all of them are taken from big five-hundred-page saga novels.

Robert Wise is a director of importance who came to movie making from editing (he was chief editor to Orson Welles on *Citizen Kane* and *The Magnificent Ambersons*). The first film he directed, *The Set-Up*, attracted considerable attention, and, as we look back, his succeeding films, *Born to Kill* and *Blood on the Moon*, probably did not get enough attention. Using his own particular strength, Wise has made a kind of masterpiece from this long melodrama. His power as a director leads us to overlook the rather simplistic psychology of his characters. Selena is an exemplary figure, the magnificent mother with perfect dignity; she reminds us of Jouhandeau's mother. The emotion is contained throughout, but this very reserve is an added cleverness of the *auteur* calculated to encourage the tears the women in the audience apparently cannot restrain. There's not a lot more to say about this film; fifty years of cinematographic know-how have created a kind of total technique in terms of the screenplay's construction, the direction of the actors, and the superb camera work. *So Big* raises the classic, traditional Hollywood style to its highest degree of effectiveness.

—1954

Destination Gobi

June 1945: A commander in the American Navy and seven sailors are on a mission in the heart of the Gobi Desert. The leader of a caravan of Mongols makes a deal to cooperate with the Americans in exchange for sixty saddles. Washington is consulted, the matter is discussed and it is decided to fly the saddles over. What happens to them, how they come to be traded for eight camels, sold, stolen, recovered, confiscated, and how they eventually save the lives of seven men is the story of this good and energetic film.

Is it an adventure film, a psychological film, or a burlesque? *Destination Gobi* is all those things and more. Every ten minutes you think you've got it figured out, and you're wrong. There's a new twist to open your eyes, confuse you one more time and move the story along.

Everett Freeman's screenplay is one of the best to come out of Hollywood in a decade. It is an important contribution to the most important effort that's being made in script-writing—breaking out of genres.

All the characters in *Destination Gobi*, both the Americans and the Mongols, are fully realized. The Technicolor, well photographed by Charles G. Clarke, brings to perfection the technique that Hathaway's *Niagara* hinted at. As Sam MacHale, the first mate, Richard Widmark has one of the best roles of his career. *Destination Gobi* is an adventure film which pirouettes away from drama. We have to think of Huston except that the playfulness and casualness are on screen rather than behind the camera. Wise's work is unusually serious, intelligent, tasteful, direct, and precise.

Ordinarily the absence of women in a film bothers me more than anything else. The fact that someone had to point that out to me about this film is a sign of how fascinated I was with it.

—1955

III

The Generation of the Talkies: The French

CLAUDE AUTANT-LARA

La Traversée de Paris

A director's highest duty is to reveal the actors to themselves; and to do that, he must know himself very well. Cinematographic failure generally occurs because there is too wide a disparity between a filmmaker's temperament and his ambitions.

From *Diable au Corps* (*Devil in the Flesh* in the United States) to *Marguerite de la Nuit*, and in between—in *L'Auberge Rouge, Le Blé en Herbe*, and *Le Rouge et le Noir (The Red and the Black)*— I have consistently attacked Claude Autant-Lara and I have always deplored his tendency to simplify everything, make it bland. I disliked the coarseness with which he "condensed" Stendhal, Radiguet, Colette. It seemed to me he deformed and watered down the spirit of any work he adapted. Autant-Lara seemed to me like a butcher who insists on trying to make lace.

But I admire, without any real reservations, *La Traversée de Paris.* I think it's a complete success because Autant-Lara has finally found the subject he's been waiting for—a plot that is made in his own image, a story that his truculence, tendency toward exaggeration, roughness, vulgarity, and outrage, far from serving badly, elevates to an epic.

During the Occupation, two Frenchmen spend the night walking around a studio-set Paris in a wartime blackout, carrying a pig clandestinely to the black market. The film simply reproduces their journey and their conversation, a dialogue both banal and theatrical, and the best that's been heard in a long time in a French film. French movies have been circling around *La Traversée de Paris* for ten years without finding it.

It's more like a filmed play, artfully given some space by the happy idea of the long walk before a mobile backdrop. In film terms, it is a series of transparencies. *La Traversée de Paris* is adapted from a short story by Marcel Aymé. The audacious (for cinema) language wouldn't be at all so on the stage, in a play like *Waiting for Godot*, but films rarely give us an opportunity to listen to the "average" Frenchman, a character who is ordinarily flattered in movies, since he's the one who pays to see them.

The character of Bourvil, a little man crushed by life, a tiny fall guy, innocent and guilty at the same time, represents an absolute truth. As Jean Gabin plays him, he is a synthesis of the painter Gen Paul (in the spirit of Marcel Aymé), Jacques Prévert, and of the anarchical ambitions of Jean Aurenche and Claude Autant-Lara. The character remains somewhat literary and contrived, but nevertheless possesses great power.

The authors could have further deepened their portrait of wickedness, and probably wanted to, but we only think about that afterward, when our astonishment has worn off. A verve much like Céline's and an insistent ferocity dominate the movie, but it is saved from meanness by a few emotional notes that overwhelm us, particularly those in the final scenes. If the whole gives the impression of more subtlety and more power than the combination of a film by Claude Autant-Lara, a play by Marcel Aymé, and dialogue by Aurenche and Bost would suggest, it is because these four personalities fuse in a particularly fortunate way in the service of a subject that becomes a common denominator. The situation the film describes tempers Autant-Lara's leftist anarchism, Aymé's rightism, and lets Aurenche and Bost set the tone. Thanks to them *La Traversée de Paris* is not trivialized by having political, social, or ideological labels attached to it.

Don't laugh too loudly when you see *La Traversée de Paris*, first of all so your neighbors can hear the dialogue—but even more because Martin and Grandgil could be you and me.

—1956

En Cas de Malheur

En Cas de Malheur (In Case of Accident), one of Simenon's best novels, is also one of Claude Autant-Lara's best films. It's not a new theme; it's the same one as in *Nana* and *La Chienne:* a mature man's love for a girl too young and frivolous for him who represents the eternal feminine. I'm reminded of *La Chienne* because of Renoir's wonderful introduction to the film where he has marionettes sing: "It's the eternal story: she, he, and the other. She is Lulu, a fine girl; she's always sincere; she lies all the time." It fits perfectly the character of Yvette as played by Brigitte Bardot.

Yvette has committed a holdup with the help of a friend. Before she is arrested, she gets the idea of asking a famous Paris trial lawyer (Jean Gabin) to take on her defense. The first time she visits his office she tries to seduce him, hiking up her dress to show him she's not wearing anything underneath. He rebuffs her but agrees to defend her and, by his slick defense, gets her off. Then, having become her lover, he installs her in his apartment with the tacit agreement of his wife, who is responsible for his social success. Yvette has nothing to do so she sleeps around and in short order falls in love with a strange and passionate boy, "a worker by day, a student by night." He tries to teach her the few absolute principles of morality before he kills her, which is what the attorney, Gobillot, would probably have done in the same situation thirty years earlier. I want to stress the daring of the plot. Yvette has recently discovered that she's pregnant by the lawyer and she's happy about it, even though she is carrying on a lesbian relationship at the same time with a young maid who is responsible for looking after her—in Gobillot's presence, even with his cooperation.

Ordinarily, Aurenche and Bost adapt novels by turning them into theater pieces rather than screenplays, using standard dramatic procedures: cuts and summaries, ellipses, three acts, ingenious flashbacks, commentaries, etc. Compared to the quality of the original work, the director's ambition and the producer's desires can produce the worst kind of matinee theater *(Le Blé en Herbe, Le Diable au Corps, Le Rouge et le Noir)*, or, on the other hand, left-bank avant-garde theater *(La Traversée de Paris)*, or as in this case, something in between, a kind of Champs-Elysées comedy.

En Cas de Malheur has been turned into the sort of play that Jean Anouilh might have written. We come out of it with a mixture of disgust and admiration, a sense of satisfaction that is real enough but incomplete. It is 100 percent French, with all the virtues and vices that implies: an analysis that is at once subtle and narrow, a skill that is mixed with spitefulness, a spirit of unflinching observation directed at the sordid, and talented sleight-of-hand that delivers a liberal message in the end.

A number of years ago, when I was twenty and innocent, I would have condemned it angrily. I feel a bit bitter today when I find myself, somewhat to my own surprise, admiring, even moderately, a film that's more intelligent than beautiful, more adroit than noble, more artful than sensitive. But if I have put some water in my wine, so have Aurenche and Bost and Autant-Lara added wine to their water and made it quite a bit stronger. If their names endure in the history of cinema, it will not be so much because they've done anything to move cinema forward as that they have moved the public forward. A filmmaker like Ingmar Bergman has for fifteen years been making films that are as daring and frank as *En Cas de Malheur*—films that make no concessions and do not sink to vulgarity. But it is because of films like *En Cas de Malheur* that the general public may come to understand Bergman.

Like Anouilh, Aurenche and Bost are clever at managing ingenious ellipses so that the director can shoot fifteen scenes of equal importance and interest without dead moments or laborious transitions and tedious connections. Their dialogue is like Anouilh's, always facile and seductive, but at the same time familiar and very effective. In terms of simple spectacle, they have achieved a certain perfection.

In Autant-Lara they have found the ideal partner. Without a moment's hesitation and without touching a single comma, he produces each of their brainstorms; he is as conscientious, hard-working, and upright as Pierre Bost, and as sharp, narrow, and vengeful as Jean Aurenche. He skirts nothing when he deals with his characters, emphasizing all their weaknesses and failings. A goodness that I believe I see in Simenon's work, a compassion that softens the worst indecency, is nowhere to be found in the film; it is full of vengeance. If I like it anyhow and go to the trouble of defending it, it's because I think it comes down on the right side of the battle against complacency.

Let me give you another example—another film of Bardot's, *Une Parisienne*. It is precisely against the state of mind that inspired *Une Parisienne*, and against its fans, that Aurenche, Bost and Autant-Lara struggle. Let me see if I can make that more concrete. The film opens with a television commentary about a visit by the Queen of England. Taking advantage of the fact that the entire Paris police force is preoccupied with the royal visit, Bardot robs a jewelry shop. All the while we hear a bombastic TV commentary: the Queen goes here, does this and that. . . . In the evening, Gobillot and Edwige Feuillère, his wife, are at a dinner in honor of the Queen at the Elysée Palace. Gobillot's secretary, modeled closely on the one of Ornifle—which was also played by Madeleine Barbulée—stuffs an enormous sandwich in her mouth as she watches the Queen pass by on a sightseeing boat.

The idea is simple but strong: a crowned head moves around Paris under spotlights seeming to symbolize grace, beauty, woman, fortune, happiness, and at the same time a beautiful penniless girl knocks over an old man for a few watches. It's the girl who interests us and preoccupies us, not an anachronistic queen. It is precisely because Bardot is a girl who represents her time absolutely faithfully that she is more famous than any queen or princess. That's why it's too bad she played *Une Parisienne* or *Les Bijoutiers*. And it's why *En Cas des Malheur* is her best film since *Et Dieu créa la Femme*—an anti-*Sabrina*, anti-*Roman Holiday*, anti-*Anastasia* movie that is truly republican.

We could list a lot of things about the film that are bold, even though each foray is balanced by small concessions. But the essential thing is that in this film you hear talk about miscarriages, tiny holes in hotel bedroom doors, a complacent wife, "games" that are, if not four-sided, at least triangular, voyeurism—everything, in fact, that smacks of original sin (which I suppose Aurenche believes in, but not Lara).

The crucial things are said clearly, avoiding the confusions, sentimentality, and the sheer physical seduction that make nine out of ten films unbearable. What of its compromises? We notice them when we compare the movie with the novel. The character of the wife, for example, is too sentimental in the film; she was much earthier in the book. But the compromises are usually visual rather than verbal,

Autant-Lara's rather than the scenarists'. For example, it is scandalous that they did not dare to film Bardot and Gabin kissing each other on the mouth; both the situation and dialogue demand it. Did they try it out and then hesitate because they were afraid it would be shocking? If the answer is yes, that would be enough to condemn the film. And if not, why did they back off, what was the reason for a self-censorship which contradicts the film's spirit?

Autant-Lara is making progress technically: his camera spins as he follows his constantly moving characters. His technique is less cluttered as he has become less theatrical. Accelerating on Bardot and Gabin, slowing down on Edwige Feuillère, it's perfect. With *La Traversée de Paris* and this film, Autant-Lara has outclassed Henry-Georges Clouzot and René Clément. But like them he closes himself off to poetry and therefore to great cinema.

—1958

JACQUES BECKER

Casque d'Or *

In Ernst Lubitsch's *To Be or Not to Be*, a group of German officers pull at each other's mustaches for several minutes in order to unmask the imposter in their midst. It would be pointless to subject the characters in *Casque d'Or* to such a test; each hair of Serge's Reggiani's mustache is guaranteed real in this celebration of authenticity.

Casque d'Or is the only film that Jacques Becker—who is ordinarily very finicky, absorbed by detail, obsessive, restless, and at times uncertain—ever made in one stroke, very quickly, straight through from beginning to end. He wrote the colloquial and absolutely natural-seeming dialogue so economically that we have the impression that Reggiani doesn't say more than sixty words.

Those of us who love *Casque d'Or* are clear in our minds that Simone Signoret and Serge Reggiani had their best roles ever in it, even if the French public (but not the English, decidedly more subtle) was cool to this paradoxical coupling, so beautiful precisely because of its contrasts—a little man and a large woman, the little alley cat who is made of nothing but nerves, and the gorgeous carnivorous plant who doesn't turn her nose up at any morsel.

If you're at all interested in how stories are constructed, you cannot fail to admire the ingenuity of the plot, particularly the strong, oblique, unexpected way it gets abruptly to Manda's execution in a scene

* This article, written in 1965, is not a review of *Casque d'Or* (which came out in 1952), but an introduction to the publication of the script in the collection *L'Avant-Scène*.

that is as beautiful as it is mysterious, as the Casque d'Or arrives in the middle of the night at a disreputable hotel. When I or any of my fellow scenarists are in trouble, we often say to each other, "How about a '*Casque d'Or* solution'?"

Casque d'Or is primarily a film of personalities, but it is also a visual tour de force: a dance, a brawl in the backyard, an awakening in the countryside, Manda's arrival at the guillotine supported by a priest—these images are like magazine covers. This visual enchantment confirms me in my conviction that cinema is a popular art, and that it deceives itself when it tries to bring the paintings of the masters to life.

Casque d'Or, at times funny, at times tragic, proves that we can surpass parody; we can look at the picturesque and bloody past and evoke it with tenderness and violence by means of a refined use of tone changes.

—1965

Touchez Pas au Grisbi

There are no theories about Jacques Becker, no scientific analysis, no thesis. His work, like his personality, discourages it. Which is all to the good.

Becker doesn't have any intention of mystifying or demystifying anyone; his films are neither statements nor indictments. He works outside all styles, and we shall place him therefore at the opposite pole from the major tendencies of French cinema.

Becker's films are his own; that is only one point but it is an important one. While it is generally thought preferable to write the films one directs, the reasons that are usually given are banal; and anyhow we continue to admire teams and partnerships. The fact that Renoir, Bresson, Cocteau, and Becker participate in working out the script and write the dialogue not only gives them a greater self-assurance on the set, but, more importantly, it allows them to avoid the sorts of scenes and cues typical of scenarists, and to create scenes a typical scenarist wouldn't think of. Do we need examples? To know that the scene in *Edouard et Caroline* where Elina Labourdette plays at making "doe's eyes" could be possible, one first had actually to have witnessed it, and only then thought it out as director. I don't know whether we owe the scene to Annette Wademant or to Becker, but I'm sure that another director would have cut it in editing. It doesn't move the action forward one step. It is just there, it seems to add a touch not of realism but of reality; it is there also out of some love for the difficult.

This search for a more and more exact tone is particularly noticeable in the dialogue. In *Casque d'Or*, Raymond (Bussières) enters Manda's carpentry shop (Reggiani) and says, "So, scrape, scrape, whittle, whittle, eh?" The remark could not possibly have been written—it had to have been invented on the set; that doesn't prevent it from revealing an *intelligence* (in the sense of an *understanding* with a friend) that confounds me each time I hear it.

It is not so much his choice of subject that distinguishes Becker as it is his treatment, and the scenes he selects to illustrate it. He keeps only what is essential in the dialogue, even the *essential* part of the *superfluous* (he sometimes keeps even onomatopoeias). He will skimp what another director would treat most seriously in order to linger over the characters eating breakfast, buttering a roll, brushing their teeth. There is a convention that screen lovers never embrace except in a lap dissolve. In a French movie, if a couple is shown undressing and walking around the bedroom in nightclothes, the purpose is to make fun of them. We might gather that these tacit rules are dictated by a concern for elegance. What does Becker do with such situations? His taste for the difficult, which I have remarked on, makes him go counter to the rules. In *Casque d'Or* he shows us Reggiani and Simone Signoret in nightgowns, and in *Grisbi* we see Gabin in pajamas.

His work is a perpetual challenge to vulgarity, and it is a gamble Becker invariably wins, for his films are always elegant and dignified.

What happens to Becker's characters matters less than the way it happens to them. His plots, scarcely more than pretexts, grow thinner from film to film: *Edouard et Caroline* is simply the story of one evening in the world, with a telephone and a dinner jacket as accessories; *Touchez pas au Grisbi* just recounts the transfer of ninety-six kilograms of gold. "What I find interesting is personalities," Becker says; the real subjects of *Grisbi* are aging and friendship. This theme came through clearly in Simenon's book but very few screenwriters

would have known how to bring it out, pushing the violent and picturesque action to the background. Simenon is forty-nine and Becker
forty-eight; *Grisbi* is a film about being fifty. At the end of the film,
Mac, like Becker, puts on his glasses "to read."

The beauty of the characters in *Grisbi,* even more than those in
Casque d'Or, comes from their quietness, from the economy of their
movements. They speak or act only to say or do what is necessary.
Like Monsieur Teste, Becker halts the marionette in them. All that
remains of the killers are two tomcats facing each other down. *Grisbi*
is, in my eyes, a kind of settling of accounts between tired and defeated
but still deluxe fat cats.

For those of us who are twenty or a little older, Becker's example
is both instructive and encouraging. Renoir we've known only as a
genius, while Becker was making his debut at the same time we were
discovering cinema. We were present at his first tries and experiments.
We have watched as the body of his work was put together. Becker's
success is that of a young man who could see only one path, who
chose it, and whose dedication to films has been repaid.

—1954

Arsène Lupin

If *Arsène Lupin* had been made and shown in 1954, it
would have been an "important" French film, one of those movies
that has to be systematically praised, even if it meant pretending
not to recognize its defects. But we are at a turning point of French
cinema, and *Nuit et Brouillard, Lola Montès, Un Condamné à Mort
s'est échappé, La Traversée de Paris, Courte Tête* have made us more
demanding about both the choice of subjects and their treatments.
Arsène Lupin is a pleasant film, it will give you a pleasant evening,
but there is indeed some question as to what is beyond the pleasantness.

The film's weak point is certainly the script. Becker is an intimate
and realistic filmmaker who is in love with verisimilitude and everyday
realities. On pretexts as slight as a lottery ticket or a dinner jacket,

he has given us *Antoine et Antoinette, Edouard et Caroline* and also *Touchez pas au Grisbi,* whose well-earned success focused on Max the Liar growing old, his weariness, his first pair of reading glasses, the little habits, the good restaurants, the pleasant absorption of a tired-out hooligan who dreams about retiring into middle-class respectability.

But Becker's best film, the one in which he rises above his own limitations, is *Casque d'Or,* which has unfortunately never been understood in France—a rapid, tragic, powerful film, every instant filled with strength and intelligence.

The name Arsène Lupin evokes an untouchable personality. Becker certainly has the right to consider the original out of date and to remake him in his own way, but did he simply reconstruct the personality?

Maurice Leblanc's Arsène Lupin is a strong, frantic individual. When he is in love, everything is possible. Incapable of vulgarity and meanness, Lupin was haughtier, more scornful and fiercely theatrical than the Master of Santiago himself. He was loved and admired, feared and respected.

For the Arsène Lupin of our childhood, Becker has substituted another who is only a variation on Max the Liar. But the style that defined *Grisbi* diminishes Leblanc's hero to such a degree that the once strong personality has become weak, imprecise, nebulous, I might almost say nonexistent.

Arsène Lupin returns to his home, puts a record on the phonograph, undresses, looks at himself in the mirror, hums along perhaps, treats his servants with familiarity and kindness . . . all that was also in *Grisbi* but here it bores us. It's clear that Becker, who had put much of himself into Max, has once again identified with his character, but this time it's frustrating to watch. Because he only wanted to paint a little man, a *petit français,* a fifty-year-old who is all of a piece, an innocently eccentric, indulgent father, Becker has been victimized by his own gentleness, and runs the risk of being able to get through only to a fifty-year-old audience, and, indeed, only the one that patronizes the Champs-Elysées movie houses.

I shall come back to Robert Lamoureux, who plays Arsène Lupin admirably; here I am only criticizing the conception of the character. It seems to me that Manda in *Casque d'Or* and the dressmaker in *Falbalas* were closer to the Lupin we long to see.

Since the character he has invented is unfinished and insufficiently realized, Becker, whether consciously or not, constantly shifts our interest to the episodic characters, very few of whom "work." Now that the gentleman burglar has become a sneak thief, a crafty accomplice, a little villain, more like "Arsène the Liar," we can see the limitations of a style that rests on kindness, mischievousness, bantering, the conspiratorial wink, buddyism, and we can see how limited the overlabored humor is, humor like a sledgehammer, more in the English style.

The plot consists of three adventures, three "hits," and leaves much to be desired in terms of originality. The first episode concerns the theft of some paintings and is irritatingly heavy-handed: 1. Lupin arrives at the chateau. 2. The master of the chateau tells him, "I am tremendously proud of my canvases." 3. The lights go off; Lupin steals the paintings. 4. The master says, "My paintings have been stolen." 5. Arsène Lupin pays off his accomplices. No ellipses, nothing to figure out. This sketch reminds us of those "funny" stories that are so boring because we are not spared a single detail. The second episode, the theft of the jewels through a hole in the wall, would have been original if Ernst Lubitsch *(Désirs)* and Sacha Guitry *(Le Romain d'un Tricheur)* had not already done it. The third episode, Lupin and the Kaiser, is the longest and best. It's about the discovery of a hiding place—and here the film picks up. The sets, costumes, and colors are superb, the acting is improved, but even in this episode the plot's flaws compromise the intelligence of the narrative. The film ends up as a very successful sketch set in Maxim's. It is not until then that we realize that the whole business should have been conceived and carried out the way the finale is—with loud drumbeats from the very beginning.

This too-soothing plot hasn't any more than six or eight good ideas, so clumsily introduced and developed that Becker and Albert Simonin had to invent forty peripheral scenes, which only confuse and weigh down the whole, already severely handicapped by a lack of ease and lightness.

Arsène Lupin consists of four or five hundred shots, each one more carefully photographed than the previous, all very pretty and well composed. The result nonetheless is a film that has no line, no rhythm, that doesn't breathe. We spend our time looking at the rare books, the furniture, the bath, the gramophone, the clothing. The total effect is soft, lacking vigor and strength; the important things are too light; and what should be light is too heavy.

Arsène Lupin is a bottle of mineral water; it refreshes and sparkles, it's true, but we'd have preferred champagne.

We should get to the positives. Liselotte Pulver is charming and Otto Hasse is very good. What saves the film, and justifies it absolutely, is Robert Lamoureux, who, seen here for the first time in color, is magnificent. Look at his nervous face, his lucid and profound expression. Lamoureux could have portrayed the real Lupin perfectly, with his anger and despair, energetic, alert and dynamic, ferocious, sentimental to the point of tears, vengeful and cruel, that admirable Lupin whose film remains to be made. Lamoureux is more than an entertainer. I am certain that he is a dramatic actor who would be able to fascinate and move us, who is capable of both violence and lyricism. He would be marvelous in the *Bande à Bonnot* or playing a tragic anarchist. He could have done *Casque d'Or.* He deserves good roles. It is to Becker's credit that he chose him and gave him a chance to show his mettle.

—1957

Le Trou

Jacques Becker's films always remind me of that phrase of Valéry's, "Taste is made up of a thousand distastes." When Becker talks about the next films he's going to make, the phrase that recurs most often is "Watch out." He told me on the telephone not long ago, "I'm going to make *The Three Musketeers,* but watch out, the film will have to stop when the diamond studs are returned; that will already be two hours . . ." This statement sums up Becker: the "Watch out," and the concern with length.

Le Trou is a superb film, superbly conceived, written, directed, edited, and mixed. Fortunately, it is the best of Becker's films—fortunately, because the critics who are in this instance acting as if they are lawyers can read a propitious last will and testament.

It is indeed a testament, and there are few enough films in which we can sense to such a degree the artist's reflections all through the process.

Becker was the most reflective filmmaker of his generation, and the most scrupulous; he asked himself the most questions. If criticism taught him nothing, it was because he had already assessed and reassessed all the problems in his own head. For a long time he was assistant-director to Jean Renoir, who liked to let him do cameos. In *Boudu*, Becker, young and thin, sits on a bench, puts his head in his hands, reflects, raises his arms toward heaven and declaims, "Poet, take thy lute and give me a kiss." In *La Grande Illusion*, he is an English officer who crushes his watch in rage rather than have it confiscated by the Germans.

This is Becker as revealed by Renoir, the great revealer: restless, anguished, elegant, lyrical, nervous, tormented.

In conceiving, shooting, and editing *Le Trou*, Becker had to have been very much on his guard; we feel it in each shot. What was he on guard against, this man who regards making a film as a kind of "fighting expedition" in the middle of the jungle, an enterprise fraught with obstacles and full of traps every step of the way? First of all, he was on his guard against the "small, closed group of men," a trap that has been fatal for not a few of his colleagues. The second trap: "the heavy-handedness of the tough" which might lead to exchanges of limpid looks and a reverse sentimentality. The third trap, one of the most difficult to avoid, is the "vocabulary of jail," or "poetic gutter talk."

Becker avoided all the traps, and *Le Trou* seems to be as above criticism in its details as it is in its overall conception. Some will perhaps deplore its limitations but the reproach is pointless. Becker was a limited filmmaker, deliberately so; he was a man who knew his own limits, he imposed them on himself; sometimes he tried to surpass them, often he respected them. But he always felt them and they gave us the best moments of his work (Goupi Tonkin in a tree, the suicide of Raymond Rouleau in *Falbalas*, the doe's eyes in *Edouard et Caroline*, the guillotine in *Casque d'Or*, etc.).

A naïve filmmaker has almost no script problems to resolve since he is himself easily taken in by the story he is telling; he is the first sucker, the first audience. A philosophical filmmaker who's trying to express general ideas obviously has to construct his own story so that it will be a vehicle for his ideas. Again in this case, there are few problems. But Becker was neither a naïve nor a philosophical filmmaker; he was a filmmaker, pure and simple, preoccupied only by the problems of his art.

Essentially he wanted to achieve an exactitude of tone, refining it more and more until it became evident, clear. Like all filmmakers who question themselves intensively, he eventually knew much more about what he wanted to avoid than what he wanted to get at. He hated the kind of cinema that might be called abusive: bombastic, erotically exploitative, violent, a mechanical raising of the tone of voice.

Since he was on guard against the exceptional, he constantly imagined himself in the place of his characters, and quite naturally, he began to trace his own portrait from film to film. But here again, *watch out:* even if you have to know yourself pretty well in order to film only what you know well, it doesn't make you infallible. Becker didn't realize he was Max the Liar, and that's what the power of *Grisbi* comes from; when he tried to solve the "Lupin problem" with the "Grisbi solution," he got soft and transformed a strong personality into a weak one.

Lupin was the end of a road, the death of a character whose career had begun with *Dernier Atout* (with Raymond Rouleau's features), continued with Goupi Monsieur, a mischievous offhand personality, nice, likable, a little too pleasant a Beckerian hero. Becker was obliged to start again from zero, to prospect other territory, and the result was *Montparnasse 19*, in which he freely accepted constraint in his portrait of a strong, even excessive, personality. Did the alcoholic genius Modigliani drink because he was a genius, or was he a genius because he drank?

The production problems of such a film were so numerous that Becker avoided them more than he resolved them. *Montparnasse 19* is a slalom, a work so negative that Jean-Luc Godard wrote, "This is not a film, it's a description of the fear of making a film."

All of which doesn't take away from the fact that the perfection of *Le Trou* owes much to *Montparnasse 19*, as if Becker's last film was the positive side of the earlier one. From now on we should no longer speak of cautious talent, but of genius, the triumph of something unique and fully realized that other filmmakers have not achieved: a total simplicity joined to a precision of tone that never falters. In *Le Trou* there is nothing but the exact look, the alive movement, authentic faces against neutral walls, an utterly natural manner of speaking. "Divide and conquer" is the motto of Becker's camera. It's as agile as it is careful; one by one it pulls apart and separates the difficulties it faces throughout this wonderfully controlled movie.

The notion of control seems to me to be very important. A film should not necessarily be dominated by its director; it can even dominate him at times—but the work that goes into it, particularly its length, must be controlled. *Le Trou* revolves precisely around these well-known problems of length. What moments should one film? What ellipses should one allow? In all of his films, during the writing, the shooting, and the editing, Becker had to face the problem of cutting, summarizing, contracting.

Le Trou was his perfect subject because there were no ellipses to be made—everything counted equally, everything had the same importance, the same power. One forgets one has been sitting for two-and-a-half hours because the film moves forward without any pauses or digressions. Every movement, every picture moves the action onward. For the five characters in *Le Trou,* there is only one goal and only one way to reach it. They advance toward freedom as Becker advances toward the *appearance* of pure documentary.

This documentary pretense along with the overturning of its usual proportions—we are dealing again with the question of length—is the essential mark of the modern filmmaker who is also polemicist, whose work is at least partly critical. In *Le Trou* there is, as a consequence, as there is in the best recent films, an aspect of the experimental. Let's be thankful that the experiment was conclusive and resulted in a perfect spectacle.

Becker was a film lover. You could feel, even after twenty years spent at his trade, how overwhelmed he was to have fulfilled his adolescent dream of making movies. At the end of *Le Trou* it is a moving experience to watch his son, Jean Becker, suddenly rise from the depths just as Edouard Dhermite-Cocteau emerges from the waves in *Le Testament d'Orphée.*

—1960

Jacques Becker, a Year After His Death

He invented his own tempo. He loved fast cars and long meals; he shot two-hour films on subjects that really needed only fifteen minutes; he talked on the telephone for hours.

He was scrupulous and reflective and infinitely delicate. He loved to make detailed films about ordinary things—a misplaced jacket, a lottery ticket. But he gladly and courageously moved beyond his limits several times—at the end of *Casque d'Or,* in *Montparnasse 19,* and in *Le Trou.*

He paid strict attention to all the new films and the new filmmakers; he was quick to show admiration and affection. He was a stranger to professional jealousy. He admitted readily that others could practice his craft. Yet, what worries haunted his last years!

Since he was a slow worker, given to reflection, he often went beyond his estimated budget. With his three last films, interruptions caused by illness aggravated the situation and affected his relationships with the producers.

In the final period, his wonderful face had grown as gray as steel, as the metallic color automobiles are painted.

I met him after my first film had just come out and he was completing *Le Trou.* He told me, "Listen to me, be sure to put a little money aside."

I've never had the courage to repeat my last conversation with him, on the telephone, two weeks before he died. Françoise Fabian picked up the phone. I asked her how he was and offered to do any errands or anything else. She said, "He is too sick to speak to you." I heard him say, "What's that?" and then he took the receiver. He had difficulty speaking: "Well, it's true, I'm not very well, but don't tell them. *They* won't give me any more work."

I have hesitated to tell that story but I decided to do so to show the cruelty of our profession and, indeed, the cruelty of all show business.

—1961

ROBERT BRESSON

Les Dames du Bois de Boulogne

Not quite ten years ago, on an afternoon when I was dying to be at the movies rather than in school, our literature professor came into the classroom and said, "Last night I saw the stupidest film in the world, *Les Dames du Bois de Boulogne.* There's a character in it who resolves his romantic problems by driving eighty miles an hour. I can't think of anything more grotesque." The critics were not any kinder. The public didn't come, or if they did, it was only to smirk at every one of Cocteau's lines. The producer, Raoul Ploquin, was ruined, and it took him seven years to recover.

The Cinéma d'Essai has just put Bresson's film on the program as part of a retrospective, and I hear that the attendance is greater than for any other film, that the audiences are quiet, and sometimes even applaud. To quote Cocteau, the movie "has won its case in the appeals court." After its spectacular commercial failure, *Les Dames du Bois de Boulogne* was shown in film clubs and almost all the critics made their amends. Today, now that *Le Journal d'un Curé de Campagne (The Diary of a Country Priest)* has won over the last holdouts, Bresson is considered one of the three or four greatest French filmmakers.

His first film, *Les Anges du Péché (The Angels of Sin),* from a screenplay by Father Raymond Bruckberger, with dialogue by Jean Giraudoux, won universal approval when it appeared in 1943. In *Les Dames,* Bresson started from an episode in Diderot's *Jacques le Fataliste*—the adventure of Madame de la Pommeraye and the Marquis des Arcis. The adaptation is faithful and very restrained. It is faithful to the degree that entire sentences of Diderot remain unchanged. It is common to underestimate the importance of the role of Cocteau, who was on this occasion a rewriter of genius. One example: Diderot: "The history of your heart is word by word the history of mine." Cocteau: "The history of your heart is word for word the sad story of mine." If we read the two sentences aloud, it has to be admitted that Cocteau improved on Diderot; he added the music.

In Diderot's story, all the characters are base. Madame de la Pommeraye is vengeance itself, a pure Racine character (pure in the sense that Phèdre is pure), and Madame Duquenoi and her daughter, the pious ladies, push duplicity to the point of going to confession assuming that the Marquis will corrupt their confessor and find out everything. When Diderot's hostess finishes her tale, Jacques' teacher says, "My dear hostess, you tell the story very well, but you still have a long way to go in dramatic art. If you want your young girl to be interesting, you must teach her simplicity, and show her to us as the innocent victim, against her will, of her mother and of Madame de la Pommeraye, and show us that the cruelest things are done to her. . . . When you introduce a character into a scene, his role must be singular. You have sinned against the rules of Aristides, Horace, Vida and Le Bossu." What is most astonishing about Cocteau's and Bresson's adaptation, why it is at the same time faithful and unfaithful, is that they took the observations of Jacques' teacher into account: in the film, Agnès is unequivocal, she is the innocent victim of Hélène. The lion's share of responsibility goes to Cocteau; from the very first exchange, his mark is everywhere: "Have I not succeeded in distracting you? Are you suffering?" And later: "There is no such thing as love, only its proofs." And further: "I love gold, it is like you: hot, cold, clear, somber, incorruptible." But if one doesn't know Diderot's text, this could easily be missed. Just as Giraudoux gave *Les Anges du Péché* its dynamism, Cocteau endows *Les Dames* with life. We cannot fail to be struck by the similarities between the films that Cocteau has himself made since 1945 and this one. The relationship between Paul Bernard and Elina Labourdette in *Les Dames* is exactly the same as between Josette Day and Jean Marais in *La Belle et le Bête (Beauty and the Beast)*. There is between them a love that leads to total submission and devotion. Maria Casares reminds us inevitably of Nicole Stéphane in *Les Enfants Terribles* as she pronounces those sentences that are Cocteau's trademark: "And above all, don't thank me" or "Don't pull down my supports."

To get away from the monotony of the usual labels that are applied to Cocteau, we should think hard about his realism. It starts with the "spoken" side of his dialogues, which sometimes make us smile: "I can't receive you, come in." The sharp sense of realism, when it's pushed to its limits, introduces the eccentric. Twenty years after *Les Enfants Terribles,* Cocteau can film it without changing a word of the dialogue and the actors can deliver it with extraordinary truth. An excellent example, which borders on the baroque but without being ridiculous, is a scene where Maria Casares walks down a staircase talking to Paul Bernard, who is escaping by the elevator: "Why are you leaving? I don't like the piano. . . ."

Bresson's part is not negligible, however. Though it was begun before the Liberation, the film was abandoned, then taken up again and completed to all intents and purposes, then really started again, several months later. The direction remains, despite the intervening years, very abstract. Cocteau himself remarked; "This isn't a film; it's the skeleton of a film." We are seduced by Bresson's intentions rather than by his execution. *Les Dames* is an exercise in style, like the book *Madame de. . . .* But if, with Louise de Vilmorin, our admiration is easily and facilely elicited, it is the opposite with Bresson, whose stubbornness and laborious work of refining finally commands our respect.

I think *Le Journal d'un Curé de Campagne,* in which every shot is as true as a handful of earth—the earth of Georges Bernanos, its author—is Bresson's best film. We shall have to wait for *La Princesse de Clèves,** which he's going to make next year, to know Robert Bresson's own real personality at last and assess his talent—on his own this time, without Giraudoux, Cocteau, and Bernanos.

—1954

Un Condamné à Mort S'est Échappé
1.

The importance of this film will make it worth returning to more than once in the coming weeks. I do not expect to do justice

---

* Bresson never made *La Princesse de Clèves;* it was directed in 1961 by Jean Delannoy, adapted and with dialogue by Cocteau.

to this major work with these notes written hastily after a first viewing.

In my opinion, *Un Condamné à Mort s'est échappé (A Man Escaped)* is not only Robert Bresson's most beautiful film but also the most important French film of the past ten years. (Before I wrote that sentence, I listed on a piece of paper all the films that have been made by Renoir, Ophuls, Cocteau, Tati, Gance, Astruc, Becker, Clouzot, Clément, and Clair since 1946.)

Now I regret that I wrote a few months ago, "Bresson's theories are always fascinating but they are so personal that they fit only him. The future existence of a 'Bresson school' would shake even his most optimistic observers. A conception of cinema that is so theoretical, mathematical, musical, and above all ascetic could not give rise to a general insight." Today I must disavow those sentences. *Un Condamné à Mort* seems to me to reduce to nothing a certain number of accepted ideas that governed filmmaking, all the way from script writing to direction.

In many films nowadays we find what is commonly called "a touch of bravura." What that means is that the filmmaker was thought to be courageous, that he tried to surpass himself in one or two scenes. By this token, *Un Condamné*, which is a stubborn film about stubbornness, made by a stubborn native of the Auvergne, is the first movie of utter bravura. Let us try to see how it differs from all the others we've seen over the years.

Bresson's remark, "Cinema is interior movement," is frequently quoted. Did he make the statement, rather too hastily interpreted as his profession of faith, for the pleasure of leading the theoreticians down the garden path? The commentators have decided that it is his characters' interior lives, their very souls, that preoccupy Bresson, while in fact it may be something more subtle: the movement of the *film*, its rhythm. Jean Renoir often says that cinema is an art more secret than painting, and that a film is made for three people. I haven't the slightest doubt that there are not three people in the world who don't find Bresson's work mysterious. It took a complete lack of awareness on the part of the daily reviewers to talk about the weaknesses of the actors in *Le Journal d'un Curé de Campagne*. However, the actors' work in a Bresson film is beyond notions of "correct" or "wrong." Their work essentially suggests a timelessness, a certain posture, a "difficulty with the fact of existing," a quality of suffering. Probably Bresson is an alchemist in reverse: he starts from movement in order to reach immobility, he screens out the gold to gather the sand.

For Bresson, films both past and present are only a skewed image of theater, and acting is exhibitionism. He thinks that in twenty years people will go to see movies to see how "the actors played in those days." We know that Bresson directs his actors by holding them back from acting "dramatically," from adding emphasis, forcing them to abstract from their "art." He achieves this by killing their will, exhausting them with an endless number of repetitions and takes, by almost hypnotizing them.

With his third film, *Le Journal d'un Curé de Campagne*, Bresson realized that he'd prefer to do without professional actors, even beginners, in favor of amateurs chosen for their appearance—and also their "spirit"—new creatures who don't bring any habits with them, or false spontaneity, bringing, in fact, no "art" at all. If all Bresson did was kill the life and the actor that's inside every person in order to bring before his camera individuals who recite deliberately neutral words, his work would be an interesting experiment. But he goes further. With amateur interpreters who know nothing about theater, he creates the ultimately real character, whose every gesture, look, attitude, reaction and word—not one of which is louder than the other—is essential. The whole takes on a form that *makes* the film.

Psychology and poetry have no part in his work. It's all about obtaining a certain harmony out of the various elements which act on each other, providing an infinity of relations: the acting and the sound, looks and noises, settings and lighting, commentary and music. It adds up to a Bresson film, a kind of miraculous success that defies analysis and, when it works perfectly, arouses a new and pure emotion.

It is clear that Bresson's films, because he takes a direction that is radically different from that of his colleagues, have a harder time making contact with the public than those films that arouse emotion by less noble and more facile, more theatrical means. For Bresson, as well as Renoir, Rossellini, Hitchcock, Orson Welles, cinema is spectacle, certainly, but the author of *Journal* wants his spectacle to be very particular, to have its own laws, not follow borrowed rules.

Un Condamné à Mort is a minute-by-minute account of a condemned man's getaway. Indeed, it is a fanatical reconstruction of an actual event, and Commander Devigny, the man who lived the adventure thirteen years ago, never left the set, since Bresson kept asking him to show the anonymous actor who portrayed him how you hold a spoon in a cell, how you write on the walls, how you fall asleep.

But it isn't actually a story, or even an account or a drama. It is simply the minute description by scrupulous reconstruction of what went into the escape. The entire film consists of closeups of objects and closeups of the face of the man who moves the objects.

Bresson wanted to call it *Le Vent souffle où il veut* (The wind blows where it will), and it was a perilous experiment; but it became a successful and moving film, thanks to Bresson's stubborn genius. He figured out how to buck all existing forms of filmmaking and reach for a new truth with a new realism.

The suspense—there *is* a certain suspense in the film—is created naturally, not by stretching out the passage of time, but by letting it evaporate. Because the shots are brief and the scenes rapid, we never have the feeling that we have been offered ninety privileged moments of Fontaine's sentence. We live with him in his prison cell, not for ninety minutes but for two months, and it is a fascinating experience.

The laconic dialogue alternates with the hero's interior monologue; the passages from one scene to another are carried out with Mozart's assistance. The sounds have a hallucinatory quality: railroads, the bolting of doors, footsteps, etc.

In addition, *Un Condamné* is Bresson's first perfectly homogeneous film. There is not a single spoiled shot; it conforms to the author's intentions from beginning to end. The "Bresson acting style," a false truthfulness that becomes truer than true, is practiced here even by the most minor characters. With this film, Bresson is acclaimed today by those who hissed *Les Dames du Bois de Boulogne* eleven years ago.

—1956

2.*

To the degree that *Un Condamné à Mort s'est échappé* is radically opposed to all conventional directorial styles, it will, I believe, be better appreciated by audiences who go to the movies

* This second article was written three weeks after the preceding one.

only occasionally, say once a month, than by the nonmovie-loving but more assiduous public whose sensibilities are often confused by the rhythm of American films.

What is striking when one sees the film for the first time is the constant contrast between what the work is and what it would be, or would have been, if it had been made by another filmmaker. At first all one sees are its deficiencies, and for a while one is tempted to redo the cutting and indicate additional shots so that the film would resemble "what a film is supposed to be."

Indeed, everybody pointed out the lack of any establishing shots— one would never know what Fontaine saw through his tiny window or from the roof of the prison. Thus, at the end of a first viewing, surprise might win out over admiration. And André Bazin felt moved to explain that it was easier to describe what the film was *not* than what it was.

It really must be seen again to appreciate its beauty perfectly. On second viewing, nothing any longer gets in the way of our keeping up, second by second, with the film's movement—it's incredibly swift—and walking in Leterrier's or Bresson's still-fresh footprints, whichever of them left them.

Bresson's film is pure music; its essential richness is in its rhythm. A film starts at one point and arrives ultimately at another. Some films make detours, others linger calmly for the satisfaction of drawing out a pleasant scene, some have noticeable gaps, but this particular film, once set on its perfectly straight path, rushes into the night with the same rhythm as a windshield wiper; its dissolves regularly wipe the rain of images at the end of each scene off the screen. It's one of those films which can be said not to contain a single useless shot or a scene that could be cut or shortened. It's the very opposite of those films that seem like a "montage," a collection of images.

Un Condamné à Mort s'est échappé is as free-style and nonsystematic as it is rigorous. Bresson has imposed only unities of place and action; it's not only that he has not tried to make his public identify with Leterrier, he has made such identification impossible. We are *with* Leterrier, we are at his side; we do not see everything he sees (only what relates to his escape), but never do we see anything more than he does.

What this amounts to is that Bresson has pulverized classic cutting—where a shot of someone looking at something is valid only in relation to the next shot showing what he is looking at—a form of cutting that made cinema a dramatic art, a kind of photographed theater. Bresson explodes all that and, if in *Un Condamné* the closeups of hands and objects nonetheless lead to closeups of the face, the succession is no longer ordered in terms of stage dramaturgy. It is in the service of a preestablished harmony of subtle relations among visual and aural elements. Each shot of hands or of a look is autonomous.

Between traditional directing and Bresson's there lies the same space as between dialogue and interior monologue.

Our admiration for Robert Bresson's film is not limited to his wager—to rest the entire enterprise on a single character in a cell for ninety minutes. The tour de force is not all. Many filmmakers—Clouzot, Dassin, Becker, and others—might have made a film that was ten times more thrilling and "human" than Bresson's. What is important is that the emotion, even if it is to be felt by only one viewer out of twenty, is rarer and purer and, as a result, far from altering the work's nobility, it confers a grandeur on it that was not hinted at at the outset.

The high points of the film rival Mozart for a few seconds. Here, the first chords of the Mass in C Minor, far from symbolizing liberty, as has often been written, give a liturgical aspect to the daily flushing of the toilet buckets.

I don't imagine that Fontaine is a very likable personality in Bresson's mind. It isn't courage that incites him to escape but simply boredom and idleness. A prison is made to escape from, besides which, our hero owes his success to luck. We are shown Lieutenant Fontaine, about whom we shall know nothing more, in a period of his life when he is particularly interesting and lucky. He talks about his act with a certain reserve, a bit like a lecturer telling us about his expedition as he comments on the silent movies he has brought back: "On the fourth, in the evening, we left the camp. . . ."

Bresson's great contribution clearly is the work of the actors. Certainly James Dean's acting, which moves us so much today, or Anna Magnani's, may risk our laughter in a few years, as Pierre-Richard Wilm's does today, while the acting of Laydu in *Le Journal d'un Curé de Campagne* and of Leterrier in *Un Condamné* will grow more forceful with time. Time always works for Bresson.

In *Un Condamné* the Bresson style of directing achieves its finest results. We are no longer offered the quiet voice of the little parish priest of Ambricourt, or the gentle look of the "prisoner of the holy

Agony," but the clear, dry diction of Lieutenant Fontaine. With his gaze as direct as that of a bird of prey, he hurls himself on the sacrificial sentinel like a vulture. Leterrier's acting owes nothing to Laydu's. "Speak as if you were talking to yourself," Bresson commanded him. He exerts all his effort to filming the face, or, more accurately, the seriousness of the human countenance.

"The artist owes a great debt to the countenance of man; if he cannot manage to evoke its natural dignity, he should at least attempt to conceal its superficiality and foolishness. Perhaps there's not a single foolish or superficial person on this earth, but simply some who give that impression because they are ill at ease, who have not found a corner of the universe in which they feel well." This marvelous reflection of Joseph von Sternberg's is, to my mind, the most apt comment on *Un Condamné*.

To think that Bresson will be an influence on French and foreign contemporary filmmakers seems highly unlikely. Nonetheless, we clearly see the limitations of the *other* cinema to the advantage of this film. The risk is that it may make us too demanding of the cruelty of Clouzot, the wit of René Clair, the carefulness of René Clément. Much remains to be discovered about film art, and some of it can be found in *Un Condamné*.

—1956

RENÉ CLÉMENT

Monsieur Ripois

It's been some time since the public stopped being preju-
diced against films made from famous novels. Today it accepts a
lack of fidelity to the spirit of the original, as well as to the letter
(Le Diable au Corps, La Symphonie Pastorale). It is taken for granted
that there is no problem in adapting literary works. Nevertheless, it
seems to me that if a filmmaker declares that he is inspired by a
book to make "something quite distinct," what he makes should be
marked by the same degree of *ambition* displayed in the original work
(as in *Le Journal d'un Curé de Campagne*). It is not permissible to
diminish the work one adapts; but this is the only criterion I would
suggest.

Raymond Queneau was the first to have the idea of basing a film
on Louis Hémon's *Monsieur Ripois et la Némésis*. René Clément
read the book, didn't like it very much, agreed to shoot it after much
hesitation, and entrusted the adaptation to Jean Aurenche. Unfortunately I don't know anything, nor will I ever, about Aurenche's treatment. Clément didn't like it and decided to do the treatment himself
with Hugh Mills, an English scenarist, leaving the dialogue to be
edited by Queneau. In the course of the work, the novel's title was
cut in half—the goddess of vengeance was relegated to the closet
and Monsieur Ripois appeared sans Nemesis.

This is the scenario: Monsieur Ripois (Gérard Philipe) is a Frenchman who has moved to London and is on the point of getting a
divorce. Taking advantage of his wife Catherine's absence, he has
persuaded a young woman, Patricia (Natasha Parry), and a friend of

hers (Valerie Hobson) to come to his wife's apartment. When Pat resists the idea of a flirtation, he starts a long confession of his love affairs. There was Anne (Margaret Johnston), his office manager, whom he seduced just to have peace during his working hours: all he did was create an office atmosphere in his private life. Next there was Mabel (Joan Greenwood), whom he promised to marry but then moved out on three days after their engagement. Next came a French prostitute, Marcelle, a good girl whom he lived off for a while until one day he took off with her savings. There was also Diana (Diana Decker), a neighbor, and then Catherine, whom he married for her money, and now finally there is Patricia, who is still resisting him. Just as she is about to give in, Ripois fakes a suicide and accidentally wounds himself. Catherine will be made to think that he only wanted to die because of her. For the rest of his life, she will push the wheelchair from which Ripois can do nothing but watch the women go by.

Hémon's book is a kind of masterpiece. It makes us think of Queneau, the Queneau of the great days, of *Odile*. Who is Amédée Ripois? He is the opposite of Don Juan; women do not appeal to him, there is nothing of the seducer about him, yet he has had numerous affairs. Ripois is the opposite number of Drieu la Rochelle's Gilles, a manic, obsessed, quintessential philanderer. Gilles's behavior toward women is built on the mechanism of seduction; his sexual life operates as murder does with Landru-Verdoux. Instead of hearts, they have computers; strictly organized filing systems that keep track of their loves. Louis Hémon, on the other hand, had enough heart and soul for two. Behind all that is sordid, pitiless, and cruel in his book, there is something even greater than generosity: the goodness of a man who was also a great writer. This goodness, Hémon's true and real feelings, and his vision are expressed by a marvelous character, a young girl named Ella, whose suicide leads Ripois to become aware of what a failure his life has been. Probably out of a snobbish fear of creating melodrama, Clément dropped this character, evidently thinking it more sophisticated to adopt the tone of ironic comedy à la Alec Guinness.

Just as the portrait of Dorian Gray grew uglier as its model lost his purity, so Ripois' problems become more numerous and increasingly grave as the list of women he has humiliated grows longer. *Monsieur Ripois et la Némésis* is a book about intrinsic justice: Ripois could not bring himself to pity Winifred when she was poor and starving, so he in turn will know the pangs of hunger.

At the sight of all the luxury on display in London society, Ripois asks himself, "How come I haven't got my share?" Later, "You've had more than your share of love. And what have you done with it?" I could give many examples to show that *Monsieur Ripois et la Némésis*, like *The Red and the Black*, is constructed in two parts: the themes in the first half are reexamined in the second. A careful reading shows convincingly that without its second part the novel would lack all meaning.

In remaining faithful only to the first half of the book, Clément has committed a fatal error, just as if he had cut one of its two verses out of a poem. He has torn off the fly's wings and then is surprised that it can't fly any more. His initial mistake was to change the first names. When Amédée Ripois becomes André Ripois, he loses the essence of his power and truth. Hémon's Ripois was a monster, Clément's is a cynical buffoon. (It brings to mind the pleasant film *Kind Hearts and Coronets*, by which Clément is a bit too obviously inspired.) Clément has confused cruelty and cynicism, mistaken the container for the content. Drawing the portrait of a man with no soul, he forgot to include any part of his own. *Monsieur Ripois* (*Knave of Hearts* in the United States) is a Ripois film; like its chief character it has no soul.

The dulling of the cutting edge of the story is matched by the film's writing style. Whereas the style of the novel was graceful, incisive, rapid, the film's is ponderous, plodding, sometimes heavy-handed. (I am thinking about how poverty in London is painted in an extraordinary passage in the book, and also the part about the prostitute, Marcelle.)

Clément's talent is as an imitator. *La Bataille du Rail* was an imitation of sobriety (Malraux's *L'Espoir* [*Man's Hope*] multiplied by ten), just as *Le Château de Verre* was an imitation of rigor and elegance (a second *Dames du Bois de Boulogne*). *Jeux Interdits* (*Forbidden Games*) imitated the cruelties of childhood.

When in his adaptation he suppressed everything that was moving in Hémon's book, Clément behaved like the pseudo-intellectuals with which French cinema is overpopulated, half-educated scholars for whom the height of genius is to remove from art anything that comes from the heart. The result is a vogue for grayish, thin soup on the order of *Les Orgueilleux* (*The Godless*), *Jeux Interdits*, *Thérèse Raquin*, *Le Blé en Herbe*—formless films in which the absence of any directive idea qualifies them to be called by our critics phenomenological, demystifying, indictments, merciless social investigations.

Faithful to the policy of the frog who wants to make himself bigger than the bull, René Clément didn't try to set straight the journalists who saw in Louis Hémon a second-rank author whose famous folk tale *Maria Chapdelaine* had won him fame. Hémon's *Journal* has not been published in France, although it appeared in England, but he wrote several books, including *Battling Malone* and *Colin-Maillard.* I believe *Monsieur Ripois et la Némésis* is the masterpiece of this melancholy, alcoholic Frenchman who killed himself by walking onto the railroad tracks before an oncoming train in the Canadian countryside.

Having betrayed Hémon, Clément betrayed Queneau. He included only a few of the exchanges of dialogue that Queneau wrote, notably a scene in which Ripois is giving a French lesson without noticing that his English pupil is quoting Mallarmé to him.

Audiences who haven't read Hémon's novel will find in Monsieur Ripois (sans Nemesis) a brilliant and enjoyable film, but they won't be able to measure the contrast in subtlety, intelligence, and, above all, in sensitivity that separates the novel from its adaptation. They won't know that the filmmaker was tinkering with a masterpiece.

—1954

HENRI-GEORGES CLOUZOT

Le Mystère Picasso

Of the two or three French films presented at Cannes, Henri-Georges Clouzot's *Le Mystère Picasso* is naturally the best.

Clouzot, whose avocation is painting, has wanted to make a film with his friend Pablo Picasso for a long time. They were held back as long as they were by a fear of having to respect the conventions of the "art film"—didacticism, dissection of canvases, the recounting of anecdotes, of being boring by having repeatedly to show first the artist at work and then his finished canvas.

A special ink made in America that was sent to Picasso by some friends settled this last problem. Clouzot was able to place the camera, not behind Picasso's back or next to him, but behind the canvas. Instead of watching Picasso paint, as would a visitor to his studio, we are present during the pure creative act without the intrusion of any external or picturesque element. This purity, this respect for the artist and his material, is pushed so far that there is no commentary to "instruct" or distract us. Only the music of Georges Auric accompanies the canvases. Planned as a ten-minute short subject, the film finally expanded to an hour and a half. *Le Mystère Picasso* begins in black-and-white on a normal screen; then it uses color; and finally the screen is expanded to show us the large canvases in CinemaScope.

The film, unique both in conception and realization, was photographed by Claude Renoir. It is his most beautiful work since he filmed his uncle's unforgettable *Carrosse d'Or*.

Clouzot has deliberately removed himself from this film, which will not be perceived by the general public as the *tour de force* it is. He has placed his cinematographic expertise at the service of one of today's greatest painters, along with his painstakingly achieved and self-confident technique. All their substance is at the disposal of the artist's achievements.

Le Mystère Picasso is a film that serves painting in general, and modern painting in particular. Once they've seen it, Picasso's detractors will no longer be able to say, "I could do as well," or, "A really fine draftsman, but no painter. . . ."

The paper Picasso is going to draw or paint on becomes one with the rectangle of cloth we are seated in front of. Indeed, it all takes place as if the artist were working in the movie house, behind the screen, at the very moment that we are watching the film. The experience one has of being present not at the showing of a film, but at a creative act in process, is raised to that level by the fact that Clouzot, as he directed the camera shots, didn't know what Picasso was going to draw or what place on the cloth he would touch with his brush.

When he discovered how to eliminate everything external to the work of art, to show nothing of Picasso, not even his arm or hand, Clouzot probably thought he was increasing the documentary value of his film. On the contrary, he was turning away from the neat sort of documentary, the "art film," and showing us a grouping of images as abstract as Norman MacLaren's drawings on film.

What is striking from the first image on is that we are precisely in the presence of an animated drawing, more beautiful than the ordinary, unusual and poetic but also unreal, and bearing no relation to what we expected, what had been announced, or anything we had known about the great painter. The Picasso mystery remains unsolved, which is why we are by turn amazed and left with a slight feeling of having been deceived. A work by Picasso created before our very eyes—that is a miracle which, if need be, would justify the greatness of cinema. What firmness in the drawing, what perpetual inventiveness, what verve, what a sense of humor; what a pleasure it is to see Picasso erase, begin over again, change, enrich. We imagine Jean Cocteau working on one of his poems doing something very like that: crossing out, substituting words, language pouring forth, images "arriving" as the colors do on the cloth. The film is about poetry and we feel overwhelmed by it.

Wouldn't we be even more so if Clouzot, aware of this poetry, had treated his film as a documentary? Why didn't he ask Georges

Auric to write a score worthy of *Sang d'un Poète (Blood of a Poet)*, instead of a mixture of comic opera tunes that deafen us?

Clouzot said that he rejected the idea of commentary because painting "cannot be explained in words." All very well, but wouldn't he have been wise to devote ten of the ninety minutes to show older or more recent canvases which had been more carefully worked out, were more successful, which would have contrasted with the drawings and canvases the painter had to execute in haste before the camera, in working conditions more like those of a music-hall caricaturist?

Along these lines, the scene where Clouzot is watching over Picasso, getting him to "beat the clock"—that is, complete a painting before the counter on the camera indicates that there is no more film in the chamber—is not in the best taste. It's a circus act in the midst of a concert.

Despite these reservations, which come to mind only on reflection, not during the film, *Le Mystère Picasso* is a great work by reason of the calm genius of its character, by the beauty of the film's material, and because of the filmmaker's ingenuity.

Le Mystère Picasso was shown at the Festival at seven-thirty and at ten-thirty. At the first showing there were some hostile outbursts and whistling. For fear of widespread booing at the main showing, the publicity director telephoned Saint-Paul-de-Vence at nine o'clock and asked Picasso to come as a reinforcement. He was in his nightshirt getting ready to go to bed, but he agreed to come to Cannes, and he arrived wearing a melon-colored hat.

The reception at the second showing was courteous but reserved, though Picasso and Clouzot were applauded for a long while by the guests when they left.

—1956

JEAN COCTEAU

Le Testament d'Orphée

Do we still have to prove how important a filmmaker Jean Cocteau is? I would first remind us of his attitude toward other people's work and toward the public.

His willingness to sign petitions, manifestos, to write prefaces and forewords, even advertising slogans for any work of distinction, was amazing, sometimes shocking. Mainly, I see it as a sign of humility. A proud man is determined not to display himself often; he seldom goes out, he exposes himself very little, and wants to be in demand.

Cocteau, on the other hand, was everywhere, and everything interested him. He helped everyone and all kinds of work. Did that take away from the value of his judgments? I don't think so. Whether written or spoken, his slogans had poetic precision; they were more than descriptive; they were true to the work or to the artist he supported.

Cocteau was well aware that most persons who came asking for his support were minor talents, but I imagine that what he thought to himself was, "The most mediocre artist is worth more than the best spectator." He exposed himself constantly, he deliberately chose that role.

Cocteau had a genuine cynicism combined with a basic generosity. An artist through and through, right to the ends of his tucked-up jacket sleeves, he was determined unconditionally to support other artists. Where was the cynicism in that? It was in his extraordinary contempt (never articulated) for the public and the critics—really, for everyone *in* the theater, for *all* the spectators, for those who faced the stage or the screen and passed judgment without running any of the risks that those who face them run all the time.

He was kind to everyone and he expected everyone to be kind to him. The slightest criticism wounded him: "I don't ask them to be sincere, I only ask them to be polite."

As to Cocteau's last film, Le Testament d'Orphée (The Testament of Orpheus), the critical notices—copiously worked out by Cocteau himself with his friends—were, most often out of simple kindness, unanimously favorable. They were no less unanimously insincere. The upshot commercially was just what would have happened if the film had been generally panned. It was as if the public could read between the lines. The rejection of Le Testament d'Orphée would appear to have been a collective and unconscious revenge on a man who, unlike the businessmen of show business, thought the public was always wrong. In this case, the public was wrong. Le Testament d'Orphée is worthy of admiration—it is an admirable film.

It is a remake, thirty years after, of Sang d'un Poète, the very same essay on poetic creation looked at afresh and revised. Indisputably, the most beautiful scene in Le Testament, and the most successful, is the meeting of the poet with Oedipus (Jean Marais). But I prefer to stick to three short scenes following one another in the last fifteen minutes of the film, which show that Cocteau, like all great filmmakers, practiced his art totally and worked to satisfy himself, which is the only way to make a good film. The direction is a critique of the scenario and the editing is a critique of the direction.

First Example: The Meeting with Myself

THE POET: I meet this character whom they have turned me into and the character only looks at me when I turn my back. I complain about him to my adopted son who makes fun of me a little.

CEGESTUS: You have been complaining everywhere that if you met him you wouldn't even want to shake his hand.

THE POET: He hates me.

CEGESTUS: He has no reason to love you. He's taken enough insults and beatings for you. . . .

THE POET: I'll kill him.

This beautiful scene, when the poet encounters his double, is, by Cocteau's testimony, the film's "hinge," its spinal column. The first plan was to shoot it on the parapet of Villefranche. Because of the weather, it was switched to the Rue Obscure, under the arches.

Here is a perfect example of an invention that was probably intoxicating. The idea is strong and beautiful. Whether it occurs to the filmmaker a year or six months or a week before the camera's first turn, it is an enormous satisfaction even before he's begun production.

At last, though, when it comes down to the routine reality of shooting, an idea of this kind doesn't turn out to be terribly enjoyable to shoot. Only the result counts. The scene has to be broken up enough so that the intention is clear, and you don't get bogged down with constantly freezing your characters in motion, or with freezing the moving camera or the glances of the actors. Cocteau had to change clothes with his stand-in (a meteorologist named Belloeil). It is hard, unsatisfying work.

When shooting such a scene, there is no room for improvisation, nothing must be left to chance. It is simply a matter of filming the eight or ten shots that have been planned in the clearest and cleanest way possible.

Here we are dealing with the cinema of efficiency—Hitchcock cinema—the impeccable execution of visual ideas constructed in a succession of predetermined and virtually sketched-out images. It would be very easy, in fact, to imagine Hitchcock shooting this scene of the "encounter with the double" in a spy story that involved look-alikes.

The happy moment for Cocteau in this case didn't come when the shooting began, but at the moment the idea was born . . . "Ah, I will shoot a scene showing the poet encountering himself."

As a literary concept the idea is uninteresting. As a work of plastic art, yes, it makes us think of Dali's canvases, but above all it is a great cinematic idea. Its effectiveness on the screen brings back the joy of the very moment when the invention was born, and its beauty is compensation enough for the laboriousness of the shooting.

Second Example: The Intellectual Lovers

A close shot of the poet and Cegestus. We see what they see: a young couple in a loving embrace. Each notes down his impressions in a notebook on the other's back.

Here is another beautiful idea, whose interest isn't evident when formulated merely in words. In contrast to the scene preceding it, this one is exciting to film because it can be improved a thousand percent during the shooting.

First, there is the choice of the couple, which can make the idea lovelier, then there is the setting, and finally, the small gestures and the mimicry that add humor. Once again, the clarity of the idea is essential, but this time it will be achieved less by the relations of the scenes to each other than by each individual construction. Clarity and exactness in this case can be verified on the spot, not just a week later on the editing table.

This is also a plastic idea but one which owes nothing to painting. It brings to mind a witty drawing because of the verve of the treatment and its satirical aspects. In his great days, Frank Tashlin made this kind of movie—which had first belonged to Jean Renoir—a cinema of jubilation. In this kind of filmmaking, the first rehearsal is always muddy and unclear; only with about the fifth does it begin to clarify, to become purer and at the same time acquire depth. The entire team around the director follows the work, participates in it, understands it; now improvisation is in the driver's seat, and the undertaking moves toward the most alive expression possible.

Third Example: The Death of the Poet

Minerva has refused the resuscitated hibiscus that the poet offered her. He draws back: I'm sorry . . . I'm . . . I'm sorry. *Scarcely has he begun to move away than Minerva brandishes her spear and throws it. A shot of the poet walking. The spear pierces him in the back, between the shoulders.*

A frontal shot. The spear has passed through the poet's body and protrudes from his chest. He brings his hands to it and falls on his knees, then lies on his side, groaning several times over: How horrible! . . . how horrible . . . how horrible. . . .

There isn't even any need to discuss the idea of this scene: it's the underlying idea of the whole film. At the end of *Le Testament d'Orphée,* the poet's blood must flow.

An unpleasant scene to shoot, the least enjoyable in the film. First of all, Minerva's costume, which appears to be inspired by the rubberized suits of frogmen, was no simple matter. Then there was the matter of the special effects for the spear. It was made of rolled paper, weighing sixty grams, composed of two tubes, one inside the other and fixed so that it would contract by forty centimeters when it reached its target, that is, Cocteau's back. He was protected by a piece of metal under his jacket. The spear was thrown by its inventor, M. Durin.

The shooting was endless, the workers went into overtime, and there was anxiety and emotional upheaval among the team. And, at the end of work like this, there may be satisfaction at the success of the planned shots, but no deeper satisfaction. At the end of this sort of scene, the special effects, impossible to forget for those who have watched the shooting, give the director pangs of conscience, or at least doubts: Does it work? Will it look foolish?

The stroke of genius that makes this scene work was, in the end, the addition of sound. The enormous roar of a jet taking off accompanies the spear-throwing. The poet will die in the inhuman noise that everybody is familiar with at airports.

I'm not suggesting that he got this idea after the shooting; on the contrary, Cocteau, like all great directors, knows that ideas by themselves are never sufficient, that they must be *imposed*—"led along," always with the public in mind. That is why, just before the poet fails to enter Minerva's hall, we hear the voice of a stewardess saying, "Please fasten your seat belts and put out your cigarettes." The idea of planes is already present—already, one might say, in the air.

So, since we are discussing the satisfactions in shooting a film, in this scene of the death of the poet, the great moment of joy for the director took place, I'd think, in the editing room, when Cocteau was able to see the flying spear accompanied by the screech of the jet. The quality of this joining of sound and image should have set to rest any doubts he had about the emotional power of the scene. He should have been happy; he should have been, and I believe he was.

—1964

JULES DASSIN

Le Rififi Chez les Hommes

Le Rififi (*Rififi* in the United States), the first French film by the American filmmaker Jules Dassin, who came to cinema from directing in the theater, is structured like a classical tragedy. Act I: Preparation for a holdup; Act II: "Consummation" of the holdup; Act III: Punishment, vengeance, death.

It isn't necessary to point out the modest production budget of *Le Rififi* before I say that I liked the film and intend to praise it, but it may serve some purpose, if only to demonstrate that a film's success depends more on its director than on massive production resources or the participation of world-renowned actors.

Out of the worst crime novels I have ever read, Jules Dassin has made the best crime film I have ever seen. In fact, this is not a minor genre. Dassin shot the film on the street during high winds and rain, and he reveals Paris to us Frenchmen as he revealed London to the English *(Night in the City)* and New York to the Americans *(Naked City)*. It would be unfair not to credit also the chief cameraman, Agostini, who truly worked miracles under very unusual conditions: the interior shots in actual dark bistros, nighttime exteriors without lights, the platform of the Port-Royal subway station, tiny details of decor, etcetera.

Everything in *Le Rififi* is intelligent: screenplay, dialogue, sets, music, choice of actors. Jean Servais, Robert Manuel, and Jules Dassin are perfect. The two failures are the female casting and the specially written song, which is execrable.

The direction is a marvel of skill and inventiveness. *Le Rififi* is composed of three bits of rigorously developed bravura. Every shot answers the viewer's question, "How?" Dassin remains faithful to his style of combining the documentary approach with lyricism. For the past week, the only thing being talked about in Paris was the silent holdup, splendidly soundtracked, in which objects, movements, and glances create an extraordinary ballet around an umbrella placed over a hole pierced through the ceiling of a jewelry store alive with security systems.

Beyond that, the real value of the film lies in its tone. The characters in *Le Rififi* are not despicable. The relative permissiveness of the French censors allowed Dassin to make a film without compromises, immoral perhaps, but profoundly noble, tragic, warm, human. Behind the smiles of the three actors—Jean Servais' bitter, Robert Manuel's sunny, and Jules Dassin's sad though with bursts of gaiety—we divine the filmmaker, a tender, indulgent man, gentle and trusting, capable of telling us one of these days a more ennobling story of characters who have been better served by their destiny. That is what we must not forget and why we must thank Jules Dassin. It is this consideration that amply justifies the presence at the Cannes Festival of *Le Rififi chez les Hommes*.

—1954

Celui Qui Doit Mourir

Jules Dassin considers *Celui qui doit mourir (He Who Must Die)* the "film of his life," the first film he really chose to make, and made with complete freedom, a film in which he succeeded in expressing himself totally. Its failure is all the more disturbing since Dassin, in Hollywood, London, and Paris, often earned our admiration by "saving" films that were made to order, little detective stories that he endowed with unusual nobility.

This time there is nothing but nobility, nobility, and more nobility— too much nobility for a film that displays an intellectual confusion seldom equaled in the history of cinema.

Let us take it all in order: at Lycovrissi, a Greek village ruled by

the Turks, the villagers are preparing their annual reenactment of
the Mystery of the Passion. The priest (Fernand Ledoux) assigns the
roles: the local prostitute will be Mary Magdalene; the stuttering
shepherd will be Christ; the blacksmith will be Judas; the son of
the local landowner, the saddler and the café owner will be respectively
Peter, James, and John.

The people of another village that was recently burned by the
Turks arrive, led by their priest (Jean Servais). They are dying of
weariness and hunger. Fernand Ledoux chases them away, saying that
they have cholera. They settle nearby on the Sarakhina and try to
build a village, assisted by some of the inhabitants of Lycovrissi who
act in the spirit of the characters they have been chosen to personify
in the Passion. Everything ends exactly as we had foreseen from the
first reel, with Christ being stabbed by Judas. This awakens the population to the universality of human conscience and calls them to a
better future of justice and peace.

I must admit that this kind of subject, in which everyday people
must transcend themselves by identifying with characters they personify, irritates me because it is so theatrical and so obvious. Knowing
in advance what is going to happen, that Judas is going to betray
Christ, we pay attention only to how the blacksmith will betray the
shepherd. Our inevitable disappointment is heightened since the trail
is all the more obvious by being shown to us in closeups. A story
interests me far more if I figure out for myself that a particular character is a Christ figure. The references are telegraphed ahead of time
in this film that proves—what? That good faith is better than bad?
That well-ordered charity begins with others?

The fact is that Dassin is a child. Since children are more spirited,
have livelier fantasies, and are more intuitive than adults, Hollywood
is a hundred times livelier than our cinema. But when children imitate
adults, the result may be Mozart, but it may also be Minou Drouet!

Celui qui doit mourir, adapted from Nikos Kazantsakis' *The Greek
Passion* by Jules Dassin and Ben Barzman goes beyond the limits of
naïveté, simplification and sentimentality. What a waste of energy,
courage, and generosity! What a lack of discrimination in this film,
influenced by Pudovkin, in which not a single frame attains the grandeur of any randomly chosen shot from Malraux's *L'Espoir.*

This plaintive and sorrowful work drips with sentimentality to the
point of indecency, as happens when someone tries to make a strong
point but gets it backward. Jules Dassin says, "I think everyone should

eat all he wants," without realizing that thus stated this is an obscenity. I know exactly what Dassin would answer: "In today's world, men and women and children die of hunger every day." I also believe that it is crucial to make films which show that people still die of hunger, but it is my conviction that misery should be filmed without "ornaments," filmed as it is, as brutally and cruelly as possible, without any Biblical pretext, without commentary and proof. Instead of filming misery directly, Dassin slaps us with a sermon so heavy that at certain moments the film becomes hateful because of its stupidities—for example, when Maurice Ronet, playing the son of a rich landowner, offers his comrades who are preparing to fight each other some pieces of cheese on a wooden tray. Marie-Chantal registering in the Communist party would do the same thing.

During the film, which I saw twice, I noted this sentence in the dialogue: "The human brain is a fragile machine; one turn too many and it breaks down." Jules Dassin gave one turn too many to his film; he has mixed everything up, tangled it all together, preaching and plasticity, reflections in mirrors, the lack of bread, rejected lovers, and children who die of cold.

In Paris, yes, in Paris, men and women spend the entire winter sleeping on the sewer grates in the middle of the sidewalks; every year, old people kill themselves when faced with tax statements that they cannot even understand; families of six live in a single room; sick children die for lack of care. And Jules Dassin, an American filmmaker who has emigrated to Paris, Jules Dassin who is gentleness itself, who can burst into tears at a warm handshake, when he had 350 million francs to make the film of his life, went to Greece to make a film about misery there, taking with him a handful of former students of the Cours Simon. And he made a film full of symbols and folklore, a film that went beyond Manichaeism, a film in which the good people are thin and stutter or have tuberculosis and the wicked are fat, healthy, and laugh too loud.

The whole thing is slow-moving, solemn and heavy, complaining. André Obey's dialogue is theatrical and often vulgar: "You give an account, St. James, of the post office," or "Your speech was perfect on the spiritual level," or again, "Cholera . . . a symbol."

Almost all the actors are bad, overacting or taking the wrong tack, except for Teddy Bilis, René Lefêvre, and Lucien Raimbourg, who bring a bit of life to their roles. Jules Dassin did considerable work on Pierre Vaneck but I fear that this young actor is going to inherit all of Gérard Philipe's terrible roles: melancholy consumptives with soft voices and misty eyes. Max Douy's sets are very successful; Jacques Natteau's photography very heavy. Apparently, nature—grass, stones, trees, clouds, and water—refused a part in this film, which suffers from a lack of carnality, sensuality, flesh and blood, and from being overly intellectual and theoretical.

Many artists who lack clarity surpass their limitations thanks to good instincts and temperament. But when one of their works is based precisely on clarity, it falls apart and its failure is total.

—1957

SACHA GUITRY

Assassins et Voleurs

Assassins et Voleurs is firmly situated on the side of immorality: the immorality of a cynical plot and script that glorify adultery, theft, injustice, and murder; and, even more, the immorality of its double financial and artistic success, which defies all the rules of good sense and experience. Its success is paradoxical and almost scandalous, as we shall see.

In contrast to all the films that we defend in *Les Cahiers du Cinéma*, *Assassins et Voleurs* is innocent of any esthetic ambitions. It possesses not the slightest indication of professional conscience: a boat scene supposed to be taking place in the open sea has obviously been shot on the sand; a hotel elevator does not ascend any more than the boat floats; the same setting is made to do for several locations; the long dialogue between Poiret and Serrault, which is divided into ten or twelve segments, was clearly filmed in a single afternoon with two cameras, and so sloppily, to boot, that if we strain a bit we can hear the buses passing by the studio-hangar and the stagehands on the next set chatting cheerfully over their lunch.

Written hastily by an old man confined to a wheelchair, directed in turn by the director, his assistant, and the film's producer (in other words, not directed at all), *Assassins et Voleurs* was patched together in a few weeks and judged unshowable by the Parisian distributors. "We can't put it out here, it's absolutely unwatchable. Let's hold the premiere in Vichy." The Vichy theater operator, flattered at first, screened the film and then indignantly refused to show "that" to "his public," which is the most indulgent in all France. The gentlemen from Paris raised their voices; the premiere was held, and the evening was a triumph. It broke box-office records everywhere in the provinces. It was decided to show it in Paris only at the end of its French run, so that the critics, who certainly would not fail to run the turkey down, could not sabotage the miraculous catch.

The rest is history. Scheduled for two weeks in six large first-run houses, *Assassins et Voleurs* got good reviews and ran for four weeks (even longer than its run on the Champs-Elysées), and, with more than 80 million francs in receipts, it is one of the ten winners among the year's feature films, beating out Carol Reed's *Trapeze*, Jean Negulesco's *The Rains of Ranchipur*, Henri Decoin's *Folies-Bergères*, Yves Ciampi's *Typhoon Over Nagasaki*, and a number of international productions.

This is the end of the paradoxes. Sacha Guitry's film may be a patchwork but that doesn't mean that it doesn't have verve, imagination, swiftness, and a rich inventiveness that we wouldn't mind finding in more costly and more ambitious productions.

Because some films arrive at a certain moment of time, and may bring together certain relevant elements, they become for the critics—though their authors may not have intended any such thing—symbolic standard-bearing works. Arriving after about ten polished (overly polished), costly (overly costly), ambitious, and indulgent French films, *Assassins et Voleurs*, with all its imperfections, symbolizes the movie that has been sanely produced, conceived, and directed. Its charm makes up for its lack of means. It doesn't depend on extravagance as do so many bad films of the time.

The production is very neat because out of necessity there could not be thirty-six ways of shooting any particular scene. Stubborn overcarefulness, too many hesitations, obsession with detail, too many rehearsals and reshots, and too many backup shots can kill any comic sense and freeze any smile. A casual and lighthearted film has to be made with a certain casualness and lightness. That's why *Assassins et Voleurs* triumphs at a time when Marcel Carné's *Le Pays d'où je viens*, Gérard Philipe's *Till l'espiègle*, and Jacques Becker's *Arsène Lupin* failed.

This curious film proves that success does not necessarily depend on complication. A really funny and insolent work without too much vulgarity, played by good actors who are not stars and who virtually direct themselves, a film shot almost without a director, which is economical to the point of austerity, is welcome in the midst of productions bogged down in timidity, cowardice, illusions of grandeur, snobbism, and ingrained distrust of the audience.

—1957

Sacha Guitry the Villain

The "in" Parisians don't like mixtures, role swapping, amateurs: Jean Renoir has written a play? It is declared cinematographic, anti-theater. Likewise, Jean Cocteau can only be an acrobat, a jack-of-all-trades, and, if I can believe the tale, the novelist Jean Giraudoux was threatened with being denied an opportunity to write for the theater. These taboos and prohibitions, these narrow labels are the work of mediocrities, fools who are jealous of their own little specialties. In the case of cinema, the fact that it requires complicated equipment is what is most frequently brought up to discourage artists who come from other disciplines.

Sacha Guitry had no such complexes, luckily for French cinema, which owes about a dozen good films to him, the best of which (among those I have managed to see) are: *Ceux de chez nous, Le Roman d'un Tricheur, Faisons un Rêve, Désiré, Remontons les Champs-Elysées, Ils étaient neuf Célibataires, Deburau, Assassins et Voleurs,* and the last of all, *Les Trois font la Paire.* Guitry was a quick, once-over-lightly worker; he disliked taking too much time fooling around with a film. He was content with his scripts and sure of his actors; he liked to shoot as quickly and conveniently as possible, sometimes with two cameras running at the same time, taking for granted that a spectacle had to be cinematographic, since it was recorded on film. The expression "filmed theater" was invented to stigmatize directors who dare film a play without inserting street scenes, a chase over rooftops, two speeding automobiles, and a bolting horse. *Celui qui doit mourir,* by Jules Dassin, adapted from a novel and filmed entirely outdoors, is more a piece of filmed theater than *Faisons un Rêve,* an absolutely perfect play that could not be improved even by transferring it to the screen.

"It's either a movie or it isn't" is the constant refrain. What foolishness! Hasn't anyone noticed that Italian neorealism—dirty laundry washed in public in Neapolitan alleys—is a direct descendant, not of the films of Carné or Feyder—both "realistic" directors—but of the filmed theater pieces of Marcel Pagnol.

In 1936, Sacha Guitry made four films. Think of it—four films in a single year. Luckily I know all four. *Le Nouveau Testament* is a comedy of manners about a gigolo and a broken date, and we find out that there are three statues of Joan of Arc in Paris—the source of a whole flood of hilarious misunderstandings. *Le Roman d'un Tricheur*, rightly considered to be Guitry's masterpiece, is a picaresque film, two-thirds commentary and full of unedited, or never reedited, brainstorms. *Faisons un Rêve*, which I have already referred to, is wonderfully acted by Sacha Guitry, Jacqueline Delubac, and Raimu in a single setting. *Le Mot de Cambronne* is a medium-length film, remarkable for its inventiveness and humor.

Seeing these films again today and holding them up against the false masterpieces of the same period is an instructive lesson. Guitry was a true filmmaker, more gifted than Duvivier, Grémillon, and Feyder, funnier and certainly less solemn than René Clair.

Guitry weaved through the history of cinema making fun of various fads and proclivities; he never practiced poetic realism, psychological realism, or American-style comedy. He was always Sacha Guitry; that is, he embroidered on themes that were personal to him, and always with a droll sense of a discovery: the benefits of inconstancy in love, the social usefulness of the asocial . . . thieves, murderers, gigolos, whores . . . he always dealt with life's paradoxes and, indeed, because life *is* paradoxical, Sacha Guitry was a realistic filmmaker.

Cinema survives and/or kills itself by depending upon a certain number of clichés that complicate the task of the scenarists, who are always boxed in in advance. Currently a thief cannot be a likable person unless he robs out of heroism and generosity like Mandrin, Cartouche, or Arsène Lupin. Likewise, an adulterous woman must necessarily be antipathetic unless her husband is a real shit or a cipher, or her lover is a prestigious leading man. If so many films are exasperatingly bad right from the start, it is because of a servile observance of rules that are supposedly dictated by the public's habits. In the face of this, a viewer doesn't have to be subversive, merely civilized, to react in reverse and sympathize with the characters the authors wanted us to find odious, so affected and labored are the so-called sympathetic characters.

With Guitry, as with Renoir (with whom he coincides on certain points, for example, a loving misogyny that grows from year to year— the idea that the only thing that counts is the soft skin of the woman you love), the whole notion of sympathetic or antipathetic personalities gives way before a more indulgent but also a clearer view of life as it is: a comedy with a hundred different acts, of which the screen is well suited to offer the most exact reflection.

Renoir's secret is sympathy, Guitry's is naughtiness. Their films have much in common in the originality and frankness with which they treat the primary universal subject, the relations between men and women, as well as the second great subject, the relations between masters and servants. Guitry and Renoir share a simplicity that justifies all their fantasies, a sense of realism that adds poetry to all their casualness, never abandoning either of them, a solid pessimism that is scarcely masked and without which a proclaimed love of life renders any work suspect.

The dialogue, love scenes, the emotional relationships in most films are unbelievably false. In Guitry's films the truth leaps at us suddenly at the end of each scene with such power that we almost jump out of our seats. In *Le Nouveau Testament* the young gigolo who has been invited to dinner arrives early; the husband may appear at any moment but the gigolo suggests to the old woman, "Come on, let's make love. Behind the door, very quickly; I swear we have time." The same character, in *Le Roman d'un Tricheur,* is an elevator opera- tor; in the elevator, Marguerite Moreno notices him. The elevator disappears from the frame on its way up; downstairs everybody awaits its return but it doesn't come down. Finally, when it appears, the little operator is gazing at a beautiful new watch he has just been given. Guitry is Lubitsch's French brother.

After two frankly mediocre films *(Toa, Aux Deux Colombes)* Guitry gave us a nice surprise, *La Poison.* The idea is based on an unusual news item: Having decided to kill his wife, a man (Michel Simon) consults a lawyer and leads him to believe that the murder has already been committed. Armed with the "sucker's" many pieces of free ad- vice, he stabs his wife after arranging all the false clues possible, and to our great joy he is acquitted.

Here is Sacha's habitual theme: Commit in cold blood, cynically, what is generally done in drunkenness or anger, twist the law and set oneself right with society by playing its game. This time the central thing is the scenes of home life between two old married people, scenes so harsh and cruel that they make us think at certain moments of the best of realistic cinema: *L'Atalante* by Jean Vigo and Stroheim's *Foolish Wives*. The wife, the "poison," insults Michel Simon, treats him like a fool, like dirt; her churlishness is set off ten times more dramatically by his calm before the murder: here is an outcome whose crudity—literally—is stupefying.

In *Les Trois font la Paire*, which the dying Sacha Guitry did not even direct, there is no question that Sophie Desmarets, Darry Cowl, Philippe Nicaud, Clément Duhour, and Jean Rigaux gave their best. Why? Quite simply because the dialogue was so right, so true that it couldn't be spoken badly, and the actors, left to themselves, found the correct tone quite naturally—it was the tone in which the text had been written. It is instructive to recollect the farcical scene in which Jean Rigaux is lying on his deathbed, dressed as a high army officer, in the costume of his favorite role. They called Sacha Guitry pretentious and foppish; yet he knew how to make fun of himself and even of death.

We have a quite recent proof of Sacha Guitry's delicacy and humanity in the scene in *Si Paris nous était conté*, when the stand-in for Henry IV, who risked his life every day by "doubling" for his king, returns home after Ravaillac's crime and is received by his wife in tears. As she kisses him, she says, "At last, we are delivered from this nightmare."

Finally, as compensation for the immense derision of love that is present in all his work, there is an overwhelming reverence for friendship and admiration. Sacha Guitry's first film, *Ceux de chez nous*, "silently" shows us the artists whom the young Sacha admired most: Mirbeau, Auguste Renoir, Claude Monet, Rodin, Dégas, Saint-Saëns, Anatole France. In his final film he renders homage to Simenon, Alfred Jarry, and Michel Simon. The last cinematographic image we have of him is in the prologue of this film, when he telephones his old friend Albert Wilemetz and says goodbye to him, holding his face to one side so that its thinness will not move us too much.

Two years ago, during the shooting of *Assassins et Voleurs*, I wanted to interview Sacha Guitry. His secretary told me that it would be possible on condition that I prepare my questions and submit them to the master beforehand. Stupidly I refused. What an idiot I was!
—1957

ALBERT LAMORISSE

Le Ballon Rouge

I saw *Le Ballon Rouge (The Red Balloon)* three times in the space of six months, so there's nothing mysterious to me about the unfailing enthusiasm it arouses. I know that if I criticize it severely I risk offending my most faithful readers and singling myself out in the worst possible way. When a work is universally admired, one hesitates to run counter to popular opinion. One might be tempted to pretend so as not to stand all alone.

There's no question that *Le Ballon Rouge,* a love story about a little boy and a balloon which follows him around everywhere like a puppy, is a carefully made film, and admirably photographed, if not well directed; also, the boy mugs as little as possible. Having said that, there is, in my opinion, neither poetry nor fantasy nor sensitivity nor truth in this film—not *real* poetry, fantasy, sensitivity, or truth.

When Walt Disney bestowed human speech and reactions on animals, he cheated the animals and the human beings as well. He betrayed La Fontaine by caricaturing him—but then no one takes Disney for a poet.

I believe firmly that nothing poetic can be born derivatively; we should despise modern artifacts which resemble something else: pens that are really cigarette lighters, leatherbound books that are cigarette boxes, etcetera.

Like Walt Disney's animals, Lamorisse's *Crin Blanc* is a counterfeit horse, his reactions are human. *Le Ballon Rouge* pushes transference to its ultimate. The red balloon that willingly follows the little boy acts like a puppy that acts like a human being. This is Walt Disney to the nth degree. What is wrong with this pretense is precisely that it *is* artificial, and it sinks deeper into the conceit as the film goes on.

Albert Lamorisse's films have none of the emotional truth that make Perrault's *Contes* or *Beauty and the Beast* what they are, works that are poetic and moral, both realistic and human. The fact that everything in *Le Ballon Rouge* is manufactured and phony isn't so bad as long as it is a matter of being amusing; basically, anything that makes us laugh is all right, even the most facile and vulgar tricks. Where things go wrong is when the director undertakes to move us. Not only does Lamorisse have no respect for the basic rules of fairy tales, he flies in their face in an attempt to give his films a breadth their basic premises never pretend to.

In a fairy tale everything is resolved humanly, things are returned to an earthly order in accord with proven dramatic law. With Lamorisse it's a different matter. At the end of *Crin Blanc*, the horse sinks into the sea with the little boy. In *Le Ballon Rouge*, the balloons carry the child off into the air. These endings are simply means of getting rid of unwieldy premises while trying to give the impression that the idea has been pushed to the ultimate.

Lamorisse believes he is showing us a balloon that is behaving like a *friend* to the little boy; in fact, it is shown as a *servant;* it travels three paces behind.

The intervention of the "villains" in both *Crin Blanc* and *Le Ballon Rouge* is consummate bad taste. In most of his films, out of fear of being dismissed simply as an "enchanter," Lamorisse shifts the focus and pretends to raise his fantasy to the level of tragedy. I find the mixture of these genres unacceptable. To make us love his poetic hero more, he has him persecuted by psychological bullies. It is all too simple.

This abuse of power, this overdoing of the pathetic, is causing havoc in every area nowadays. Edith Piaf may be supported by choruses and may force her voice through an echo chamber, but she will never be able to make us believe that a song about a boy and girl who have just committed suicide in a bistro is a Greek tragedy. She sings, "I dry the glasses in the back of the café," but it isn't Sarah Bernhardt singing Bach to Racine's words. I would remind you of Jack Palance's remark to the producer in *The Big Knife:* "Hasn't anyone ever told you that your bombastic statements are out of proportion to what you have to say?"

Yes, Lamorisse, everybody knows that it's better to tell a serious story lightly than to relate light matters gravely.

In dramatic art, a "telegraphed" effect is the one that comes from a distance and can be seen coming a long way off. The poetry in *Le Ballon Rouge* is consistently telegraphed, as is the effect of the tearing of Folco's pants in *Crin Blanc*. "Anything that isn't raw is merely decoration," Cocteau wrote. Lamorisse, who avoids anything raw, never moves beyond decorative art.

Once you understand the formula, it's quite easy to "make a Lamorisse." All it takes is to oppose a nice little boy against a few villains, with, as the object of conflict, an appealing little animal or a pretty little "something."

The child must have something of the animal about him, and the animal something of the child. I suggest the following: A little Laplander loses his white reindeer and, after he has found it again despite the wicked polar explorers, he disappears into the snow on the neck of his animal. Or: The little Brazilian whose sack of coffee has been ripped open by villainous soldiers. The coffee rolls into the sea and the child disappears forever when he jumps into the sea to recover his little treasure. How about the little Chinese who loses his paganism? The little street urchin who loses his breeches? . . . ! But this is already too much fantasy for Lamorisse.

We know Cocteau's cruel but accurate remark: "Every child is a poet except Minou Drouet." *Le Ballon Rouge* is like a film of Minou Drouet made for *Marie-Chantal*.

I would be remiss if I failed to point out that *Le Ballon Rouge* is one of the most beautiful color films ever made, thanks to the extraordinary work of Edmond Sechan.

—1956

JEAN-PIERRE MELVILLE

Les Enfants Terribles

When this Cocteau-Melville film appeared in 1950, it wasn't like anything else being done in French cinema at the time. But *Les Enfants Terribles* brought back the profound, powerful, bewitching charm of the novel, interpreted faithfully, a novel in which all those who were young in the 1930s had recognized themselves.

It's smart to reissue *Les Enfants Terribles* now when young audiences are attuned to the poetic cinema of the "children" of those "children," Jean-Luc Godard, Philippe Garrel, Carmelo Bene and others.

Over the years I continue to admire Nicole Stéphane, who spills rather than speaks the role of Elizabeth from her incredibly generous mouth. I also like the wan gravity of Edouard Dhermit as her brother Paul. His acting, as controversial at the time as Nora Gregor's in *La Règle du Jeu,* still moves me.

"To love and be loved, that is the ideal . . . provided, that is, that both involve the same person. The opposite often happens." In *Le Grand Ecart,* Jean Cocteau announced six years before the fact the profound subject matter of *Les Enfants Terribles.*

There is no need to carefully distinguish what is Melville's and what is Cocteau's in this four-handed concerto; the former's calm strength is well served by the latter's spirited writing. These two artists worked together like Bach and Vivaldi. Jean Cocteau's best novel became Jean-Pierre Melville's best film.

The drama of *Les Enfants Terribles,* one of the few truly olfactory films in the history of cinema (its odor is of children's sickrooms), progresses and rises in bursts, like a disturbing broken line on a temperature chart. This hospital poetry will never grow out of date, not so long as young and old alike remain capable of being struck by love sickness.

—1974

MAX OPHULS

Lola Montès

The cinematographic year now ending has been the richest and most stimulating since 1946. It opened with Fellini's *La Strada*, and its apotheosis is Max Ophuls' *Lola Montès.*

Like the heroine of its title, the film may provoke a scandal and arouse passions. If we must fight, we shall; if we must polemicize, so be it.

It is whole cinema that must be defended today, a cinema of *auteurs* which is also a visual pleasure, a cinema of ideas where inventiveness informs each image, a cinema that does not borrow from the prewar period, a cinema that breaks new paths too long forbidden.

Let's put a brake on our enthusiasm and proceed in orderly fashion, trying to stay objective no matter how little we want to.

The way the narrative is constructed, the way it hurries the chronology, reminds us of *Citizen Kane*, though now we have the benefits of CinemaScope, a process here used to the maximum of its potential for the first time. Instead of simply leaving his actors to the inhuman framework of the large screen, Ophuls tames the image, divides it, multiplies it, contracts or dilates it according to the needs of his amazing conception. The structure is new as well as daring; it could well confuse the viewer who lets himself become distracted or who comes in the middle. Too bad. There are films that demand undivided attention. *Lola Montès* is one of them.

At the end of her dramatic life, Lola Montès acts and mimes her Passion, a few episodes of an unusual love life. The atmosphere of the circus is nightmarish and hallucinatory. Three episodes take us away from this scene: the end of an affair with Franz Liszt; her youth; and a royal love affair in Bavaria just before she joins the circus. The fourth episode shows us Montès in the circus. Peter Ustinov plays the roles of ringmaster, tormentor, and final lover.

In fact, at the end of her life, the real Lola Montez (an Irish adventuress and courtesan despite her Spanish pseudonym) was engaged by an American circus as the star of a spectacle based on her life. Rather than condense into two hours film material that would justify a sixteen-part serial, Ophuls opted to recreate the spectacle of a circus and interject scenes from Lola's past. Peter Ustinov, the ringmaster-biographer, manages his show with the same bad taste, vulgarity, and unconscious cruelty that govern television broadcasts. If important actors have more prestige than the TV stars, it is because art imitates life—and embellishes it not a little.

Max Ophuls' film is about the underbelly of success, about turbulent careers and the ways scandal is exploited. Montès, it is often pointed out, cannot sing or dance; she simply knows how to please, she provokes, she causes scandal. The ringmaster tells us that she is a femme fatale and, if she has moved around a great deal, it is because "femmes fatales cannot stay put." But the flashbacks into Lola's past that show us her girlhood, her marriage to a drunken brute (Ivan Desny), her adventure with a solemn and foolish Franz Liszt, and her artistic disappointments belie his condescending statements. Lola was a woman like all the others, vulnerable and unsatisfied, only she did "all the things that women in the street dream about doing but don't dare." But she lived at an accelerated pace, and following a marvelous last interlude with an anachronistic king in Bavaria (Anton Walbrook), she must die every evening in an American circus, mimicking her own passions.

Ophuls doesn't forget that it took several weeks to cross a country a hundred years ago, so a central part of the film is set in coaches as they crisscross Europe. By the end of her breakneck life, Lola is wasted, used up prematurely: "I have examined her," the physician says. "Her heart is giving out and the disease in her throat is perhaps even more serious." The physical, earthy remarks tell the story: "For me, life is movement." The king of Bavaria asks her one evening, "Don't you want to stop, to rest, to be still for a bit?"

The film is constructed rigorously; if it throws some viewers off, it's because for fifty years most films have been narrated in an infantile way. From this point of view, *Lola Montès* is not only like *Citizen*

Kane but also *The Barefoot Contessa, Les Mauvaises Rencontres,* and all those films that turn chronology around for poetic effect.

The result is less a matter of following a story than contemplating a portrait of a woman. The image is too full and too rich to see it all at once. The author clearly intends it that way, going so far as to allow us to listen to several conversations at once. Clearly, Ophuls is interested less in the strong moments of intrigue than in what occurs *in between* them. The story that we grasp in scraps—what we perceive of it helps us to reconstitute the rest, as in real life—is brilliantly laconic. The characters do not sum up situations with elegant formulas; when they suffer, it is seen, not articulated. Surely this is the most intelligent and precise dialogue heard in a French film since Jean Vigo's *Zéro de Conduite*—strictly empirical dialogue: Pass me the salt . . . Here . . . Thank you. And yet, what spirit he manages to get into each exchange. The only character who is careful to fashion his phrases and make a stab at eloquence is Peter Ustinov, but he searches for the right words, stammers, repeats himself, just as in real life. If Ophuls were an Italian filmmaker, he might say, "I have made a neorealist film." He has indeed given us a new kind of realism here, even if it is the poetry, above all else, that draws our attention.

Lola Montès, made in three languages, is played by actors of many nationalities including Peter Ustinov (Russian-English), Anton Walbrook (Austrian-English), and Oskar Werner (Austrian). For the French version, the one that interests us here, these actors speak French with a more or less pronounced accent. Add to this that the dialogue sometimes offers us two or three conversations simultaneously, as well as whispers and dropped phrases, and you end up with a sound track that is about 20 percent unintelligible on first hearing.

Because I was fascinated and intrigued by the dialogue, I obtained a script in order to compare it to the final sound track. The dialogue in the written continuity is good, but that of the film is extraordinary because the actors were not able to deliver it according to the text, and because of changes on the sound stage. This sentence from the script, "A wild beast a hundred times more deadly than those you have just applauded in our menagerie," is declaimed by the scatterbrained genius Peter Ustinov as "A wild beast a hundred times more deadly than those in our menagerie." All the dancing master's lines were replaced during shooting by little cries and murmurs that are extremely effective. Ophuls deliberately retained shots that were flawed by accidents in preference to others that were perfect in his final edited version—for example, a scene where Ustinov's whip gets tangled in the fringe of a prop. Also, the king of Bavaria at the theater: "I was going to your home, Madame . . . no, that's not right—" he moves a piece of the scenery and picks up again—"I was going to your home, Madame, so as to spare you the inconvenience." The marvelous "No, that's not right" undoubtedly came when Walbrook lost his place during the shooting. With this kind of ongoing improvisation, all of it geared to improve the film, all directed toward a more authentic truth, Ophuls joins the Jean Renoir who made *Le Crime de Monsieur Lange.*

The two- and even threefold slippage that constantly crops up in *Lola Montès* between the characters and their remarks, and between their delivery and the text, creates an enchantment similar to the hesitations of Margaritis in *L'Atalante. Lola Montès* is the first film that stutters, a film in which the beauty of a word (the velvety voluptuousness with which Walbrook adorns the word "audience") consistently gives the cue for the meaning of a sentence. Jean Vigo again comes to mind, with his taste for versified text which he shares with Ophuls. My heart is split between this tiny poem from *L'Atalante:*

Ces couteaux de table	These table knives
Aux reflets changeants	With their shifting reflections
Sont inoxydables	Are unoxydizable
Eternellement.	Forever.

and this one declaimed by Ustinov:

A Raguse	At Ragusa
Robe exquise	An exquisite gown
Qu'on refuse	We refused to donate
A l'église.	To the church fair.

Lola Montès is a film that breaks all the records: the best French film of the year, the best CinemaScope to date; Max Ophuls is declared the best French technician of the day as well as the best director; for the first time, Martine Carol, as Lola, is really satisfactory, Peter Ustinov is sensational, and so is Oskar Werner; Anton Walbrook and Ivan Desny are excellent.

Max Ophuls is markedly a nineteenth-century filmmaker. We never have the impression that we are watching an historical film, but rather that we are 1850 spectators, as if we were reading Balzac. The portrait of the woman in this work is a synthesis of all his previous women: Lola Montès has all the emotional mishaps of the heroines of *Sans Lendemain, Letter from an Unknown Woman,* and *Madame de.* . . .

I'm well aware that it's probably not a good idea to attack films I don't like in order to defend a film I love, but in the end I am frankly obliged to think that if the public was cool to *Lola Montès,* it is because it has been scarcely educated to see really original and poetic works. The "best" French films (I am thinking of *Le Rouge et le Noir* of Claude Autant-Lara, and of *Diabolique* by Clouzot, and of *Les Grandes Manoeuvres* by René Clair) were made to order to please, to flatter, and to stroke the public.

A rave for a film one has reveled in five times in one week could go on forever. Let me end it by describing the beauty of the last scene: In the menagerie, Lola offers her hand to be kissed through the bars of a cage; as the camera moves backward, the circus spectators move forward at the bottom of the screen and we mingle with them. For the first time, the exit from a movie theater happens on screen. The entire film is thus put under the patronage of Pirandello, as is all of Ophuls' work.

Lola Montès is presented like a box of chocolates given to us as a Christmas present; but when the cover is removed, it comes out as a poem worth an untold fortune.

—1955

Max Ophuls Is Dead

We had thought he was cured of the rheumatic heart disease he developed while directing *The Marriage of Figaro,* which he translated and adapted himself, at the Schauspiel Theater in Hamburg. A German critic wrote that, through Beaumarchais, Ophuls resurrected the spirit of Mozart and the Commedia dell'Arte in this production. His habitual frantic drive stamped a breakneck rhythm on it. This *Marriage of Figaro* is composed of some thirty dizzying tableaus. The premiere was held January 6, but Ophuls, confined to his hospital bed on the other side of the city, could not be present at his triumph. The crowd went wild, forcing the actors to return for forty-three curtain calls.

He died on the morning of March 26, 1957.

He was born in Saarbrücken on May 6, 1902. After the 1914–18 war, at the time of the plebiscite in the Saar, Ophuls opted for French citizenship. This detail is not widely known and he was often described as a "Viennese working in our midst." In fact, Ophuls lived in Vienna for only ten months in 1926.

A stage actor and then a director, he came to films after he'd fallen in love with an actress whom he followed to Berlin. When talking pictures were first being developed, new filmmakers were sought from among theater people. Between 1930 and 1932, Ophuls directed four German-language films about which we know almost nothing. In 1932, he made *La Fiancée Vendue*, based on Smetana's opera, and more importantly, *Liebelei*, from Arthur Schnitzler's play, his most famous film and the one he himself preferred. When *Madame de . . .* , which he made four years ago, came out in Paris, no one noticed that Max Ophuls had adapted Louise de Vilmorin's short story to make it *Liebelei's* mate. The last half hour, the duel and the finale, is a remake pure and simple. When Ophuls fled Germany at the advent of Nazism, his name disappeared from the credits of *Liebelei.* When he went back a year and a half ago, he had the opportunity to see the film again, after twenty-five years. Before the showing, a local celebrity rose to explain that there was nothing to be proud of in the doctored list of credits. There was a moment of silence, then the film was shown and applauded at length.

Once in a while the Cinémathèque Française shows us the very lovely film which followed *Liebelei, La Signora di Tutti,* shot in 1934 in Italy, and based on a serial novel that oddly anticipates *Lola Montès.* It is a drama about an aging star, who after a suicide attempt, under the influence of anesthesia administered in a hospital, reviews the saddest episodes of her love life. Isa Miranda, twenty years before Martine Carol, was the pathetic heroine of this admirable work.

Of the half dozen films that Ophuls made in France before the war, *Divine* is perhaps the best. Starting with a situation straight out of Colette—a good country girl comes to Paris where she is caught up in the life of the music hall—he offers us his first inside portrait of the backstage world. If we are already made to think about *Lola Montès,* it's because Ophuls, forced to use Simone Berriau as his star, juggles her to play up all the secondary roles and to accumulate a mass of details, both whimsical and realistic. Along with *Le Plaisir*, *Divine* is the film in which Ophuls is closest to Jean Renoir.

Less successful was *La Tendre ennemie (The Tender Enemy)*, again with Simone Berriau. It is a ghost story full of René Clair special effects, but there is a good deal of tenderness as well in this fable.

Next Ophuls made *Yoshiwara*, which he didn't much like, *Le Roman de Werther (Werther)* which he thought OK, *Sans Lendemain (Without Tomorrow)* which he liked a little more, and in 1939, *De Mayerling à Sarajevo (Mayerling)*, which he finished in uniform, having been mobilized into the Algerian infantry.

After he was mustered out, he began shooting *L'Ecole des femmes* with Louis Jouvet and Madeleine Ozeray in Geneva. After three days the producer was tearing his hair. The first scene opens in a theater with the curtain still lowered. Jouvet comes down from the ceiling, lands on the stage, and the show begins. Ophuls' camera follows the actors when they leave the stage, it goes behind the scenes, into the wings. We will meet this Pirandello-likeness again in *La Ronde*, *Le Plaisir*, and most particularly in *Lola Montès*.

As unwilling in 1940 in Paris as in 1932 in Germany to meet the Nazis, Ophuls, accompanied by his wife and son, departed for New York. He bought a car to save train fare and arrived in Hollywood broke. For four years he hoped each day to begin work the next. Finally, in 1948, he made an excellent film, produced and starred in by Douglas Fairbanks, Jr., *The Exile*. Then came *Letter from an Unknown Woman*, an incredibly beautiful adaptation of a story by Stefan Zweig, and *Caught*, which has never been distributed in France.

In 1950, Ophuls returned to France to make *La Ronde*. Though it was booed at its premiere, it became one of the greatest successes of the post-war world. Then came *Le Plaisir*, based on three stories of Maupassant, the most misunderstood of his films; *Madame de . . .* ; and finally *Lola Montès*, about which all has been said and written. These four films demonstrate Max Ophuls' success in safeguarding his freedom of expression within that most difficult of categories—major European productions aimed at a world market.

Max Ophuls' taste for luxury really masked great modesty. What he sought—tempo and sweep—was so fragile and yet so precise that it had to be sheltered in a disproportionately huge wrapping, like a precious jewel enclosed in fifteen cases, each one large enough to contain the preceding one.

In his inside pocket, Ophuls carefully kept a small scrap of cardboard on which he'd written the titles of the films he dreamed of making. He showed it to me one day. *Egmont* by Goethe, *Adolphe* by Benjamin Constant, *La Belle Hélène*, to be adapted from Offenbach, *The Love of Four Colonels* by Peter Ustinov, a life of Catherine the Great for Ingrid Bergman, Pirandello's *Six Characters in Search of an Author*, and some others that I cannot remember.

In his contracts he always reserved the right to stop work on a film right up to the eve of the shooting if he wasn't allowed to proceed according to his own ideas. This happened, for example, with *Mam'zelle Nitouche*, which was passed on to Yves Allégret a week before the shooting was scheduled.

The main problem he encountered concerned the treatment of scripts. Ophuls was less interested in real things than in their reflections; he liked to film life indirectly, by "ricochet." For example, the first treatment of *Madame de . . .* , rejected by the producers, planned that the story, which we all know, be seen entirely in mirrors on the walls and ceiling.

That is why, since with *Lola Montès* he was dealing with feckless producers who only cared about the validity of the checks they wrote, he had carte blanche for the first time in a long while to fulfill his old dreams—the play within the play, Lola's life in nonchronological flashbacks, in fragments of the three-ring circus act.

Ophuls had lived so closely with these ideas for such a long time that it did not cross his mind that *Lola Montès* would explode like a bomb, make him the standard-bearer of the profession, and bring him new, unsuspected admirers—Jean Genêt, Audiberti, Rossellini.

Ophuls' bursts of laughter, joyful and contagious, were famous; his conversation was extraordinary, generous, enthusiastic, rich in musical allusions. Rhythm was his predominant preoccupation—the rhythm of a film, of a novel, the novelty of someone's walk, of a performer's acting, the rhythm of a life—Lola's . . . breathless. He dreamed pauses, stops, rests. After *Lola Montès* came out, to escape his telephone which bombarded him incessantly with both insults and praise, he went to Baden-Baden to "think."

Before his departure he had categorically refused to modify his editing of the film. I wired him in Baden that, taking advantage of his absence, they were cutting *Lola* in a Paris lab. He answered immediately: "I cannot imagine that French technicians would do such work behind a filmmaker's back. There must be a misunderstanding. I am attempting, all too unsuccessfully, to escape from this *Lola*, which is going through the same storms in Germany as in France, panic, despair, enthusiasm, hope. . . ." We know the rest.

There are two kinds of directors: those who say that "making a film is very difficult," and those who claim that "it's very easy; all you have to do is whatever comes into your head, and have a good time doing it." Max Ophuls belonged to the second group. But since he preferred to discuss Goethe and Mozart rather than himself, his intentions remain a mystery and his style is poorly understood.

He was not the virtuoso, or the esthete or the decorative filmmaker he has been called. He didn't make ten or eleven shots with a single sweep of the camera merely to "look good," nor did he run his camera up and down stairs, along façades, over railroad platforms, and through bushes. Like his friend Jean Renoir, Ophuls always sacrificed technique to the actor. Ophuls thought actors were at their best and least theatrical when forced to some physical effort—climbing stairs, running through the countryside or dancing throughout a long single take. When an actor in one of Ophuls' films is still, just standing or sitting—rare enough—you can be sure that something, a stove or a transparent curtain or a chair will be between the face and the camera. It's not at all that Ophuls did not recognize the expressiveness of the human face, but that he wanted the actor, knowing his face was partially hidden from the lens, to force himself to instinctively compensate for it, and to affirm himself by his tone. The actor then has to be more accurate, more exact. Ophuls was obsessed with verity and exactness. He was a filmmaker of realism; in the case of *Lola Montès*, even a neorealist.

We don't register all sounds or all conversations equally. This is why Ophuls' films annoyed the sound engineers so much; only about a third of the sound track could be heard distinctly; the rest was meant to come through only vaguely, as in real life. Dialogue was often merely sound.

Women are the principals in Ophuls' work: the hyper-feminine woman, victim of every kind of man—inflexible soldiers, charming diplomats, tyrannical artists, idealistic young boys, etcetera. Because Ophuls treated only this eternal subject, he was accused of being out-of-date, anachronistic. He showed the cruelty of pleasure, the trials of love, the traps of desire in his films; he was the director of "the sad tomorrow that follows the sprightly ball" (Victor Hugo).

If he received so many letters from young filmmakers after *Lola*

Montès, and if the cinema clubs discovered him, it's because, for the first time, he superimposed contemporary preoccupations onto his perennial theme of the woman burned out prematurely: the cruelty of modern forms of entertainment, the abusive exploitation of romanticized biography, indiscretions, quiz games, a constant succession of lovers, gossip columns, overwork, nervous depression. He confided to me that he had systematically put into the plot of *Lola Montès* everything that had troubled or disturbed him in the newspapers for the preceding three months: Hollywood divorces, Judy Garland's suicide attempt, Rita Hayworth's adventure, American three-ring circuses, the advent of CinemaScope and Cinerama, the overemphasis on publicity, the exaggerations of modern life.

Lola Montès is the greatest satirical film ever made, but rather than coming out like a laboratory test case, like Ionesco's *The Chairs,* for example, it is a superproduction within everyone's grasp. Peter Ustinov wrote an article about its phenomenal disproportion: "[Ophuls] was the most introspective of directors, a watchmaker who had no other ambition than to make the smallest watch in the world and who then, in a sudden burst of perversity, proceeded to place it on the tower of a cathedral."

Disturbed by the financial failure of *Lola Montès,* the producer, who was preparing a film on Modigliani, forced on Ophuls as collaborator a blasé, formerly prestigious scenarist, Henri Jeanson, a man of consummate skill. His role was to restrain Ophuls' enthusiasm and channel it. The extraordinary and moving thing about the affair is that, once he had come in contact with Ophuls' effervescence, Jeanson recaptured his own former verve. The beautiful script of *Modigliani* is the result of an unexpected but effective collaboration, the combination of two enthusiasms that turned out to be less contradictory than had been expected.

Max Ophuls was counting on the success of *Modigliani* to enable him to start an independent production company with Danielle Darrieux. Their first film was to have been *L'Histoire d'Aimer,* based on the novel by Louise de Vilmorin.

For some of us, Max Ophuls was the best French filmmaker, along with Jean Renoir. Our loss is immense, the loss of a Balzacian artist who was an advocate of his heroines, an accomplice of women, our bedside filmmaker.

—1957

JACQUES TATI

Mon Oncle

Movies are accused so consistently of being enslaved by money interests that there must be some truth to it. The one thing money can't buy, however, is time. Stars are the darlings of the moment, and so are the more numerous technicians. Even the fabulous movie studios don't last. This is why chance is so important in creating cinema—on the side of the gifted and against the rest.

Some filmmakers will not allow chance to play any part in their work; they want control over every detail; they reshoot a spoiled shot or a bad scene twenty times. For them, the key to success is time, all the time it takes. The only way they can afford such time is by reducing shooting costs twenty or thirty times by doing without both stars and studio.

Only two filmmakers follow this policy of absolute control: Robert Bresson and Jacques Tati. The point is that nowadays, given the haphazard, confused, and sloppy way films are made, a film by Bresson or Tati is necessarily a work of genius *a priori*, simply because a single, absolute authority has been imposed from the opening to "The End." In theory, of course, such authority ought to control any work of artistic pretensions.

This is why *Mon Oncle* can only be judged in terms of Tati's other films. Let us admit that *Mon Oncle* didn't live up to our hopes at Cannes; before it was shown, everyone accorded it a probable Grand Prix; afterward, only a possible Grand Prix.

Tati's humor is extremely restricted, first of all because he limits himself to comedy based on observation and rejects all the recent so-called discoveries that only amount to burlesque. Even within the restrictions of this comedy of observation, Tati rejects anything that is not believable. In addition, he refuses to use observations fitted to the personalities of his characters, since he rejects editing in the classic sense, the dramatic construction of scenes, and the psychology of characters. His comedy bears only on a slightly twisted picture of current life, but always within believable situations.

At the beginning of his career this was probably unconscious and intuitive. Of three gags, Tati preferred the most probable, the least fabricated, but he filmed all three. Now, his repugnance for pure fantasy, his taste for the true—the truly believable—has become systematic, analyzable, and criticizable like all systems. One may have loved or hated *Les Vacances de Monsieur Hulot (Mr. Hulot's Holiday)*, but it was impossible to be neutral about this logical, dense film, this beautiful, integrated whole. With *Mon Oncle*, on the other hand, this harmony has not been achieved, and the charm is not total. We admire one sequence and suffer through another; the repetitions grate; we are impatient to leave the Arpel factory to get back to Saint-Maur. In the darkness of the movie house our attention wanders.

Like Chaplin with *Modern Times*, and René Clair with *A nous la Liberté*, Tati presents his ideas in a film that concerns our time, but without saying so. The two worlds it sets in opposition are the world of twenty years ago and the world of twenty years hence. The whole Saint-Maur part, the life of the little people on the street, the market, the children, is completely charming, pretty, pleasant to watch, truly successful. The modern part, the Arpel family's house, the factory, is sometimes annoyingly overinsistent, undoubtedly because Tati was determined to press things to their ultimate conclusions. The plot is bare pretext; sometimes it even gets in the way: the ultra-modern kitchen is funny the first time, somewhat less so the second, not at all the third. Tati cannot stand ellipsis, which leads to an excess of details that spoil the thrust of the film. Thus, the metal fish that automatically spits out water whenever anyone but Mr. Arpel comes by is superfluous during the two-thirds of the film that comes after we have grasped the principle and what it means. Nevertheless, Tati cannot remove the fish from the scene or stop using it: *that would be logical.* It could just quietly disappear, but this is impossible within Tati's style, which uses only large, still shots corresponding to the vision of the visitor; no closeups because "in real life we don't stand on top of people's noses."

Likewise, the squeaking of Mme. Arpel's shoes is amusing at first, and almost maddening by the end. It's not just that Tati uses gags and keeps striking the same chord. His esthetic position and insane logic lead to a totally deformed and obsessive world view. The closer he seeks to get to life, the farther away he moves, because life is not logical (in real life we get so used to noises we don't hear them). In the end he creates a mad, nightmarish, overly concentrated universe which paralyzes laughter rather than engendering it.

I would be heartsick if anyone saw any malice in what I have written; my strictness is a measure of my admiration for Tati and *Mon Oncle*. His art is so great that we would like to be with him 100 percent. His film is basically so successful that we are struck with consternation before this documentary about tomorrow.

Tati, like Bresson, invents cinema as he makes a film; he rejects anyone else's structures.

—1958

IV
HURRAH FOR THE JAPANESE CINEMA

KENJI MIZOGUCHI

The Street of Shame

Mizoguchi, whose sudden death we learned about in the middle of the Venice Festival, was the author of the best Japanese films of recent years: *The Brave Life of O'Haru, Tales of the Hazy Moon,* and others. *The Street of Shame,* which is being shown at the Festival, seems at first more Western than his others because of its contemporary subject matter and its episodic nature. It's about the misadventures of six prostitutes who are threatened that they may have to leave the bordello where they are employed. I gather that the public was disappointed by this film, though I liked it as much as Mizoguchi's others. Mizoguchi, like Ingmar Bergman, is fascinated by luxury and the moral rot that develops in its wake. A good thirty shots show us money being passed from hand to hand, the wages of sin. Notice that the Japanese prostitutes drive around in a 4 CV (Citroen Quatre Chevaux) and talk from evening to dawn about Marilyn Monroe. The scene where the heroine (the girl Mizoguchi clearly prefers, made a pet of, fussed over) offers herself to her father is the best scene in this beautiful movie.

—1956

KON ICHIKAWA

The Burmese Harp

This Japanese military tale relates the story of a corporal of an elite regiment who plays a kind of Burmese harp during the Japanese invasion of Burma in 1945, and evokes salutary, peaceful, amazing results.

Like the Pied Piper who charmed first the rats and then the children, Mizushima plucks the strings of his instrument and charms the enemy, who stop fighting in order to sing. To his comrades, who owe their lives to him several times over, he is a man of great prestige. When the war ends, he leaves his company to carry the news to the soldiers who are still fighting in the mountains. Along the way he passes decaying corpses which he buries or incinerates. He has to work constantly to overcome his disgust, and he who had been so lighthearted meditates on horror all the time. When he takes the robe off the corpse of a Burmese bonze, he gets the idea that the habit makes the monk, so he puts it on and withdraws from the world. One day, his comrades cross his path, and he turns his head away and continues walking. The soldiers wonder aloud: Was it he or not? They send him a parakeet that repeats over and over the phrase it has memorized: "Let's go, Mizushima, return to Japan with us." A few days later, Mizushima, on one side of a barrier, his friends on the other, offers *them* a parakeet which repeats: "No, I cannot go back, no, I cannot go back." The prisoners sing "Home, Sweet Home," and Mizoshima accompanies their song briefly on his instrument, bows low, and disappears.

It's a curious film which pleased some members of the Venice

Festival jury enough last year that they came close to awarding it the Golden Lion. The sincerity of the enterprise is somewhat dubious. In any case, it is always hard to know where one stands about Japanese films. If I have the feeling that the reputation of *The Gates of Hell, All the Birds Knew, Shadows in Mid-day* is unjustified, I also think, on the other hand, all the Japanese films I've had the opportunity to see are strikingly beautiful and intelligent.

The Burmese Harp undeniably seduced me, even if I find fault with it for resembling a bit the sort of postwar works that purposely try to soften up the conquerer, fawn on him, titillate his curiosity.

Indeed, I loved those wonderful Japanese prints, above all for their plastic beauty; the emotion progressively overwhelms us, all the more powerfully because it is diabolically repressed by the authors. The extraordinary dignity of the personalities and the great nobility of the subject capture our interest, as long as a bit of literature and a touch of sentimentality don't frighten us off. Pervading the whole story there is an immense tranquillity and a mysterious charm that carry the film—which is not to ignore a decorative leisureliness possibly explained by the same legend that holds that any self-respecting Japanese needs at least seven hours to make love.

—1956

YASUSHI NAKAHIRA

Juvenile Passion

Apparently *Juvenile Passion* was directed by Yasushi Naka-hira, about whom we know absolutely nothing, rather than by someone named Ishihara, who, as it happens, is the screenwriter as well as the brother of one of the male stars, Yujiro Ishihara. If you add to that that the two actors in the film play two brothers, and that it's impossible to tell which of the two is the screenwriter's brother, you must agree that I have to be terribly fond of this film to publish this hazy review.

The one person whose biography no longer holds any secrets for me is the writer, Shintaro Ishihara, who was born in 1933, and is already at such a young age a thoroughbred in the René Julliard stable. The publishing house presents the author of this roguish saga as the Japanese equivalent of Françoise Sagan, if you please.

I read his *The Season of the Sun* in a French translation by Kuni Matsuo, published in the Collection Capricorne. This too was a collection of short stories that are very filmable, four novellas in which the spirit of *Juvenile Passion* is already evident.

In 1956, Ishihara won the Akutagawa literary prize—the Japanese Goncourt—and it caused a scandal. It is true that Ishihara writes with his feet, which may be irrelevant, even though the Japanese wash theirs more often than we do. We know that old refrain—it's sung just as often in the West. Certain faded guardians of the public morals suggested that Ishihara, under the pretext of realism and novelty, courts scandal and publicity by perverting the young, attacking sound morals, and exalting violence and sex. "The Sunshine Race" is an expression that was invented by some commentator to pillory these depraved young people. One story, "The Season of Sunshine," answers the charge, and it is a bitter answer indeed. Ishihara feels akin to Hemingway, and like him is concerned with speed, ellipses, allusions. Within a few months, five successful films have been based on his stories, and Ishihara, a handsome lad who stands about five feet three inches, has played in several of them.

In short, you will have guessed, Ishihara is called in Poland the Marek Hlasko of Japan, and in France the Sagan/Vadim/Buffet of Japan. The second is certainly warranted, since it seems clear that *Juvenile Passion* was influenced by *And God Created Woman (Et Dieu créa la Femme)*, which played in Japan at the same time it was released in France.

As in Vadim's first film, we are shown two brothers who are successively the lovers of a young woman unhappily married to an American. I find the Japanese film superior to its French model from every point of view: script, direction, acting, spirit.

The character of the young woman is remarkable. In the beginning, when the two boys meet her on the railroad platform, she is wearing a white corsage, a wide skirt, dark glasses, and we really believe along with them that she is a famous minx, inaccessible. Later, we guess that she is in love with Haruji, the timid brother, but we'd gamble our head that he is a virgin (if I had been taken at my word, I would have to take a leaf from Ishihara's book and write this article with my feet). Only later will she marry; this scene is played so finely that we will reproach ourselves for not having figured out the truth. To buy the brash brother's silence, she gives herself to him, and then she will give herself also to the timid one, who loved her from the start. There is nothing of the hussy about Elri. We can readily accept that she is unhappily married; she is in love with the timid Haruji for the purity of his heart; she is also in love with the rash Natshuhisa because he excites her physically. There is nothing either aggressive or paradoxical about the situation. Vadim is defeated on his own turf, for director Nakahira effortlessly allows us to sympathize with each of his characters in every circumstance.

The direction is to be admired for its inventiveness and nonconformism. Almost all the transitions are awkward as shots that do not at all resemble each other follow one another. It would seem clear that there was a great deal of improvisation; the shooting is full of ideas that could not have been foreseen; the ideas that spring up in the acting could not possibly have been indicated in a script.

In most films, one beautiful shot is introduced by two uninteresting ones and followed by two more; the idea is that the whole meshes harmoniously, flows into the film's mold like a smooth cooking sauce. Nakahira works entirely differently. When he's about to film a couple lying on the sand, he first shows us the girl as we would see her if we were lying behind her: an oblique perspective of her body, a little glimpse of her breasts through the gap in her bathing suit, very pretty, and not edited out for the screen. Having filmed that view, now he frames the faces vertically; two glances: the boy looks at the girl, whom he believes to be asleep; he is euphoric; next the girl glances at the boy, who has closed his eyes; then the camera returns to its original position behind the couple on the ground; the girl's hand moves slightly from her thigh and brushes against the boy's hand; a shot of the boy's body, lightly turned on his side, and a discreet glimpse of his bulging trunks.

All of this, which I explain more or less well, has absolute simplicity and clarity on the screen. These are, all of them, full, rich shots because each has equal value; none is there merely to introduce the next one. Obviously, such shots do not and cannot intertwine, since it is the actual taking of the first shot that suggests the next one in a certain way to the filmmaker, and then one more in another way. When he edits his takes, he finds one more beautiful than the other and sets them in succession to serve the scene and the film as well as possible.

We should understand that there are two ways to make films, and this way is not in any sense inferior; it is Vigo's method, and sometimes Bergman's and Fellini's. It is always a matter of sacrificing the film to the film, and everything depends on what we mean by the film— whether it means expressing the greatest number of ideas with the minimum of elements or whether it means showing the greatest number of elements with just enough ideas.

One would have to say that the greatest filmmakers are over fifty, but it is important to practice the cinema of one's own age and try, if one is twenty-five and admires Dreyer, to emulate *Vampyr* rather than *Ordet*. Youth is in a hurry, it is impatient, it is bursting with all sorts of concrete ideas. Young filmmakers must shoot their films in mad haste, movies in which the characters are in a hurry, in which shots jostle each other to get on screen before "The End," films that contain their ideas. Later on, this succession of ideas will give way to one great, overriding idea, and then the critics will complain about a "promising" filmmaker who has grown old. So what?

Mr. Tessonneau, the general administrator of the Institut des Hautes Etudes Cinématographiques, should buy a copy of *Juvenile Passion* and show it to his flock on the first Monday of each month to keep them from acquiring the mentality of assistants. And what is the assistant's mentality? It can be summed up: "I am finally going to make my first film; I am terrified of falling on my face; I have allowed a script and actors to be imposed on me, but there is one thing I won't give in on, and that is time; I demand fourteen weeks of shooting, thirteen of them in the studio, because if I can use time and film as much as I want, I will be able, if not to make a good film, at least to prove that I can make a film."

Juvenile Passion was shot in seventeen days.

—1958

KEISUKE KINOSHITA

The Legend of Nayarama

We know that quite a large part of Japanese film production is intended for export. This was the case with *Gate of Hell*, for example, which the Japanese critics quite rightly did not find important. The confusion about the first Japanese films to be released in France, with the worst mixed indiscriminately with two or three masterpieces, all of them being presented as masterpieces, has compromised their distribution in France in the art and experimental theaters. The most beautiful Japanese film that we have been able to see, indeed one of the most beautiful films in the world, Mizoguchi's *Tales of the Hazy Moon*, which has French subtitles, is still waiting for some distributor with perspicacity enough to show it commercially in Paris.

The Legend of Nayarama, by Keisuke Kinoshita, is a film that is difficult to distribute in Europe. It is less plastically beautiful than the Mizoguchis we have seen at the Cinémathèque or at the festivals, although in the same tradition. It reminds us of Ophuls through its daring use of CinemaScope, colored projectors, and, extravagantly, of moving cameras.

When the old people of a certain village where a bowl of rice feeds a man for several months reach seventy, they are left on the summit of Nayarama mountain so they will no longer burden their families. When the moment comes, and she asks, the dutiful son must carry his aging mother there on his back. The hero of this film, too, must carry his father to the mountain top on his back like a mountaineer's knapsack. He puts the old man down in a crevice in the rocks and descends to the village, lighter in his body, if heavier in his heart. Vultures begin to fly around the summit. When it begins to snow, the hero, filled with remorse, turns and goes back to find his father dead, frozen, turned into a statue. It is a sight we don't see every day.

The astonishing thing is that this cruel and inhuman legend is treated only in its most human aspect. There are evasions, exceptions, procrastination. The old man doesn't want to go to the mountain and so again and again he delays his departure. The old woman wants to go, but before she does she breaks her teeth on a stone so that she will no longer be able to eat solid food. We are reminded irresistibly of Beckett's *Endgame* and last meals of gruel when we confront this grandiose and terrible portrait of human ruin. Indeed, these are not pictures we want to look at from five to seven, but later in the night, before we go to sleep . . . perhaps forever. My God, what a beautiful film!

—1958

V
SOME OUTSIDERS

INGMAR BERGMAN

Bergman's Opus

It's common knowledge that Ingmar Bergman, who is forty this year, is the son of a minister. Before he started to make films in 1945, he had written some plays and novels and was already deeply involved in directing a theater company—which he still is. He had mounted a broad range of plays by Anouilh, Camus, and masterpieces of French and Scandinavian classical literature.

This prodigious activity hasn't stopped him from making nineteen films in thirteen years, a fact all the more dizzying in that he usually creates them entirely, writing the screenplay as well as the dialogue, and directing them as well. Out of the nineteen, only six have been released commercially in France: *L'Eternel mirage, Summer with Monika, Smiles of a Summer Night, Sawdust and Tinsel, The Seventh Seal,* and *Sommarlek (Summer Interlude).* But thanks to the prizes that Bergman has amassed during the past three years and to the fact that his films are finding a growing public in an increasing number of "art houses" (there are now eighteen in Paris), a number of his older films will open in first-run houses next season. I would think that those most likely to find as wide an audience as, for example, *Smiles of a Summer Night* did are *A Lesson in Love* (a stunning comedy in the style of Lubitsch); *Waiting Women; Journey into Autumn,* a comedy tinged with bitterness. Two other films, more ambitious, but uneven, might enjoy the kind of success that *Sawdust and Tinsel* had: *The Prison,* the story of a film director whose old mathematics teacher has just proposed that he make a film about hell; and *Thirst,* in which a couple of Swedish tourists traveling across war-torn Germany just after World War II become aware of their own double standards.

In Sweden, Ingmar Bergman is now considered the preeminent film director, but it wasn't by any means always that way. His first contact with cinema was in 1944 when he wrote the screenplay for *Torments* by Sjöberg (who also directed *Miss Julie*), the story of the "torments" that a Latin teacher named Caligula inflicts on his pupils. (Just before that, Bergman had mounted Camus' *Caligula.*) The next year he made his first film, *Crisis*, about the woes of a young girl who is fought over by her natural mother and her adoptive mother. After that came *It Rains on Our Love* and *Port of Call.*

Bergman's first films shocked audiences because of their pessimism and rebelliousness. They were almost always about a couple of adolescents searching for happiness in escapades, at odds with middle-class society. These first movies were generally badly received. Bergman was treated like a subversive, blasphemous, and irritating schoolboy.

The first film which brought him real success was *Music in Darkness* (1948), the story of a pianist who goes blind during his military service. Once back in civilian life, he is patronized because of his infirmity until a rival in a love affair strikes him in anger. He goes mad with joy, simply because someone has finally treated him like a normal person. By 1951, Bergman had become fairly well recognized, but because of a crisis in the Swedish film industry no films were being made, and, in order to live, he made nine film commercials extolling the merits of a particular brand of soap.

The next year he went back to his real work with increased ardor, and made *Waiting Women*, which was probably influenced by Joseph Mankiewicz's *A Letter to Three Wives.*

Bergman's work is the labor of a born moviemaker. When he was six, he began to play with a tiny projector, using the same film strips over and over. In his film *Prison* he lingers lovingly over this childhood memory, showing us a movie buff who runs, in his attic, an old burlesque film in which a sleepwalker in a nightshirt, a policeman, and the devil himself chase each other in accelerated speed. Now, Bergman has a private film library of about 150 movies reduced to 16 mm. that he often shows for his collaborators and actors.

Bergman has seen a lot of American films, and he appears to have been influenced by Hitchcock. One cannot help thinking of *Suspicion* and *Rich and Strange*, when in *Thirst* one sees Bergman drawing out a dialogue between a man and a woman by the use of almost imperceptible but revealing gestures, and the interplay of precise and rather stylized glances. Starting in 1948, the year *The Rope* was released, Bergman stopped chopping up his footage and began to concentrate on moving his camera and his actors around more in order to construct longer uninterrupted episodes.

But unlike Juan Bardem, each of whose films is influenced by a different director and who has never succeeded in stamping his work with his own personality or sensibility, Bergman has perfectly incorporated in his own work the elements he admires in Cocteau, Anouilh, Hitchcock, and the classical theater.

Like Ophuls and Renoir, Bergman's work centers on woman, but it evokes Ophuls more than it does Renoir, because the creator of *Sawdust and Tinsel*, like Ophuls, adopts the viewpoint of his female characters more spontaneously than that of his male characters. Specifically, one could say that Renoir beckons us to view his heroines through the eyes of their male partners, whereas Ophuls and Bergman tend to show us men through women's eyes. This is palpable in *Smiles of a Summer Night*, where the men are stock characters and the women are drawn with great subtlety.

A Swedish journal once noted that "Bergman is much wiser about women [than men]." Bergman replied, "All women move me—old, young, tall, short, fat, thin, thick, heavy, light, beautiful, charming, living, dead. I also love cows, she-monkeys, sows, bitches, mares, hens, geese, turkey hens, lady hippos, and mice. But the categories of female that I prefer are wild beasts and dangerous reptiles. There are women I loathe. I'd like to murder one or two, or have myself killed by one of them. The world of women is my universe. It's the world I have developed in, perhaps not for the best, but no man can really feel he knows himself if he manages to detach himself from it."

An increasing amount is written about Bergman and that's to the good. The critics who don't indulge in a tirade about the deep pessimism of the Bergman opus usually go on about his optimism, both of which are true enough in terms of his overall work because he is a lover of truth. Bergman pushes stubbornly in all directions. This line of dialogue from *Smiles* sums up a philosophy of caring that is, nevertheless, tinged with Audiberti's mechanism: "What finally pushes us to the inaction of despair is that we cannot protect one single being from a single moment of suffering."

Bergman's early films pose social problems; in his second period the analysis becomes more personal, a purely introspective look into the hearts of his characters; and for the last few years, he has been preoccupied with good and evil and with metaphysics—which dominate *Sawdust and Tinsel* and *The Seventh Seal.* Thanks to the freedom allowed him by his Swedish producers (practically all his films have been released by them in Scandinavia), Bergman has raced ahead, producing in twelve years a cycle of creative work that took Hitchcock and Renoir thirty years.

There is a great deal of poetry in Bergman's work, but we become conscious of it after the fact. Rather, the essential elements are to be found in the search for a truth, which is always a more fruitful method. Bergman's preeminent strength is the direction he gives his actors. He entrusts the principal roles in his films to the five or six actors he loves best, never type-casting them. They are completely different from one film to the next, often playing diametrically opposite roles. He discovered Margit Carlquist in a dress shop and Harriet Andersson, dressed in black tights, singing in a provincial revue. He rarely asks his actors to redo scenes, and he never changes a line of his dialogue, which he writes in one draft without any preestablished plan.

At the beginning of one of his films, the viewer has the feeling that Bergman himself doesn't yet know how he'll end his story and that may indeed sometimes be the case. With Renoir also one almost always has the impression of helping to shoot the film, of watching it as it becomes what it is going to be, of a kind of collaboration with the director.

It seems to me that the best proof of Bergman's success is that he impresses on us with such power characters born in his own imagination. So natural is the dialogue he gives them that it is both eloquent and, at the same time, sounds the way people talk. Bergman often cites O'Neill, concurring with him that "dramatic art that does not impinge on the relationship between man and God is without interest." This judgment perfectly describes *The Seventh Seal,* though I admit that I prefer *So Close to Life. The Seventh Seal* is an inquisitive meditation on death. *So Close to Life* is a meditative inquiry into birth. It amounts to the same thing; both are about life.

The action of *So Close* takes place in a maternity ward during a twenty-four-hour period. I can't improve on the description of the story and the meaning of the film given by Ulla Isaksson, who wrote it together with Bergman.

Life, birth, death are secrets—secrets for which some are called to live, while others are condemned to die.

We can assail both the heavens and the sciences with questions—there is only one answer: Wherever life is lived, the living are rewarded with both anguish and happiness.

The woman who thirsts for tenderness is deceived by her desires and must accept her sterility. The woman who is bursting with life is not allowed to keep the child she waited for so passionately. The young woman, so inexperienced in life, is suddenly surprised by it when she is thrown into a crowd of women in childbirth.

Life touches them all—without posing questions or offering answers—it goes on its way without interruption toward new births, new lives. Only human beings ask questions.

In contrast to *The Seventh Seal,* which is inspired by medieval stained-glass windows and filled with tableaux, *So Close* was shot with the utmost simplicity. The background is always secondary to the three heroines, and, by the same token, Bergman intrudes as little as possible on Ulla Isaksson's story. Eva Dahlbeck, Ingrid Thulin, and above all Bibi Andersson, are remarkably accurate and feeling in their portrayals. There is no musical accompaniment; everything is geared to a purity of line. What is most striking in Bergman's latest films is their lack of frills. Anyone born into this world and living in it can understand and appreciate them. I think Bergman reaches an enormous audience around the world because he speaks with such astounding simplicity.

—1958

Cries and Whispers

It begins like Chekhov's *Three Sisters* and ends like *The Cherry Orchard* and in between it's more like Strindberg. *Cries and Whispers,* Ingmar Bergman's latest film, was a tremendous success in London and New York, and the sensation of the Cannes Festival last week. It will open in Paris in September. Unanimously considered a masterpiece, *Cries and Whispers* is going to bring back to Bergman the public that has been avoiding him since his last great success, *The Silence*, in 1963.

Yet there has been no body of work of the caliber and integrity of Bergman's since the war. Between 1945 and 1972 he made thirty-three movies. His name became well known with the success in Cannes in 1956 of *Smiles of a Summer Night*, his sixteenth film. Ten years earlier the first Bergman film to be shown in France had been noticed by only one critic, André Bazin, who congratulated the young Swedish director for "creating a world of blinding cinematic purity" (Review of *L'Eternel mirage* in *L'Ecran Français*, September, 1947).

Since 1957, almost all of Bergman's films have eventually come out in France, though not in the right order. The most famous are *Sawdust and Tinsel, The Seventh Seal, Wild Strawberries, The Virgin Spring, The Silence,* and *Persona;* the most touching are *Sommarlek, Summer with Monika, Les Communiants, The Rite.* Let's speak briefly about *The Rite.*

For the past few weeks, this extraordinary film, shot by Bergman in black and white for Swedish television, has been playing in Paris. The theater of the Studio Galande is tiny, and the eighty spectators who come each day to see it don't cover the costs of showing it. In a move of real stupidity, *The Rite* was closed the day before Bergman arrived in Cannes; his arrival was an event we've been hoping for for fifteen years. Taking *The Rite* off the bill last week is like taking an author's book out of the bookstore window the day he receives the Prix Goncourt. What a mess! And a mess for which the Paris critics have to bear some responsibility. A film of extreme inner violence, *The Rite* shows us three artists executing a judge—in other words, a critic. It is curious, then, that the press chose to ignore this film.

Bergman is a stubborn, shy man. He devotes his whole life to the theater and movies, and one has the sense that he is only happy when he's working surrounded by actresses, and that in the near future one won't see a Bergman film without women. I think he's more involved in the feminine principle than in feminism. Women are not seen through a masculine prism in his films, but are observed in a spirit of total complicity. His female characters are infinitely subtle, while his male characters are conventions.

Instead of squeezing four hours worth of material into an hour and a half as most contemporary directors do, Bergman works with short stories—a few characters, very little action, little in the way of stage effects, a brief time frame. Each of his films—it's fascinating to see them together in a week-long retrospective or at a festival—reminds us of a single painting in an exposition. There are Bergman "periods." The present period is more physical than metaphysical. The strange title *Cries and Whispers* stays with you as you come away from watching the film, having been cried to and whispered to.

Bergman's lesson is three-fold: freedom in dialogue, a radical cleaning of the image, and the absolute priority of the human face.

As far as freedom of dialogue goes, the text of his films is not meant to be a piece of literature but simple spoken words—actually spoken and unspoken words—confessions, and confidences. We could also have learned this lesson from Jean Renoir, but curiously it comes through with greater weight by means of a foreign and cinematically virginal language. This has been evident since *Sommarlek*—the film of our salad days, of our twenties, of our first loves. As we watch a Bergman film, our senses are strongly involved. Our ears hear Swedish—it's like a piece of music or a dark color—and we read the subtitles which simplify and reinforce the dialogue. If you are interested enough to compare Buñuel's Mexican or Spanish films with the ones he made in France, you can reflect on this phenomenon of shifted communication.

Consider the cleanness of his images. Some filmmakers allow pure chance to enter into their images—the sun, passersby, a bicycle (filmmakers like Rossellini, Lelouch, and Huston) and others want to control every square inch of the screen (Eisenstein, Lang, and Hitchcock). Bergman started out like the first group and then changed camps. In his latest films you never see a chance pedestrian; your attention will never be distracted by an extra object in the setting, even a bird in the garden. There is nothing on the canvas except what Bergman (who's anti-pictorial, like all true filmmakers) wants there.

The human face. No one draws so close to it as Bergman does. In his recent films there is nothing more than mouths talking, ears listening, eyes expressing curiosity, hunger, panic.

Listen to the words of love that Max von Sydow addresses to Liv Ullmann in *The Hour of the Wolf.* Then listen to the hate-filled words the same couple hurl at each other in *The Passion of Anna,* three years later. What you hear is the most mercilessly autobiographical director working in movies today.

His most rueful film is *Now About These Women.* It's ironic to realize that Bergman's finest work is precisely involved in bringing out the dormant genius in each of the actresses he's chosen to work with—Maj-Britt Nilsson, Harriet Andersson, Eva Dahlbeck, Gunnel Lindblom, Ingrid Thulin, Bibi Andersson, Liv Ullmann. They are not kittens or dolls but real women. Bergman films them as they look out at the world, their gazes increasingly intense with toughness and suffering. The results are wonderful movies that, like Renoir's, are as simple as saying hello. However, is saying hello so very simple?

—1973

BUÑUEL THE BUILDER

I sometimes wonder whether Ingmar Bergman really finds life as hopeless as his films of the past decade would indicate. One thing is sure: he doesn't tell us how to go on living, as Renoir does. Rightly or wrongly, it seems to us that an optimistic artist—at least if it's not a question of smugness but of transcending pessimism—is greater, or at least more helpful to his contemporaries, than the nihilist, or the artist who has succumbed to despair.

Luis Buñuel is, perhaps, somewhere between Renoir and Bergman. One would gather that Buñuel finds mankind imbecilic but life diverting. All this he tells us very mildly, even a bit indirectly, but it's there in the overall impression we get from his films. Even though he has very little stomach for "messages," Buñuel did manage to make one of those rare, truly antiracist movies, *The Young One* (1960), the only film he has shot in English. It succeeded because of his masterful ability to intertwine sympathetic and unsympathetic characters and to shuffle the cards in his psychological game while he addresses us in perfectly clear, logical language.

The antipsychological Buñuelian scenario functions on the same principle as the hot-and-cold shower—alternating favorable and unfavorable signs, positives and negatives, reason and nonsense. He puts these elements to work on both the action and the characters in his films. Anti-bourgeois, anti-conformist, Buñuel is as sarcastic as Stroheim but he has a lighter touch; his world view is subversive, happily anarchist.

Before the French uprising in May 1968—everything has been more complicated since—the substance of Buñuel's films suited those who demand that movies be committed. Yet, André Bazin was perfectly correct to write, after *Los Olvidados*, that "Buñuel has passed from revolution to moralism." Buñuel is a cheerful pessimist, not given to despair, but he has a skeptical mind. Notice, he never makes films *for,* always *against,* and none of his characters ever appear to be very practical. Buñuel's skepticism extends to all those whom he finds playing too neat a social game, those who live by accepted opinions.

Like the writers of the eighteenth century, Buñuel teaches us how to doubt, and I think Jacques Rivette is quite right to compare him to Diderot. Catherine Deneuve, who played in his *Tristana,* wrote an article about what it's like to work with Buñuel behind the camera. "Buñuel's lens, even when he's filming a grim story, is always focused on black humor. He is a deliberate joker, malicious but very funny. Thanks to him, you're constantly amused on the set and it's clear that in the character of Don Lope, magnificently acted by Fernando Rey, he produced a synthesis of all the men he's portrayed from those in *Archibaldo de la Cruz* to those in *Viridiana,* by accumulating a mass of cruel, funny, and often very intimate details."

I suspect that when Buñuel invents the character of a mature man, rather than a young buck, it amuses him to pile on all the ideas he finds most stupid, and then counterbalance them with true, deep, and rational ideas—his own thoughts. That's what creates paradox; that's how he leaves the merely psychological and approximates real life. He mixes judgment and autobiography.

In *Tristana,* two friends of Don Lope come to ask him to act as second in a duel, but when he hears that the combat will stop with the first wound, the first drop of blood, he ushers them out: "Gentlemen, never come again looking for me to witness a travesty of a duel where honor counts for so little."

This example neatly illustrates the way Buñuel shatters the psychological. If Don Lope were a complete idiot (even within a context where the idea of dueling is an act of idiocy) he would never react that way. On the other hand, the idea that blood must be spilled to satisfy some convention no doubt constitutes another form of idiocy, but a madness more appealing for being mad, as opposed to the sham duel. Buñuel's effort to smash common sense, to circle around meaning and divert it often leads to real innovation.

Once, when I had gone to Spain for a film premiere, I decided to go on to Toledo, where Buñuel was shooting *Tristana.* I knew he regretted not having brought along some cartons of filter Gitanes, which he prefers to Spanish tobacco, so I was doubly welcome on the set, where a particularly interesting scene was being blocked out.

The screenplay of *Tristana* calls for a young deaf-mute, Saturno, to circle about Tristana like a moth around a candle. He continues to desire her even when she comes back to live with Don Lope after having had her leg amputated. In the script, at a certain moment Tristana and Saturno pass each other in a corridor, exchange looks, and after a pause, Tristana leads the boy to her bedroom. Buñuel was nervous as he got ready to shoot the scene. He thought it was too brutal, too obvious, too blunt, in a word, and he decided to modify it. So this is how it came out: Saturno is prowling in the garden just under Tristana's window. He throws some pebbles at the window pane. In her bedroom, Tristana is evidently getting undressed, though all one sees is her underwear thrown on a bed, where her artificial leg is lying. The camera turns on Tristana as, having heard the pebbles, she is wrapping herself in her robe and walking on crutches toward the window. Then we see Saturno gesturing to Tristana to open her robe. She complies and we merely conjecture Saturno's reaction as he backs away into the garden staring at the window.

As I watched this scene being shot, I thought of an interview Buñuel had given me in 1953, the first time I'd ever interviewed a film director. Replying to a question about whether he had ever imagined a film that would be impossible to make, he told me, "I'd answer no, but I can tell you about a film I dream about because I'll never make it. It's inspired by Fabre's work. I would invent the same kind of characters as in my usual films, but they'd each possess the characteristics of certain insects. The heroine would act like a bee, the hero like a beetle, and so on. You see why the project is hopeless."

This "instinctual movie" that Buñuel has never made, even if he has never stopped playing with the idea, is instructive in helping us understand the singular way he makes his characters live and move. Contrary to what many of his admirers believe, Buñuel's screenplays and his preparation for shooting are extremely rigorous, reflected on at length, and constantly reexamined. Like all great artists, Buñuel knows that his first priority is to make the film as interesting as possible, and that while there are always any number of ways to do things, there is only one way which is best.

Too many commentators refer to Buñuel as a poet of hallucination who follows the caprices of his fantastic imagination, while in reality he is a brilliant screenwriter very much concerned with dramatic construction. As Catherine Deneuve describes him in the article already cited, "Buñuel is first and foremost a marvelous storyteller, a calculating plotter who works endlessly on his scripts to make every single piece of business intriguing and accessible. Buñuel will say that he never dwells on what the public thinks of him, that he makes his movies for a few friends. I rather think, however, that he sees those few friends as hard to please and demanding. And because he goes to such lengths to capture their attention, he succeeds in reaching a larger public of film devotees the world over who admire and love his films."

I am absolutely in agreement with Deneuve's point of view. She has, after all, played his heroines in *Belle de Jour* and *Tristana.* Let's look at how he constructed a much earlier film, *The Criminal Life of Archibaldo de la Cruz (Archibald of the Cross),* which he made in Mexico in 1955. He was not then universally recognized as a genius, and he was working in a country in which the censors would have prohibited him from showing a murderer who is not only likable but goes unpunished into the bargain.

As *Archibaldo de la Cruz* opens, the hero is a small boy. As he watches, his governess dies just as he switches on a music box. As a matter of fact, the woman has been killed by a stray bullet fired by revolutionaries in the street. But when we see Archibaldo again, thirty years later, he is in a hospital run by nuns and has just finished telling the story of his childhood to a sister who is nursing him through a convalescence. He is staring at his razor. The idea of committing a murder seems to come over him, or perhaps it's just an empty longing. Whatever the case, the nun is terrorized and she runs out into the corridor to the elevator. Not stopping to look, she steps through the door—the elevator is not there, she plunges six stories down the shaft. In due course, there is a police investigation and either Archibaldo confesses to her murder or he accepts an accusation made against him. His testimony constitutes a flashback to the recent past, probably only a few weeks before the episode.

Archibaldo has been in an antique store, where he discovers his old music box at the very moment that a rather strange couple are on the verge of buying it. The gentleman is a little old man with a goatee and the dark young woman with him is, we'll soon find out, a tourist guide. Archibaldo explains that it's a souvenir from his youth, and he manages to buy the box himself and take it away. A short time later, he's on his way to visit his fiancée when he encounters a beautiful, sensual, but emotionally disturbed woman. (I have to call your attention to these characters as they pass because we'll see them again. They are the fishhooks on the lines that Buñuel is throwing out one after another as he goes along.) If my memory doesn't deceive me—unfortunately, I don't have any documentation; the script was never published—we learn before the hero does that his fiancée is cheating on him, that she is, to her mother's great despair, the mistress of a married man, an architect. On this day, during his visit, Archibaldo and his fiancée talk about their coming marriage.

When we see Archibaldo again, he is in a casino, and at the same gambling table is the distraught woman with whom he had exchanged provocative looks that afternoon on the street. The man with her is apparently her lover, but she behaves badly and he refuses to replace her chips. They argue, there is an uproar, they separate. Archibaldo leaves the casino, and the woman, who has just cracked up her car, asks him to take her home.

Now we are at the woman's home. In the purest tradition of the commercial novel, she changes her dress and reappears in "something comfortable." In the bathroom, as he waits for her, Archibaldo *thinks* for a moment of killing this woman who both attracts and repels him. We see the murder as Archibaldo imagines it, and needless to say, we hear the tune of the music box. Archibaldo gets hold of himself, returns to reality, and at that moment the woman's lover returns and Archibaldo steals away. The next day, the police find the lovers' bodies covered with blood. Archibaldo has had nothing to do with this tragedy of passion. The unhappy couple could neither live with nor without each other, and they chose to die together.

Archibaldo then invites his fiancée to dinner but she refuses—perhaps she has something better to do, more probably a final farewell to make. Archibaldo goes off to kill time in a cabaret, where he again encounters the pretty dark woman he'd seen in the antique store as she had been about to buy the famous music box. Remember, she is a guide for American tourists. The little elderly man with the goatee, with whom we'd seen her in the beginning, hovers around, and I believe she introduces him first as her uncle and later as her fiancé— a device that is in the same romantic tradition as any number of components in this story. Archibaldo loses sight of the woman, but she has given him an address where he can find her.

When he arrives there the next day, he sees it is a dress shop. He stops abruptly in front of a wax mannequin that looks exactly like the dark young woman who so preoccupies him. He looks around the place, quickly finds the real woman, and invites her to visit his pottery studio the following Saturday. I've forgotten to mention that

Archibaldo, who is well-to-do, is a dilettante potter.

Saturday. Archibaldo has devised a charming stage setting. He has gotten hold of the wax mannequin and has set it in an armchair. He's waiting for the flesh-and-blood woman. When she arrives, she is both astonished and amused. The presence of the woman and her double allows Archibaldo to josh about clothes, underclothes, etcetera. At the moment when something finally happens between the two (the fact that I can't remember whether the act is sexual or criminal demonstrates that it's the same thing) the doorbell rings. It's a group of drunken tourists whom the young woman had briefly abandoned. She has played a good trick on him, and when she leaves Archibaldo is very upset. He's been left alone—but he doesn't quit. He drags the mannequin along by the hair, opens the kiln, which is going full blast, and, as we watch, the only real murder in the film is committed. Just as in Charles Trenet's song, "The King's Polka," we see the wax mannequin literally melt before our eyes, tortured before being licked by the flames. It is a sinister vision that evokes the Nazi crematoria.

We're still at Archibaldo's as his fiancée and his future mother-in-law arrive to pay him a visit. He has to hastily push a woman's shoe under the sofa (it is, in fact, the mannequin's shoe which had fallen off as he dragged it across the room). Just then, Archibaldo receives an anonymous letter revealing the affair between his fiancée and the architect. That evening, hiding in his rival's garden, he sees them together. Actually they are saying goodbye, but Archibaldo, a window between him and the lovers, has no way of knowing that. I believe something happens to indicate that the architect had sent the anonymous letter in hopes of preventing the marriage, which was breaking up his affair.

Now, as we have come to expect, we see a new murder plan. Archibaldo imagines forcing his fiancée to kneel before him—we don't need to draw in the details—then the usual music, and we are brought back to the real world.

The day of the wedding. Archibaldo and his bride, all in white, pose for a photograph. As in Hitchcock's *Foreign Correspondent*, Buñuel creates a moment of confusion between the flash of the camera and a gunshot. Of course, it's the rejected architect. His bride is killed right before Archibaldo's eyes.

Buñuel brings us back to the present. For more than an hour we've been so involved in a flashback that we've lost track of the beginning.

We are in the police commissioner's office, where we started out. He's been diverted by Archibaldo's life story and he has evidently come to the conclusion that Archibaldo has committed no crime.

When Archibaldo leaves the police station, he throws the cursed music box in the lake. He takes a walk in the park, considers for a moment crushing an insect with his cane, rejects the idea, and just then runs into the dark young guide-mannequin, smiling as always. They wander off together.

I'm not familiar with the literary sources of *Archibaldo de la Cruz*, but the cinematic inspirations are clear—Hitchcock's *Shadow of a Doubt* (1948), which tells the story of a man who murders widows (Joseph Cotten) set against the musical theme of *The Merry Widow;* a film by Preston Sturges, *Unfaithfully Yours* (1948), in which an orchestra conductor played by Rex Harrison imagines three different ways of killing his wife as he conducts a symphony; and, above all, Chaplin's *Monsieur Verdoux* (1947). The distraught woman whose path Archibaldo keeps crossing is obviously related to the extraordinary Martha Raye (Captain Bonheur's wife) whom Verdoux-Bonheur never quite succeeds in murdering.

But the true interest of *Archibaldo* lies elsewhere—in the ingenuity of its construction, the audacious handling of time, the expertise of the cinematic narrative. If you question the audience at the end of *Archibaldo*—remember, its full title is, mischievously, *The Criminal Life of Archibald of the Cross*—almost everybody will tell you that they've just seen the story of a likable guy who kills women. It is absolutely not true; Archibaldo has killed no one. He's been satisfied simply to wish, after the death of his governess when he was a little boy, for the deaths of the nun who was a nurse in the hospital, the beautiful disturbed woman, the sultry guide, and his unfaithful fiancée. Four of the five women have died in one way or another shortly after Archibaldo has expressed his desire. We have anticipated these deaths as fantasies (flashes forward), and then we've seen certain of them really occur, but only as recounted by Archibaldo in flashback.

In the hands of most film writers, *Archibaldo* would have become a series of sketches, but Buñuel and Eduardo Ugarte were able to intertwine the individual episodes by introducing us to all the female characters early in the story, and then, in the second half of the film, gathering them delicately for their ten-minute scenes to show them as real women.

Archibaldo is one of those rare films so finely constructed, written with such a sense of how to put images on a screen, that reading the screenplay gives only a weak idea of the result, maybe even a completely inaccurate impression. Just as it is impossible to get an accurate description of Archibaldo from the posters at the exits of the movie house, I think that merely reading the screenplay would be a painful affair. The same is true with almost all Lubitsch's films, principally *To Be or Not to Be*. If one simply recounted its scenes literally, it would seem ridiculous. Lubitsch and Buñuel are the masters of the invisible flashback, the flashback that interrupts without breaking the story line and, on the contrary, refreshes it when it threatens to flag. They are also masters at bringing us back to the present without startling us. They both use a two-pronged hook with which they jerk us backward and forward. The hook is almost always a gimmick—comic in Lubitsch's work, dramatic in Buñuel's.

Too many screenplays are conceived for their literary effect, and they end up as novels written in pictures. They are pleasant to read, they make easy promises, and they deliver on them, presuming the director and the actors have as much talent as the writer. I'm not out to criticize the straight story-line movies—of which *Bicycle Thief* is one of the most beautiful examples—but to suggest that the talents of the scenarists who wrote *The Big Sleep, North by Northwest, Heaven Can Wait*, or *Archibaldo de la Cruz* are far greater. The discipline of film has its own rules, which have not yet been fully explored, and it is only through works such as those of Buñuel and the other great director-writers that we will one day realize them fully.

—Presentation at the Ciné-Club of la Victorine, 1971

NORMAN MacLAREN

Blinkety Blank

Blinkety Blank is a four-minute color film that was shot without a camera. Right on the film itself MacLaren drew a number of designs and abstract figures to create an erotic ballet of male and female elements encountering each other. The sound is also printed directly onto the film. What is so extraordinary about it, aside from the beauty of its designs and their brilliance, is that MacLaren had the whole theater laughing at simple curves that were glimpsed for less than half a second accompanied by a few synthetic noises.

Blinkety Blank is an absolutely unique work which bears no resemblance to anything that has been made in sixty years of filmmaking. In this "great little film" that's only four minutes long, there is all the fantasy of Giraudoux, the mastery of Hitchcock, and the imagination of Cocteau.

In the nighttime of a dark theater, *Blinkety Blank,* with colored flashes of summer lightning and synthetic clicks and clacks, creates a new myth—the goose with the golden eyes.

—1957

FEDERICO FELLINI

The Nights of Cabiria

Fellini's *The Nights of Cabiria*, the most eagerly awaited film of the [Cannes Film] Festival, was also the only one to arouse much comment at the exits. Till three in the morning, in the bars near the Palais, the role created by Giulietta Masina was the subject of violent argument. In this vein, let us deplore the fad that seems to be shared equally by the audience, producers, distributors, technicians, actors, and critics who fancy that they can contribute to the "creation" of the films being shown by deciding how they should have been edited and cut. After each showing, I'd hear things like "Not bad, but they could have cut a half-hour," or "I could have saved that film with a pair of scissors."

A pair of scissors in his hand, each one of them discovers his vocation as a filmmaker. I find it despicable. No question that there are soft spots in Fellini's film, but however little one may love cinema, there's more pleasure and profit to be had in that extra "half-hour" than in the whole of the two English films that were shown.

I believe in either attacking or defending a film in its entirety. The sense of it, its tone, style, its life are more important than a niggardly inventory of good and not so good scenes. It's possible that *The Nights of Cabiria* is Fellini's most uneven film, but its strong moments are so intense that I find it his best.

Fellini has taken a lot of risks in pushing *The Nights of Cabiria* in so many directions, renouncing unity of tone right from the start in order to test many difficult possibilities. What a healthy man he is, good-natured on the set, and what quiet mastery and entertaining ingenuity he displays.

Masina is Cabiria, the droll little Roman prostitute, naïve and trust-ing, battered by life, mistreated by men, but always honest. Fellini's creation of Cabiria is a logical conclusion of Gelsomina in *La Strada,* but the way the character and the effects are worked out here is strictly Chaplin.

The character of Cabiria will exasperate audiences who demand something from films other than strong, raw emotion. For all that, even if Masina becomes a coquette some day, she will have carved out for herself a particular "moment" in cinema, as James Dean and Robert Le Vigan did. I love Fellini, and since Giulietta Masina inspires him, I love her too. This creation is a comic overview which constantly spills over into grotesque contrivance. Not to attach too high a price tag to such comic observation, what touches me most in the film is the final moment of each episode as events speed by and farce turns into tragedy. The end of the film is bursting with power and strength, and the most intense suspense.

—1957

8 1/2

Films about medicine annoy doctors, films about aviation exasperate fliers, but Fellini has managed to please filmmakers with *8½* which is about the difficult pregnancy of a director who is getting ready to shoot a film. If you believe Fellini, a director is first of all a man whom everybody bothers morning, noon, and night. They ask him questions he either doesn't know how to answer or doesn't want to answer. His head is reeling with a thousand conflicting ideas, impressions, feelings, and budding desires, and yet everybody is de-manding certainties, precise names, exact figures, places, and schedules from him.

Anyone can appreciate why his sister-in-law's skepticism—Hello! How are you, joker?—makes him sick. The only way he can revenge himself is to force her into his erotic dreams, for example, in the harem scene where she will join, among others, an unknown beauty whom we, the audience, had glimpsed in the hotel lobby making a telephone call, but whom we could have sworn that Mastroianni-Guido hadn't noticed. All the problems which can sap a director's energy before the shooting begins are carefully enumerated. It is to the preparation of a film what *Rififi* is to planning a robbery.

Certain actors want to know more right away "in order to live with my character." Set designers ask, "Where shall I put the fire-place?" There are sententiously literary writers who are never satisfied, paternalistic producers who display such patience and confidence that they only add to Guido's anguish.

Directors who have acted, or actors who have gone to the circus a lot, directors who have written scripts or know how to construct a set, almost always have something extra to offer. Fellini has been an actor, a screenwriter, a circus buff, a designer. His film is as whole, as simple, as beautiful, and as honest as the one that Guido, in *8½*, wants to make.

—1963

ROBERTO ROSSELLINI PREFERS REAL LIFE

When I met Rossellini in Paris in 1955, he was utterly discouraged. He had just finished a film in Germany, *Angst (Fear)*, based on a play by Stefan Zweig, and he was seriously thinking of getting out of movies. All his films since *Amore* had been commercial failures, and they had also been panned by the Italian critics. The admiration of the younger French critics for his recent films, particularly the most rueful, *I Fioretti, Stromboli, Voyage to Italy*, comforted him somewhat. The fact that a group of young journalists who wanted to be directors had chosen him as their teacher broke through his feeling of isolation and reawakened his enormous enthusiasm.

It was at that time that Rossellini suggested to me that I come work with him. I agreed, and although I continued to work as a journalist, I was his assistant for three years. During that time he did not shoot a single foot of film. Even so, there was plenty of work and I learned a great deal from him.

After a conversation with someone he had an idea for a film. He phoned me to say, "We'll start next month." Immediately I was to buy every book that had anything to do with the subject, make a summary, get in touch with a lot of people; we had to "get going."

Then one morning he telephoned me. The previous evening, at a night club, someone had been telling him about the theatrical misfortunes of Georges and Ludmilla Pitoëff. He was enraptured. He wanted to start "the" film in several weeks. He could identify with this character. He would show Pitoëff as he searched for roles for pregnant women because Ludmilla was expecting a baby, hanging the curtain himself an hour before curtain time, entrusting an important role to the daughter of the cloakroom attendant at the last moment, being made fun of by the critics because of the accents of the actors he used, money worries, debts, tours, etcetera.

A month went by and he had forgotten all about the Pitoëffs. A producer in Lisbon had invited him to discuss making a film of *La Reine Morte.* He had just spent a day with Charlie Chaplin at Vevey and he was to meet me in Lyons. We drove to Lisbon in a Ferrari, Rossellini at the wheel day and night. I had to keep telling him stories to keep him awake, and every time he saw me dropping off he'd hand me a mysterious bottle to sniff.

The fishermen in Estoril didn't seem real. They looked as though they were staging a pageant for tourists; one of their boats was named *Linda Darnell.* Roberto didn't like Portugal. We drove back across southern Spain, and in Castile the controls of the Ferrari gave out as we were traveling at top speed. In a tiny village, the mechanics put together a part for the car overnight and we were able to go on. Inspired by the talent, tenacity, and know-how of the garagemen, Roberto decided that he would come back to Castile and film *Carmen.* We returned to Paris and Roberto started to make the rounds of the distributors. At the Spanish ballet, he had discovered a dark little dancer, only fifteen—the perfect Carmen. The distributors, even in France, were suspicious of Roberto and all his plans and they demanded to see a script. Armed with three copies of a cheap edition of Prosper Merimée's *Carmen,* a pair of scissors and a good supply of Scotch tape, I manufactured a cut (literally and figuratively) of *Carmen.* Of necessity, it was faithful to the letter.

Now the distributors wanted a star; they suggested Marina Vlady, who is as fair as a wheatfield. In the meantime, Roberto had lost interest.

For some time he'd been meeting a mysterious character who never came to his hotel, nor did Roberto go to his place. They'd meet in the street, at a different location each time. The man was a Soviet diplomat. Indeed, Rossellini had now conceived the idea of making a Soviet *Païsa,* a collection of six or seven stories typical of life in modern Russia. Every day Roberto had *Pravda* translated; he read basketfuls of books and began to compose his stories. Right off the bat, Rossellini had a run-in with the diplomat over a story the man thought too flippant. This is it: In a street of a small city, a Russian man catches a glimpse of his wife, who seems to be on her way to an assignation. Crazed with grief and jealousy, he follows her, losing sight of her again and again. Several times he thinks he has found her—always on the arm of another man. The denouement is that the largest store in the city has just gotten in hundreds of dresses, all the same model. That particular day, all the women were dressed alike.

So he had to abandon the project after all. And once more Rossellini found himself without work, this time the victim of political rather than commercial imperatives.

When Rossellini writes a script, he doesn't bother about story development. It's enough to have a point of departure. Given such and such a person with a particular religion, occupation, nationality, drive, it follows that he will have certain needs and longings, and a limited number of possibilities of fulfilling them. Any gap between his needs and desires and the possibilities for satisfying them will inevitably create a conflict, provided you accept his historical, ethnic, social, and geographic realities. There are no problems in bringing the film to a conclusion: the end is dictated by the sum of the parts of the conflict; it is either optimistic or pessimistic. For Rossellini, it's a matter of rediscovering the man that so many opposing fantasies have made us lose sight of. He approaches him first by a simple documentary method and then thrusts him into the most ordinary difficulty, the easiest to relate.

By 1958, Rossellini was well aware that his films were not like those of other people, but he very sensibly decided that it was the others who ought to change. "The movie industry in America," he remarked, "is based on the sale of projectors and their wide use; Hollywood films cost too much to be profitable and are deliberately too expensive, in order to discourage independent production. It would be madness for Europe to imitate American films; if movies are really too expensive to be conceived and made with any degree of freedom, then let's not make any more; let's just do outlines and drafts."

That's how Rossellini became, as Jacques Flaud called him, "the father of the French new wave." And it's true that every time he came to Paris, he'd meet with us, have our amateur films projected, read our beginners' scripts. All those new names, which took the French producers by surprise in 1959 when they read them each week on the lists of films in production, had long been known to Rossellini: Rouch, Reichenbach, Godard, Rohmer, Rivette, Aurel. In fact, Rossellini was the first to read the scripts for both *Le Beau Serge (Handsome Serge)* and *The 400 Blows*. It was he who inspired Jean Rouch to make *Moi, un Noir* after having seen *Les Maîtres Fous*.

Was I influenced by Rossellini? By all means. His severity, his seriousness, his thoughtfulness freed me from some of the complacent enthusiasm I'd felt for American movies. Rossellini detests clever titles, especially with scenes preceding them, flashbacks, and everything in general that's included simply for decoration, everything that does not serve the film's intention or the character development.

In some of my films I've tried to follow a single character simply and honestly in an almost documentary manner, and I owe this method to Rossellini. Aside from Vigo, Rossellini is the only filmmaker who has filmed adolescence without sentimentality, and *The 400 Blows* owes a great deal to his *Germania Anno Zero (Germany Year Zero)*.

What's made Rossellini's career so difficult, I think, is that he's always treated the public as his equal, while he is himself an exceptional man, extraordinarily intelligent and ardent. That's why he doesn't linger over the action, never explains or amplifies. He throws out his ideas very swiftly, one after another. Jacques Rivette said that Rossellini "never demonstrates, he simply displays," but his quick mind, his thought processes, and his extraordinary ability to assimilate thrusts him out ahead of his audience and as a result he sometimes loses it. This ability to absorb so much, this thirst to clarify contemporary conditions is clear in each of his works: *Roma, Città aperta (Open City)* is about a city; *Païsa* is about all of Italy from the south to the north; *Germany Year Zero* is about a great country that has been conquered and destroyed; *Europe 51* is about our whole continent, rebuilt materially but not morally.

The last great cinematic adventure of Rossellini was his discovery of India. In six months he had seen all of the subcontinent and had reevoked it in his *India*, a film of extraordinary simplicity and intelligence, not merely a series of images of countrysides and of people, but a world view, a meditation on life, on nature, on animals. *India* is not set in time or place as his other films are. It's free verse, perhaps only comparable to his meditation on perfect joy in *The Fioretti of St. Francis of Assisi*.

I know it's a dangerous thing to say, but I believe it is true that Rossellini doesn't really like cinema particularly, any more than he cares for the arts in general. He prefers life, he prefers man. He never opens a novel, though he spends his life gathering social and historical facts. Each night he reads books on history, sociology, science. He craves more and more knowledge; he aspires to devote himself to cultural films.

The truth is that Rossellini is not an "activist" nor is he an ambitious man. He is an inquirer, a man who asks questions, who is much more interested in other people than he is in himself.

One might even wonder why he became a director, how he happened to come to cinema. It was by chance—or rather by love. He was in love with a girl who had been noticed by some producers and hired to make a movie. Purely out of jealousy, Roberto went with her to the studio and, since it was a low-budget production, and they saw him there doing nothing, and since he had a car, they sent him each day to pick up the male star, Jean-Pierre Aumont, at his home.

Rossellini's first films were documentaries on fish, and I rather think it was because of his love for Anna Magnani that he turned to making narrative films. He was spurred to it also by conditions in wartime Italy. In the end (and his only recent success, *General della Rovere*, would seem to confirm it) Rossellini's work is accepted by the public and the critics only when it is about the war. News films have accustomed us to his sort of rough and violent truths.

Are those of us who love and admire Rossellini wrong to think that he's perfectly right to film the wars that rage within families, the antics of St. Francis, and the apes of the Bengal the same way street fighting is shot, just like the news, the same way reportage has always been done?

The last time I saw him, Rossellini had me read a hundred-page screenplay on iron. He was going to shoot from it a five-hour movie for students, a three-hour film for television, and an hour-and-a-half movie for theaters. It was thrilling to read and no doubt it would have made a beautiful film, but I couldn't help wondering whether some day, in spite of everything, he would be allowed to realize his great schemes: a film on Brazil, to be called *Brasilia, The Dialogues of Plato,* and *The Death of Socrates.*

—*1963*

ORSON WELLES

Citizen Kane: The Fragile Giant

Though it was made in Hollywood in August–September 1940, and shown in the United States during 1941, because of the war *Citizen Kane* didn't make it to France until six years later. When it opened in Paris in July 1946, it was a great event for the film buffs of my generation. Since the Liberation we had been discovering American movies and were busily abandoning the French filmmakers we had admired during the war. We were even more emphatic about our disaffection with French actors and actresses as we rushed to the Americans. Out with Pierre Fresnay, Jean Marais, Edwige Feuillère, Raimu, Arletty; long live Cary Grant, Humphrey Bogart, James Stewart, Gary Cooper, Spencer Tracy, Lauren Bacall, Gene Tierney, Ingrid Bergman, Joan Bennett, et al.

We excused our radical shift on the grounds that French movie magazines, especially *L'Ecran Français,* were so devoted to corporate anti-Americanism that we were profoundly irritated. During the Occupation, because German films were so mediocre and English-language films were forbidden, the French movie industry prospered, our films were snatched up, the theaters were usually full. After the Liberation, the Blum-Byrnes accords authorized the release of a great many American films in France and the box-office receipts of French films went down. It was not unusual to see French stars and directors demonstrating in the streets of Paris for a reduction in the number of American films allowed to be imported.

Also, a taste for escaping one's own milieu, a thirst for novelty, romanticism, and also obviously a spirit of contrariness, but mostly a love of vitality, made us love anything that came from Hollywood. It was in this mood that we first heard the name Orson Welles in the summer of 1946. I rather think that his unusual first name contributed to our fascination: Orson sounded like *ourson*, a bear cub, and we heard that this cub was only thirty, that he'd made *Citizen Kane* at twenty-six, the same age at which Eisenstein had made *Potemkin*.

The French critics were full of praise—Jean-Paul Sartre, who had seen it in America, wrote an article preparing the ground. Still, a number of them were confused as they recounted the screenplay; they contradicted each other in the various journals over the meaning of the word "rosebud." Some critics said it was the name given to the glass filled with snowflakes that slips from Kane's hands as he dies. Denis Martin and André Bazin were the leaders in this journalistic inquiry and they persuaded the distributor, RKO, to add the subtitle "Rosebud" at the precise moment when a child's sled is going up in flames.

The confusion between the sled and the glass was exactly what Welles wished. The glass was filled with drops of snow falling on a little house, and twice Kane says the word in relation to the glass— first when he picks it up as his second wife, Susan Alexander, is leaving him, and then, as he is dying, drops it.

As magical for us as "rosebud" was the name "Xanadu." In France we didn't know Coleridge's poem about Kubla Khan. Even though it is explicitly quoted in the film, it was lost on our French ears in the text of "News on the March."

> In Xanadu did Kubla Khan
> A stately pleasure dome decree: . . .
> So twice five miles of fertile ground
> With walls and towers were girdled round.

It was thus reasonable to conclude that even the name Kane came from Khan, as that of Arkadin probably came from Irina Ardakina, the actress-heroine of Chekhov's *The Sea Gull*.

Citizen Kane, which was never dubbed, sobered us up from our Hollywood binge and made us more demanding film lovers. This film has inspired more vocations to cinema throughout the world than any other. This seems a little odd since Welles's work is always rightly described as inimitable, and also because the influence he exerted, if it is sometimes discernible as in Mankiewicz' *The Barefoot Contessa*, Astruc's *Les Mauvaises Rencontres*, Max Ophuls' *Lola Montès*, and Fellini's *8½*, is most often indirect and under the surface. The Hollywood productions I spoke of earlier, which we had so loved, were seductive, but they seemed unattainable. You could go again and again to see films like *The Big Sleep*, *Notorious*, *The Lady Eve*, *Scarlet Street*, but these movies never hinted to us that we would become filmmakers one day. They served only to show that, if cinema was a country, Hollywood was clearly its capital.

So, it was no doubt the double pro-and-con-Hollywood aspect that made *Citizen Kane* stir us so, as well as Welles's impudent youth and a strong European element in his attitudes. Even more than his wide travels, I think that it was his intense and intimate knowledge of Shakespeare that gave Welles an anti-Manichaean world view and allowed him to mix good and bad heroes so gleefully. I will make a confession. I was fourteen in 1946 and had already dropped out of school. I discovered Shakespeare through Orson Welles, just as my taste for Bernard Hermann's music brought me to Stravinsky, who so often was its inspiration.

Because Welles was young and romantic, his genius seemed closer to us than the talents of the traditional American directors. When Everett Sloane, who plays the character of Bernstein in *Kane*, relates how, one day in 1896, his ferryboat crossed the path of another in Hudson Bay on which there was a young woman in a white dress holding a parasol, and that he'd only seen the girl for a second but had thought of her once a month all his life . . . ah, well, behind this Chekhovian scene, there was no big director to admire, but a friend to discover, an accomplice to love, a person we felt close to in heart and mind.

We loved this film absolutely because it was so complete—psychological, social, poetic, dramatic, comic, grotesque. *Kane* both demonstrates and mocks the will to power; it is a hymn to youth and a meditation on age, a study of the vanity of all human ambition and a poem about deterioration, and underneath it all a reflection on the solitude of exceptional beings, geniuses or monsters, monstrous geniuses.

Citizen Kane has both the look of a "first film," because of its grab bag of experiments, and a film of a director's highest maturity, because of its universal portrait of the world.

I didn't understand until long after that first great encounter in July 1946 why *Kane* is what it is and the ways in which it is unique; it's the only first film made by a man who was already famous. Chaplin was only a little emigrant clown when he made his debut in front of the camera. Renoir was, in the view of the profession, just a daddy's boy keeping himself busy with a camera and wasting his family's money when he shot *Nana;* Hitchcock was only a credits designer who was being promoted when he made *Blackmail.* But Orson Welles was already very well known in America—and not only because of the notorious radio play about Martians—when he started *Citizen Kane.* He was a famous man and the trade papers in Hollywood were laying for him. "Quiet," they ordered, "genius at work." The normal course of events is to become famous after having made a number of good films. It's rare to be famous at twenty-six, and even rarer to be given a film to make at that age. This is the reason that *Citizen Kane* is the only first film to have for its theme celebrity as such. In the long run, it is clearly Welles's legend and precocity which enabled him to lay before us plausibly and accurately the span of an entire lifetime—we follow Charles Foster Kane from childhood to death. As opposed to a timid beginner who might try to make a good film in order to win acceptance in the industry, Welles, with his considerable reputation already established, felt constrained to make a movie which would sum up everything that had come before in cinema, and would prefigure everything to come. His extravagant gamble paid off handsomely.

There has always been considerable talk about the technical aspect of Welles's work. Had he acquired all that technique in a few weeks before shooting *Kane,* or had he picked it up by watching a lot of movies? The question is beside the point. Hollywood is full of directors who have made forty films and still don't know how to fade two shots into each other harmoniously. To make a good film, you need intelligence, sensitivity, intuition, and a few ideas, that's all. Welles had all these to spare. When Thatcher challenges him, "So, that's really how you think a newspaper should be run?" the young Kane answers, "I have absolutely no experience in running a paper, Mr. Thatcher. I just try out all the ideas that come into my head."

When I see *Kane* today, I'm aware that I know it by heart, but in the way you know a recording rather than a movie. I'm not always as certain what image comes next as I am about what sound will burst forth, or the very timbre of the next voice that I'm going to hear, or the musical link to the next scene. (Before *Kane,* nobody in Hollywood knew how to set music properly in movies.) *Kane* was the first, in fact the only, great film that uses radio techniques. Behind each scene, there is a resonance which gives it its color: the rain on the windows of the cabaret, "El Rancho," when the investigator goes to visit the down-and-out female singer who can only "work" Atlantic City; the echoes in the marble-lined Thatcher library; the overlapping voices whenever there are several characters. A lot of filmmakers know enough to follow Auguste Renoir's advice to fill the eyes with images at all cost, but only Orson Welles understood that the sound track had to be filled in the same way.

Before he had decided on *Citizen Kane,* Welles was preparing an adaptation of Joseph Conrad's *Heart of Darkness* in which the narrator would be replaced by a subjective camera. Something of the idea is retained in *Kane.* The investigator, Thomson, is shot from the back all through the film, which also discards the rules of classical cutting according to which one scene must be backed onto the next. The story is moved along as if it were a newspaper story. Visually the film is more aptly described as "page setting" rather than stage setting. A quarter of the shots are faked, the camera manipulates almost as if it were an animated film. So many of the shots in depth of focus— the glass of poison in Susan's bedroom, to begin with—were trick shots, a kind of "hide-and-don't-seek," the cinematic equivalent of the photomontage of sensational newspapers. One can also view *Citizen Kane* as a film of artful manipulation if you compare it to its successor, *The Magnificent Ambersons,* which is the opposite, a romantic film with drawn-out scenes, an emphasis on action over camera work, the stretching of real time.

In *The Magnificent Ambersons* Welles uses less than two-hundred shots to relate a story which spans twenty-five years (as opposed to 562 in *Citizen Kane*), as if the second movie had been shot in a fury by a different director who hated the first and wanted to give Welles a lesson in modesty. Because he's always very much the artist *and* the critic, Welles is a director who is very easily carried away but who later judges his flights of fancy on the cutting table with growing attention in his subsequent films. Many of Welles's recent films give the impression that they were shot by an exhibitionist and edited by a censor.

Let's return to *Citizen Kane,* in which everything happens as if Welles, with extraordinary arrogance, had rejected the rules of cinema, the limits of its powers of illusion and, with quick strokes and tricks—some more clever and successful than others—made his movie resemble the form of American comics in which fantasy allows the artist to draw one character close up, behind him at full length the person who's talking to him, and at the back ten characters with the designs on their ties as clear as the wart on the nose of the character in closeup. It's this singular marvel, never reedited, that is brought off fifty times in a row. It gives the film a stylization, an idealization of visual effects that had not been attempted since Murnau's films *The Last Laugh* and *Sunrise*. The great moviemakers who are conscious of form—Murnau, Lang, Eisenstein, Dreyer, Hitchcock—all got their start before the talkies, and it's no exaggeration to see in Welles the only great natural visual artist to arrive on the scene after the advent of sound.

If you see a superb scene from a Western, it could be John Ford, Raoul Walsh, William Wellman, or Michael Curtiz, whereas Welles's style, like Hitchcock's, is instantly recognizable. Welles's visual mode is his alone, and it is inimitable because, for one reason, like Chaplin's, it emanates from the physical presence of the author-actor at the center of the screen. It is Welles who comes slowly across the image; who creates a hubbub and then breaks it by suddenly speaking very softly; Welles who hurls his retorts over the heads of his characters as if he deigned to speak only to the gods (the Shakespearean influence); Welles, working against all custom, who breaks away from the flat horizon so that sometimes the whole scene spins haphazardly, the ground seeming to seesaw in front of the hero as he strides toward the lens.

Welles might well find all other films slack, flat, static, because his are so dynamic. They unroll before the eyes the way music moves in the ear.

Seeing *Citizen Kane* again today, we discover something else: this film, which had seemed extravagantly luxurious and expensive, is made up of fragments of stage tricks, actually put together out of odds and ends. There are very few extras and a lot of stock shots, lots of large pieces of furniture but a great many faked walls, and, above all, a lot of closeups of small bells, cymbals, "spliced-in" shots, newspapers, accessories, photographs, miniature portraits, a great many fade-ins and dissolves. The truth is that *Citizen Kane* is a film that if not cheap was at least modest, and was made to look sumptuous on the cutting-room table. This result was achieved by an enormous amount of work to enhance all the separate elements, and especially through the extraordinary strengthening of the visual track by the most ingenious sound in the history of movies.

When I saw *Citizen Kane* as an adolescent film buff, I was overcome with admiration for the film's main character. I thought he was marvelous, splendid, and I linked Orson Welles and Charles Foster Kane in the same idolatry. I thought the film was a panegyric to ambition and power. When I saw it again, after I'd become a *critic*, accustomed to analyzing my enjoyment, I discovered its true critical point of view: satire. I understood then that we're supposed to sympathize with the character of Jedediah Leland (played by Joseph Cotten). I saw that the film clearly demonstrates the absurdity of all worldly success. Today, now that I am a director, when I see *Kane* again for perhaps the thirtieth time, it is its twofold aspect as fairy tale and moral fable that strikes me most forcefully.

I can't say whether Welles's work is puritanical because I don't know the significance of the word in America, but I've always been struck by its chastity. Kane's downfall is brought about by a sexual scandal: "Candidate Kane found in bed with 'singer' "; and yet we've observed that Kane's and Susan's relationship was a father-daughter, protective bond. Their liaison, if one can call it that, is actually linked to Kane's childhood and to the idea of family. It's when he's coming back from a family pilgrimage (he had gone to see his parents' furniture, including probably the sled "Rosebud" stored in a shed) that he meets Susan on the street. She's coming out of a drugstore, holding her jaw because she has a toothache. He's just been splashed by a passing car. Notice that later Kane twice pronounces the word "rosebud"—when he's apparently dying and once before that, when Susan leaves him. He smashes all the furniture in his bedroom—it's a famous scene—but note that Kane's anger is only appeased when he takes the glass in his hand. At that point, it is quite clear that "rosebud," already connected to his separation from his mother, will henceforth be linked to Susan's abandoning him. There are partings which are like deaths.

What we already have found in *Citizen Kane,* and will find better expressed in other of Welles's works, is a world view which is personal, generous, and noble. There is no vulgarity, no meanness in this film, only the satirical, imbued by a fresh and imaginative antibourgeois morality, a lecture on how to behave: what to do, what not to do.

What all of Welles's films have in common is a liberalism, the assertion that belief in conservatism is an error. The fragile giants that are at the center of his cruel fables discover that you cannot conserve anything—not youth, not power, not love. Charles Foster Kane, George Minafer Amberson, Michael O'Hara, Gregory Arkadin come to understand that life is made up of terrible tears and wrenches.

—1967 (unpublished)

Confidential Report

Here is Orson Welles back with another film of uncertain nationality. The director is American, the chief cameraman French, and the actors English, American, Turkish, Russian, German, Italian, French, and Spanish. The locations are equally varied: Barcelona, Munich, Paris, Mexico. And the backers are Swiss.

Confidential Report is an admirable film. It begins badly, really quite badly, a bit like a cheap thriller. Everything looks seedy and squalid—the sets, the costumes, the grayish image; and at the outset we even dislike the young romantic lead (Robert Arden). Welles himself, so long awaited, arrives on the screen, and even he is disappointing. Ordinarily so adroit at standing aloof while he creates his character, here he seems even to have messed up his makeup. How are we supposed to find this Gregory Arkadin marvelous when his wig is coming unglued, when he looks like Santa Claus, or even more like Neptune? (Welles was so conscious of this resemblance—whether he intended it in the beginning or not—to the underwater god that one of the characters in this intrigue actually compares Arkadin to Neptune in the dialogue.)

But then the spell begins to work; we accept the film's seediness and are drawn into the action. Gregory Arkadin, as arrogant as Charles Foster Kane, as cynical as the "Third Man," as proud as George Minafer Amberson, is very much a Wellesian character. The road that led to his fortune is strewn with still-warm corpses. But Arkadin has a daughter, Raina, whom he cherishes, and he suffers terribly as he watches her being wooed by questionable characters. The latest, Van Stratten (Arden), is a young con man, a sometime blackmailer. Arkadin has made inquiries and has found out that Van Stratten is only courting his daughter to uncover something about Arkadin himself for the purpose of blackmail. Arkadin pretends to have lost all memory of his distant past and hires Van Stratten to investigate it, retracing all his far-flung travels. The old millionaire takes advantage of this circuitous operation to assassinate his old accomplices and any witnesses to his tumultuous past, as Van Stratten proceeds to uncover it. When there is nobody left to get rid of except Van Stratten, his intended victim provokes Arkadin into killing himself by convincing him that he's going to tell his daughter the truth about her father's life. Van Stratten gains nothing except his own life, for Raina, who already mistrusts him and doesn't want anything more to do with him, runs off with a young English aristocrat who's been standing in the wings.

Throughout the film we follow Van Stratten, whose investigation takes him all over the world—Mexico, Munich, Vienna, Paris, Madrid. The actors are plastered against the walls of real apartments, and Welles's camera, usually so mobile, has to calm its feverish activity and catch them in tilted shots compressed beneath the inevitable ceilings of the rooms. A Spanish fete where the guests hide their faces behind Goya masks makes us long for a time that will never return, when the all-powerful RKO gave an absolutely free hand to a young man of twenty-five to make his first film, *Citizen Kane*, exactly as he wished. That freedom was brutally lost, then patiently recovered by force of will—but today's methods are not even those of low-budget Hollywood Westerns. Even Welles is forced into making a film using the worst kind of stage tricks. But in the long run what difference does the workmanship make, if the ideas are superbly expressed? And we do admire the ideas, for they are truly excellent. All his life, Orson Welles will be influenced by Shakespeare whose lines he recited throughout his youth. He has, more than anyone, the gift of going beyond the particular action and situation and writing about the transcendence of the great, sophisticated philosophic and moral dialogues in which each sentence has a universal pertinence that rises above time and place.

Orson Welles is the only celebrity whose travels are not publicized; what you hear instead is "Welles was in New York the day before yesterday; last night, I had dinner with him in Venice; oh, I have a meeting with him in Lisbon the day after tomorrow."

At a certain moment, on the terrace of a Mexican hotel, Van Stratten is talking on the phone to Arkadin, whom he believes to be in Europe. The conversation ends with a roar of laughter from Arkadin, but Van Stratten hangs up and the roar continues. Arkadin is right there in Mexico, in the same hotel as Van Stratten. It used to be that Welles was a filmmaker of ambiguity. Now he's one of ubiquity.

One should really compare the filmmakers who stay put in one place to those who wander the world. The first make story movies— and only with great difficulty, usually at the end of their careers, do they succeed in moving from the particular to the universal. The latter gradually succeed in filming the whole world. Because their social situation keeps them sedentary, critics are as a whole unaware of the powerful beauty of the films of Renoir, Rossellini, Hitchcock, and Welles because these films are the conceptions of wanderers, emigrants, international observers. In the best of today's films, there's always an airport scene, and the best yet is in *Confidential Report* when Arkadin finds the plane full and shouts out that he will offer $10,000 to any passenger who will give him his seat. It is a marvelous variation on Richard III's cry, "My kingdom for a horse," in terms of the atomic age. It is indeed a Shakespearean inspiration that informs even the most minor sequences of the work of this astounding man whom André Bazin called, "a Renaissance man of the twentieth century." Welles's best friends lent their services more or less for nothing. They made no mistake. Never have Michael Redgrave, Akim Tamiroff, Suzanne Flon, Katina Paxinou, Mischa Auer, Peter van Eyck and Patricia Medina been better than in these brief, vivid profiles drawn from them by this inspired filmmaker, profiles of frightened people hunted down by adventurers, people who have a rendezvous with death within the hour.

In this gorgeous film, once again we find Welles's inspiration behind every image, that touch of madness and of genius, his power, his brilliant heartiness, his gnarled poetry.

There isn't a single scene which isn't based on a new or unusual idea. The film will undoubtedly be thought confusing, but certainly at the same time exciting, stimulating, enriching, a movie one could discuss for hours because it is filled with what we want most to find in any movie—lyricism and creativity.

—1956

Touch of Evil

You could remove Orson Welles's name from the credits and it wouldn't make any difference, because from the first shot, beginning with the credits themselves, it's obvious that *Citizen Kane* is behind the camera.

Touch of Evil opens on a shot of the clock of a time bomb as a man places it in the trunk of a white car. A couple have just gotten into the car and started off, and we follow them through the city. All this happens before the film starts. The camera perched on a motorized crane loses the car, finds it again as it passes behind some buildings, precedes it or catches up with it, right up to the moment when the explosion we have been waiting for happens.

The image is deliberately distorted by the use of a wide-angle lens that gives an unnatural clarity to the backgrounds and poeticizes reality as a man walking toward the camera appears to advance ten yards in five strides. We're in a fantasy world all through this film, the characters appearing to walk with seven-league boots when they're not gliding on a moving rug.

There are movies made by incompetent cynics, like *The Bridge on the River Kwai* and *The Young Lions,* movies that are merely bluff, designed to flatter a public which is supposed to leave the movie house feeling better or thinking it has learned something. There are movies that are profound and lofty, made without compromise by a few sincere and intelligent artists who would rather disturb than reassure, rather wake an audience up than put it to sleep. When you come out of Alain Resnais' *Nuit et Brouillard,* you don't feel better, you feel worse. When you come out of *White Nights* or *Touch of Evil,* you feel less intelligent than before but gratified anyhow by the poetry and art. These are films that call cinema to order, and make us ashamed to have been so indulgent with cliché-ridden movies made by small talents.

Well, you might say, what a fuss over a simple little detective story that Welles wrote in eight days, over which he didn't even have the right to supervise the final editing, and to which was later added a half-dozen explanatory shots he'd refused to make, a film he made "to order" and which he violently disavowed.

I'm well aware of all that, as well as that the slave who one night breaks his chains is worth more than the one who doesn't even know he's chained; and also that *Touch of Evil* is the most liberated film you can see. In *Barrage contre le Pacifique*, René Clément had complete control; he edited the film himself, chose the music, did the mixing, cut it up a hundred times. But Clément is a slave nonetheless, and Welles is a poet. I warmly recommend to you the films of poets.

Welles adapted for the screen a woefully poor little detective novel and simplified the criminal intrigue to the point where he could match it to his favorite canvas—the portrait of a paradoxical monster, which he plays himself—under cover of which he designed the simplest of moralities: that of the absolute and the purity of absolutists.

A capricious genius, Welles preaches to his parishioners and seems to be clearly telling us: I'm sorry I'm slovenly; it's not my fault if I'm a genius; I'm dying: love me.

As in *Citizen Kane, The Stranger, The Magnificent Ambersons,* and *Confidential Report,* two characters confront each other—the monster and the sympathetic young lead. It's a matter of making the monster more and more monstrous, and the young protagonist more and more likable, until we are brought somehow to shed real tears over the corpse of the magnificent monster. The world doesn't want anything to do with the exceptional, but the exception, if he is an unfortunate, is the ultimate refuge of purity. Fortunately, Welles's physique would seem to preclude his playing Hitler, but who's to say that one day he will not force us to weep over the fate of Hermann Goering?

Here Welles has given himself the role of a brutal and greedy policeman, an ace investigator, very well known. Since he works only by intuition, he uncovers murderers without bothering about proof. But the court system, which is made up of mediocre men, cannot condemn a man without evidence. Thus, Inspector Quinlan/Welles develops the habit of fabricating evidence and eliciting false testimony in order to win his case, to see that justice will triumph.

After the bomb explodes in the car, all that's necessary for everything to go awry is for an American policeman on his honeymoon (Charlton Heston) to meddle in Quinlan's investigation. There is a fierce battle between the two men. Heston *finds* proof against Welles while Welles *manufactures* evidence against him. After a frantic sequence in which Welles demonstrates that he could doubtless adapt de Sade's novels like nobody else, Heston's wife is found in a hotel, nude and drugged, and apparently responsible for the murder of Akim Tamiroff, who in reality has been killed by Quinlan—whom Tamiroff had naïvely helped set this demonic stage.

As in *Confidential Report*, the sympathetic character is led to commit an underhanded act in order to undo the monster: Heston records the few decisive sentences on a tape recorder, sufficient proof to destroy Welles. The film's idea is summed up neatly in this epilogue: Sneakiness and mediocrity have triumphed over intuition and absolute justice. The world is horrifyingly relative, everything is pretty much the same— dishonest in its morality, impure in its conception of fairness.

If I've used the word monster a number of times, it's merely to stress the fantastical spirit of this film and of all Welles's movies. All moviemakers who are not poets have recourse to psychology to put the spectator on the wrong scent, and the commercial success of psychological films might seem a good enough reason for them to do this. "All great art is abstract," Jean Renoir said, and one doesn't arrive at an abstraction through psychology—just the opposite. On the other hand, abstraction spills over sooner or later onto the moral, and onto the only morality that preoccupies us: the morality that is invented and reinvented by artists.

All this blends very well with Welles's supposition that mediocre men need facts, while others need only intuition. There lies the source of enormous misunderstanding. If the Cannes Festival Committee had had the wisdom to invite *Touch of Evil* to be shown rather than Martin Ritt's *The Long Hot Summer* (in which Welles is only an actor), would the jury have had the wisdom to see in it all the wisdom of the world?

Touch of Evil wakes us up and reminds us that among the pioneers of cinema there was Méliès and there was Feuillade. It's a magical film that makes us think of fairy tales: "Beauty and the Beast," "Tom Thumb," La Fontaine's fables. It's a film which humbles us a bit because it's by a man who thinks more swiftly than we do, and much better, and who throws another marvelous film at us when we're still reeling under the last one. Where does this quickness come from, this madness, this speed, this intoxication?

May we always have enough taste, sensitivity, and intuition to admit that this talent is large and beautiful. If the brotherhood of critics finds it expedient to look for arguments against this film, which is a witness and a testimony to art and nothing else, we will have to watch the grotesque spectacle of the Lilliputians attacking Gulliver.

—1958

A PORTRAIT OF HUMPHREY BOGART

The last image in *The Harder They Fall* shows Bogart at his typewriter trying to revise his confession. Rather than in this final role, where he was sloppily directed by Mark Robson, we will recall him as the movie director in *The Barefoot Contessa*. We see him standing at Ava Gardner's burial, in the rain, wearing his trench-coat; just before he leaves the cemetery he says: "Tomorrow it'll be sunny; we can get to work." In *Barefoot Contessa*, Bogart was playing Joseph Mankiewicz.

Humphrey Bogart always enjoyed telling people that he was born on Christmas Day in 1900, a year when every day was Christmas. Humphrey was his actress mother's family name, which he took as his first name. A bad student, a bad sailor, a bad husband, it took the movies to make him the best of everything.

His first mention in the newspapers was a review of a play in which he had a small part. The critic said, "To be as kind as possible, we will only say that this actor was inadequate." Humphrey ran scared. Then Leslie Howard chose him to play opposite him in *The Petrified Forest*, first on the stage and afterward in the movie. After that there were about thirty thrillers in which Bogart played supporting roles as the scoundrel-foil for the stars: Victor McLaglen, Spencer Tracy, Edward G. Robinson, James Cagney, George Raft, and even Paul Muni. Hollywood tradition demands that an actor who has become famous playing gangsters can rise in the hierarchy only by changing sides; the killer becomes a cop and his salary increases tenfold.

From 1936 to 1940, Humphrey Bogart was asleep on his feet, making films that put audiences to sleep. On January 1, 1941, he grabbed his chance with both arms and lips: the body and the mouth of Ida Lupino. He embraced the first and kissed the second in *High Sierra*, one of Raoul Walsh's best films, based on a screenplay by John Huston; Bogart played a role that had been turned down by James Cagney.

A little later, John Huston was ready to shoot his first film, *The Maltese Falcon*. To play Dashiell Hammett's wonderful character, Sam Spade, he thought immediately of George Raft. Raft turned down the part, luckily for Bogart, who agreed to search for the false falcon. If the real one exists, he's still in flight. Now the outlaw became a private eye, with a police ID in his pocket just in case. He made the switch and added up the balance: in just under forty films, he had died a dozen times in the electric chair, and had totaled more than eight hundred years at hard labor. Before that the only thing that spoke was his gun. Now, *he* spoke. And what did he say? Ladies, I'm six feet, 170 pounds; my hair is brown and I have nice hazel eyes. My first marriage only lasted eighteen months (too long) and my second eight years (also too long) and no one's going to get me back into that . . . until next time.

Walk and talk, talk and walk; that was his new job. As he went along the street, he put his hand on anything it could reach. A fire hydrant, a railing, a kid's head became so many markers along his route. Bogart adapted to life remarkably well, and grabbed hold of it. He constructed his own character; he learned to pinch his ear to express astonishment. You think he's just polishing his nails on the back of his jacket? Yes, but watch him stretch his arm out and land that sock right on the jaw: "Tell that to your boss." With Bogart, you had to know how to keep your distance.

The best film writers and scriptwriters did their best work to order for him. It is thus possible to speak of the "written work" of Humphrey Bogart. "Hi, sweetheart. The greatest thing would be a woman who could shrink to six inches, you could put her in your pocket." Or, "I ain't ever seen so many guns for such a small brain."

Did you see his death scene in Stuart Heisler's *The Big Shot*? In order to surrender he has to outdistance the motorcycle cops and get to the prison before them. He wins the paradoxical race and, as he is dying, he makes a confession to the prison warden that will clear the innocent young man. "Get married, have kids, like in the storybooks." The warden offers him a cigarette: "Do you still smoke the same junk?"

But Bogart played roles that were more serious without being less dramatic. Among them was the role of the incorruptible journalist in *Deadline*, which Richard Brooks shot in neorealist Italian fashion in the New York *Daily News* offices with the actual linotypers as extras. There was no mix, no music, only the sounds of the presses, the telephones and the typewriters. Another Richard Brooks film,

Battle Circus, equally unrecognized, offered him one of his most beautiful roles, as an army doctor who wants to love June Allyson without having to marry her.

One day, Mrs. Howard Hawks, the wife of America's most intelligent director, saw a beautiful girl with dreamy eyes on a magazine cover. It was "the look" of the future, Lauren Bacall, who thus met Hawks and subsequently Bogart. Making *The Big Sleep,* their love awakened and they decided to sleep together for life. Their meeting was Don Juan checkmated by the look. *The Big Sleep* is the bolt-of-lightning film. *To Have and Have Not* is the marriage film, replete with Bogart's entire panoply: hat, revolver, cigarette, telephone, all enriched by Betty. They got married in Louis Bromfield's home and bought Thomas Ince's Benedict Canyon ranch, which still smelled of Hedy Lamar's perfume from the time she had lived there. Their yacht was named the *Santana* and Bogart soon founded his own production company, also called Santana, for which Nicholas Ray made his masterful films *Knock on Any Door* and *In a Lonely Place.* It was Ray who was to make Bogart definitively the appealing hero, much more than an actor, a personality I shall attempt to describe.

Having shaved that morning but always in need of a shave, his brows angling toward his temples, eyelids half closed, one hand thrust forward, ready to justify or to confound, from film to film Bogart surveys the length and breadth of life's tribunal, his gait punctuated by Max Steiner's chords. He comes to a stop, spreads his legs a bit, unbuttons his jacket, sticks his thumbs inside his belt, and begins to talk. His jerky pronunciation is partial to the vowel *A* and the consonant *K;* we know how important the word "racket" sounds when he pronounces it. His clenched jaw indubitably reminds us of the grin of a cheerful corpse, the last expression of a man who is about to die laughing.

It was indeed the smile of death. A few weeks before his death, having lost forty pounds, he cracked, "I don't go out in the street any more because I'm afraid of being blown away, but as soon as I put on some weight, I'm going to make a film with John [Huston]."

What Bogart did, he did better than anyone else. He could act longer without saying a word than anyone else. He was more threatening than anyone else, and he struck his blows better. When he sweated, you could have wrung out his shirts.

Bogart was a good worker: he liked the hard work with Huston, the disputative violence of Nicholas Ray, the cold, lucid intelligence of Howard Hawks. One of his last films, *The Caine Mutiny,* showed his fascinating face in its best light. In the role of an officer who was as tough as leather, Bogy appeared as he really was, because the actors didn't wear any makeup in the old Technicolor films. For the first time we saw the scar on his upper lip that was left from a time long ago when he was in the navy and a piece of wood cut him when he broke a bottle on the bridge.

Humphrey Bogart was a modern hero. The period film—the historical romance or pirate story—didn't suit him. He was the starter at the race, the man who had a revolver with only one bullet, the guy in the felt hat that he could flick with a finger to express anger or gaiety, the man at the microphone: "Hello! Hello! calling all cars . . ."

If Bogart's appearance was modern, his morality was classic. He was much closer to the Duke de Nemours in *La Princesse de Clèves* than to Commissioner Maigret. He knew that causes are worth less than beautiful deeds, and that every act is pure so long as it goes by the rules.

—1958

JAMES DEAN IS DEAD

On the evening of September 30, 1955, against the wishes of the Warner Brothers studio executives, James Dean got behind the wheel of his sports car and was killed on a road in northern California.

The news, which we learned in Paris the next day, did not arouse much emotion at the time. A young actor, twenty-four years old, was dead. Six months have passed and two of his films have appeared, and now we realize what we have lost.

Dean had been noticed two years before on Broadway when he played the role of the young Arab in an adaptation of André Gide's *The Immoralist*. Following that, Elia Kazan starred him in *East of Eden*—Dean's movie debut. Then Nicholas Ray chose him for the hero of *Rebel Without a Cause*, and finally George Stevens picked him to play the principal role in *Giant*, the story of a man we follow from twenty to sixty. His next part was to have been the boxer Rocky Graziano in *Somebody Up There Likes Me*.

Dean worked very hard at *Giant;* he never took his eye off George Stevens or the camera. When the film was finished, he told his agent, Dick Clayton, "I think I could be a better director than an actor." He wanted to establish an independent company so he could shoot only properties he had chosen himself. Clayton promised to talk it over with the Warner Brothers executives. Then, Dean, who had been forbidden by contract to drive his car while the film was being shot, roared off to Salinas to compete in a race.

The accident: "I think I'll take a ride in the Spyder [the brand name of his Porsche]," he told George Stevens. Near Paso Robles that evening, he and his Spyder were cut off by another car coming onto the highway from a side road. Dean died from multiple fractures and internal contusions on the way to the hospital.

It was his fate to die before his time, as have so many artists.

James Dean's acting flies in the face of fifty years of filmmaking; each gesture, attitude, each mimicry is a slap at the psychological tradition. Dean does not "show off" the text by understatement like Edwige Feuillère; he does not evoke its poetry, like Gérard Philipe; he does not play with it mischievously like Pierre Fresnay. By contrast, he is anxious not to show that he understands perfectly what he is saying, but that he understands it better than the director did. He acts *something beyond* what he is saying; he plays alongside the scene; his expression doesn't follow the conversation. He *shifts* his expression from what is being expressed in the way that a consummately modest genius might express profound thoughts self-deprecatingly, as if to excuse himself for his genius, so as not to make a nuisance of himself.

There were special moments when Chaplin reached the ultimate in mime: he became a tree, a lamppost, an animal-skin rug next to a bed. Dean's acting is more animal than human, and that makes him unpredictable. What will his next gesture be? He may keep talking and turn his back to the camera as he finishes a scene; he may suddenly throw his head back or let it droop; he may raise his arms to heaven, stretch them forward, palms up to convince, down to reject. He may, in a single scene, appear to be the son of Frankenstein, a little squirrel, a cowering urchin or a broken old man. His nearsighted look adds to the feeling that he shifts between his acting and the text; there is a vague fixedness, almost a hypnotic half-slumber.

When you have the good luck to write for an actor of this sort, an actor who plays his part physically, carnally, instead of filtering everything through his brain, the easiest way to get good results is to think abstractly. Think of it this way: James Dean is a cat, a lion, or maybe a squirrel. What can cats, lions and squirrels do that is most unlike humans? A cat can fall from great heights and land on its paws; it can be run over without being injured; it arches its back and slips away easily. Lions creep and roar; squirrels jump from one branch to another. So, what one must write are scenes in which Dean creeps (amid the beanstalks), roars (in a police station), leaps from branch to branch, falls from a great height into an empty pool without getting hurt. I like to think this is how Elia Kazan, Nicholas Ray, and, I hope, George Stevens proceeded.

Dean's power of seduction was so intense that he could have killed his parents every night on the screen with the blessing of the snobs and the general public alike. One had to witness the indignation in the movie house when, in *East of Eden*, his father refuses to accept the money that Cal earned with the beans, the wages of love.

More than just an actor, James Dean, like Chaplin, became a personality in only three films: Jimmy and the beans and at the country fair, Jimmy on the grass, Jimmy in the abandoned house. Thanks to Elia Kazan's and Nicholas Ray's sensitivity to actors, James Dean played characters close to the Baudelairean hero he really was.

The underlying reasons for his success? With women, the reason is obvious and needs no explanation. With young men, it was because they could identify with him; this is the basis for the commercial success of his films in every country of the world. It is easier to identify with James Dean than with Humphrey Bogart, Cary Grant, or Marlon Brando. Dean's personality is truer. Leaving a Bogart movie, you may pull your hat brim down; this is no time for someone to hassle you. After a Cary Grant film, you may clown around on the street; after Brando, lower your eyes and feel tempted to bully the local girls. With Dean, the sense of identification is deeper and more complete, because he contains within himself all our ambiguity, our duality, our human weaknesses.

Once again, we have to go back to Chaplin, or rather Charlie. Charlie always starts at the bottom and aims higher. He is weak, despised, left out. He fails in all his efforts; he tries to sit down to relax and ends up on the ground, he's ridiculous in the eyes of the woman he courts or in the eyes of the brute he wants to tame. What happens at this point is a pure gift: Chaplin will avenge himself and win out. Suddenly he begins to dance, skate, spin better than anyone else, and now he eclipses everyone, he triumphs, he changes the mood and has all the jeerers on his side.

What started out as an inability to adapt becomes super-adeptness. The entire world, everybody and everything that had been against him, is now at his service. All this is true of Dean, too, but we must take into account a fundamental difference: never do we catch the slightest look of fear. James Dean is beside everything; in his acting neither courage nor cowardice has any place any more than heroism or fear. Something else is at work, a poetic game that lends authority to every liberty—even encourages it. Acting right or wrong has no meaning when we talk about Dean, because we expect a surprise a minute from him. He can laugh when another actor would cry—or the opposite. He killed psychology the day he appeared on the set.

With James Dean everything is grace, in every sense of the word. That's his secret. He isn't better than everybody else; he does *something else*, the opposite; he protects his glamour from the beginning to end of each film. No one has ever seen Dean walk; he ambles or runs like a mailman's faithful dog (think of the opening of *East of Eden*). Today's young people are represented completely in James Dean, less for the reasons that are usually given—violence, sadism, frenzy, gloom, pessimism, and cruelty—than for other reasons that are infinitely more simple and everyday: modesty, continual fantasizing, a moral purity not related to the prevailing morality but in fact stricter, the adolescent's eternal taste for experience, intoxication, pride, and the sorrow at feeling "outside," a simultaneous desire and refusal to be integrated into society, and finally acceptance and rejection of the world, such as it is.

No doubt Dean's acting, because of its contemporaneous quality, will start a new Hollywood style, but the loss of this young actor is irreparable; he was perhaps the most inventively gifted actor in films. Good cousin of Dargelos that he was, he met his death on the road, one cool September evening, like the young American described in Cocteau's *Enfants Terribles:* ". . . the car leapt, twisted, crashed against a tree and became a silent ruin, one wheel spinning slower and slower like a raffle wheel."

—1956

VI

My Friends in the New Wave

ALAIN RESNAIS

Nuit et Brouillard

Starting from actual documents—news clips, photos, archives—and joining them to images that he filmed last year, Alain Resnais has given us a cruel but deserved history lesson.

It is almost impossible to speak about this film in the vocabulary of cinematic criticism. It is not a documentary, or an indictment, or a poem, but a meditation on the most important phenomenon of the twentieth century.

Nuit et Brouillard (Night and Fog) treats deportation and the concentration camps with a flawless tact and quiet restraint that make it a sublime work . . . "uncriticizable" . . . almost "undiscussable."

The power of this film, which opens with the image of grass springing up by the abandoned watchtowers, crushed underfoot by police, is rooted in its tone, the *terrible gentleness* which Alain Resnais and Jean Cayrol, who wrote the commentary, were able not only to create but to maintain. *Nuit et Brouillard* is a question that haunts us all: Are we not all "deporters"? Or couldn't we be, at least by complicity?

Resnais' work, which combines color in the present with documentary black-and-white footage, subtracts from the latter all macabre theatricality, all staged horror, and thus forces us to react with our heads rather than with our nerve endings. When we have looked at these strange, seventy-pound slave laborers, we understand that we're not going to "feel better" after seeing *Nuit et Brouillard;* quite the opposite.

As Resnais' camera moves lightly over the new grass and "visits" the now empty camps, Jean Cayrol informs us about concentration camp rituals and questions himself unpityingly: "We pretend that we believe all this belonged to another time and a particular country, but we do not look around us and we do not hear people crying endlessly."

Miles and miles of film are shown every day in studios around the world. For one evening we must forget to think of ourselves as critics or moviegoers. Here we are involved as human beings who have to open our eyes and question ourselves. For a few hours *Nuit et Brouillard* wipes out the memory of all other films. It absolutely must be seen.

When the lights go on at the end, no one dares applaud. We stand speechless before such a work, struck dumb by the importance and necessity of these thousand meters of film.

—1955

ALEXANDRE ASTRUC

Les Mauvaises Rencontres

As in Alfred Hitchcock's films, there are two stories in *Les Mauvaises Rencontres*. While searching the home of an "obliging" physician who has disappeared, the police find a letter from Catherine Racan (Anouk Aimée). Suspecting that she had written to Dr. Danieli (Claude Dauphin) to get an abortion, they take her to police headquarters to be questioned by Inspector Forbin (Yves Robert). The doctor's suicide puts an end to the investigation.

This is the film's first subject, or more exactly, the underpinnings of the real subject, which is simply the story of Catherine Racan.

Three years earlier, this little cousin of Rastignac had left her home in the provinces with the man she loved, Pierre Jaegers (Gianni Esposito) to find "success" in Paris. He grows discouraged, gives up, and returns home. Then she meets Blaise Walter (Jean-Claude Pascal), the publisher of a large daily newspaper. Catherine becomes his mistress but eventually leaves him, after she has become, with his help, a fashion magazine editor. A short affair with a photographer, Alain Bergère (Philippe Lemaire), follows. Then, one evening, Blaise and Catherine meet again. Catherine is upset by the encounter and returns to Besançon to try and renew her relationship with Pierre. This fails and she comes back to Paris pregnant. This is when she has recourse to the services of Dr. Danieli.

At the end of the film she is shown leaving headquarters surrounded by news photographers, a disillusioned woman. It isn't how she had dreamed of "someday seeing her name in the papers."

There is, obviously, nothing very complicated about the plot, despite its being perhaps a little too elaborate to be completely clear at first viewing without giving it your complete attention. In three hours at police headquarters Catherine Racan relives three years of her life. These flashbacks are handled smoothly and naturally, and with considerable ingenuity. One must be there at the beginning of the film and avoid chatting with one's neighbor in order not to miss anything.

There remain the deeper intentions of the film which some consider mysterious; they were stated clearly in the June issue of *Arts* in an interview with the director: "To stay within the framework of Balzac, let us say that it's a little bit like *Les Illusions Perdues*. This girl evolves through different situations and looks around her. In terms of production, it is a large picture that brings judgment to bear on the larger scene. . . . I wanted to make a narrative film, not novelistic, but narrative. . . . I am interested in how personalities can be related to what they don't understand."

Les Mauvaises Rencontres should not be approached as if it were a detective film or a newspaper account. These characters are neither criminals nor victims; they are simply contemporary young intellectuals. If I think that *Les Mauvaises Rencontres* is ahead of its time, it is because it is the first film a) to take the confusion of young intellectuals as its theme; b) to speak of Paris from other than a tourist's view in a "Paris by Night" tour, the first to describe it in Balzacian terms—*Les Mauvaises Rencontres* is the new "scenes of Paris life"; and c) the first to speak of "success" without cynicism, mockery, or hypocrisy.

What touches me most in *Les Mauvaises Rencontres* is the accuracy of the dialogue. It is certainly literary, but after all, these are intellectuals talking. Astruc does not judge his characters; he looks at them with clarity, tenderness, and above all, absolute lucidity, since he is one of them. Blaise Walters, Pierre Jaegers, and Alain Bergères are innocent men who suffer because they cannot stay that way. They spend most of their leisure time justifying themselves, judging themselves, above all hating themselves. They are weak and vulnerable people whose preoccupations are, nevertheless, essentially moral. All this is specific to our generation; it will be a surprise that those who do not question themselves will not grasp the importance of Astruc's undertaking.

This difficult, specifically 1955 theme has been treated with a generosity to which we have grown unaccustomed in French scenarists, most of whom can only dominate the characters they create by making fun of them or caricaturing them.

It sounds more like Hollywood than Joinville. I am also pleased to add that nothing (almost nothing) technically distinguishes *Les Mauvaises Rencontres* from the kind of American film we love, that Astruc loves. "Let's go to the movies; is there an American film around?" the heroine asks. This is also the first French film shot almost entirely on a crane, and it gives the camera a suppleness we scarcely find except with Preminger or Fritz Lang. Robert Lefebvre's photography is extraordinary, as are the settings by Max Douy. Actors like Jean-Claude Pascal or Yves Robert are surprisingly well cast here; Philippe Lemaire, Gianni Esposito, and Claude Dauphin are perfect, and Anouk Aimée is unquestionably embarking on a second career.

At the Venice Festival I saw that *Les Mauvaises Rencontres* was not to everyone's taste: some of my colleagues and some viewers may have thought the film was too intellectual, literary, and overdone, while some who were indifferent to the plot may have considered it a brilliant stylistic exercise and nothing more. But one thing I noticed always. Not a single viewer under thirty was unmoved or failed to recognize himself in one of the characters.

Les Mauvaises Recontres shakes up the accepted style of storytelling and ordinary approaches; it doesn't resemble anything else being done nowadays.

To a foreign journalist in Venice who remarked to Astruc, "You have overestimated the public too much," the director replied, "One can never overestimate the public enough."

—1955

AGNÈS VARDA

La Pointe Courte

Two steps from the Vavin subway stop and the Dôme Café, almost impossible to find on a first try, but familiar to all true cinéphiles, stands the Studio Parnasse, the best "programmed" Paris movie theater for the past eight years, where one can see the most important works in any given year.

By way of exception, the Studio Parnasse will leave the "classics" for two weeks, and become a first-run house on behalf of a film that couldn't last three days in a theater on the Champs-Elysées or the other main streets.

La Pointe Courte, the first film by Agnès Varda, a photographer for the Théâtre Nationale Populaire, is a cinematic essay, an ambitious experimental work, perfectly at home on the screen of the Studio Parnasse.

According to the advertisement—which, for once, is true to the work being promoted—it is a "film essay to be read," made up of two accounts: one about a couple who have been married for four years, and another about a fishing village (La Pointe Courte, near Sète). The film doesn't try to reproduce an experience or to prove any point. It tells its stories slowly, in rhythm with the consuming, transforming passage of time, in rhythm with inexorable time, under the glow of time that is beautiful as well.

Behind the suspect simplicity of the project, a number of secret intentions are hidden, left unstated because they are almost impossible to articulate. Some might fear they bear only a distant relationship to the direction and the handling of the actors.

Since the heroine of the film is in touch only with iron, and her partner only with wood, there is an intense moment of crisis when, at a certain moment, the saw cuts into a plank of wood. That is the kind of idea—I would not have discovered this one unaided!— that recurs in *La Pointe Courte*, as images that have been a bit too carefully "framed" follow one another, accompanied by exchanges of dialogue that are straight out of the highly intellectual theater of Maurice Clavel.

It is difficult to form a judgment of a film in which the true and the false, the true-false and the false-true, are intermingled according to barely perceived rules.

Sylvia Montfort and Philippe Noiret, lying next to each other in bed, ponder the light bulb in their bedroom:

She: "Is the water from the canal on the ceiling?"

He: "Yes, because the moon is in the canal!"

In order to judge whether these statements are subtle or grotesque, poetic or pretentious, one has to see *La Pointe Courte*. I think they are simultaneously good and bad, realistic and a little too laboriously "authentic." One can't help thinking "there is a lot of muscle at work here."

If, by the nature of its ambitions, *La Pointe Courte* joins the family of films that are *outside* cinema—*Minna de Venghel, Le Pain vivant, Huis Clos*—it is nonetheless superior to these because the result matches the director's intentions. Indeed, Agnès Varda may yet one day ask herself, and confront, the essential problems in filmmaking.

The main fault with this film, which in the end, I have not understood much better than my colleagues—those who praised it and those who did not—is that it is loosely directed. I am not speaking of the technique, which is surprisongly mature for a first film, but about the completely slack direction of the actors. The acting of Montfort and Noiret (whose resemblance to Varda is perhaps not accidental) remains uncertain. Their gestures, attitudes, looks, and tones of voice remain *deliberate and theoretical.*

At the end of this report on a film (which is itself a kind of report), I notice that I have dealt with the vehicle rather than the content. It was the best way of avoiding the ponderous remarks that this very cerebral director confidently expects.

Now, I am afraid that I have not communicated a desire to see this film, and that would be a shame. Each evening, after the showing, J. L. Cheray, the director of the Parnasse, moderates a debate in which *La Pointe Courte* is praised or damned by satisfied or unhappy customers.

Also, at least once in one's lifetime, one should see *A Propos de Nice*, Jean Vigo's first film, which opens the program.

—1956

ROGER VADIM

Et Dieu Créa la Femme

Everyone is talking about it; some are complaining, "It's not even dirty!" and others, "It's indecent!" *Et Dieu créa la Femme (And God Created Woman)*, which we had every reason to worry about after the censors provided a free publicity campaign, is a sensitive and intelligent film with no trace of vulgarity. It's a film that belongs to this generation: simultaneously amoral (rejecting the current moral system but proposing no other) and puritanical (conscious of its amorality and disturbed by it). Far from being trivial, it is revealing and completely honest.

Lots of films are based on sex. Sometimes the most effective way to get the public into the movie houses has been to promise them, with posters and photos at the entrances, something new and wonderful, new flesh, young bodies, usually female. We should, however, note that female customers are not indifferent to the attractions of the masculine body. Count how many films show Georges Marchal, James Dean or Curt Jurgens barechested. (Pierre Fresnay always insists on at least one scene in which he can wear a turtleneck.)

Yet, when this new flesh appears on the screen, it is greeted with shock or sneers by a jaded public which, although secretly looking for emotional response, would rather play the devil with directors than risk being surprised with their hearts in their mouths.

To avoid this reaction a lot of directors refrain from making the erotic scenes which their screenplays imply. It's depressing when the public smirks at a daring scene that is intended seriously. French filmmakers fall back on erotic dialogue; our trivial treatment of the entire subject, unbelievably vulgar and complacent, passes for spirited satiric comedy.

The generation gap is widest of all on the subject of eroticism and sexual mores. As a result, despite the huge audience that *Et Dieu créa la Femme* will certainly attract, only the young will side with Vadim, because he sees things as they do.

Under the pretext of telling us a simple story simply depicted, Vadim presents a woman he knows very well, his wife. Something of an unconscious exhibitionist, temperamentally disposed to nudism, the child-woman—or more precisely, the infant-woman—strolls in the Mediterranean sun, her hair billowing in the breeze, arousing desire . . . troubled and unambiguous, pure and impure desire. She's a good girl; men love her either too much or not enough, or badly. All she asks is to be loved truly, definitively—and this she finally gets.

The little scandal that does hover over the film comes from the unusual frankness of the screenplay. To fool the public and leave their consciences at ease, Léonide Moguy presents "medical case histories," Cayatte "legal cases," and Ralph Habit "social cases." All one has to do to save appearances and throw the idiotic censors off the track is to show someone in a white tunic in front of a hospital. Vadim didn't want to hide behind such hypocritical procedures; he bet on realism and life, with no cynicism or provocation, and he won out with inventiveness and ideas.

Obviously the film is not perfect. The plot could have been improved; five or six of the director's remarks could go; there is no pacing and the direction is uneven. But what is good is really good. Brigitte Bardot is magnificent; for the first time she is completely herself. You have to see her lips trembling violently after Trintignant slaps her four times. She is directed affectionately, like a pet animal, as Jean Renoir directed Catherine Hessling in *Nana*.

There is no vulgarity, no failure of taste. Thirard's photography is excellent, and so are Jean André's sets. Curt Jurgens confirms the fact that he is one of the four worst actors in the world; Christian Marquand is making progress.

Et Dieu créa la Femme, an intimate film, a notebook film, reveals a new French director who is more personal than Boisrond, Boissol, Carbonnaux, and Joffé—and just as gifted.

—1957

CLAUDE CHABROL

Le Beau Serge

Everyone agreed that the best film shown outside the festival was Claude Chabrol's *Le Beau Serge (Handsome Serge)*, which will be in the Brussels competition. It was withdrawn here at the last moment by the "protectors" of *L'Eau Vive*. Chabrol is the producer, writer, and director of *Le Beau Serge*. His film starts with psychology and ends with metaphysics. It's a chess game played by two young men: Gérard Blain has the black pieces, and Jean-Claude Brialy the white. At the moment they meet, they change colors and the game ends in a tie. My interpretation may make this seem a purely intellectual work. But that is not the case. *Le Beau Serge* makes its impact through the reality of the peasant environment (the action takes place at Sardent, Creuse) and of its characters. In the role of Serge, Gérard Blain gives his best performance, and Jean-Claude Brialy, in a very difficult role, shows his dramatic gifts. Technically the film is as masterful as if Chabrol had been directing for ten years, though this is his first contact with a camera. Here is an unusual and courageous film that will raise the level of French cinema this year.

—1958

LOUIS MALLE

Les Amants

Les Amants (The Lovers) is a fascinating film—not a masterpiece, because it is not completely under control; but it is free and intelligent, done with absolute tact and perfect taste. It moves with the spontaneity of Renoir's early films. One has the feeling of discovering each thing along with the filmmaker, rather than trailing or being hemmed in by him.

Love is the subject of subjects, particularly for cinema, where the carnal cannot be separated from feeling. Louis Malle has made the film that everybody carries around in his heart and dreams of turning into a reality: the detailed story of lightning striking, the burning "contact of two skins" which only much later will reveal itself as "the exchange of two fantasies."

Much better than *L'Ascenseur pour l'Echafaud (Lift to the Scaffold)*, *Les Amants* also outclasses *Et Dieu créa la Femme*, *Le Beau Serge*, *Le Dos au Mur*. It is certainly the best film offered by an "under-thirty."

The act of sex cannot be shown in cinema because there would be too great a gap between the abstract and the concrete, between the filmmaker's inspiration and the visual presentation of his idea. It would be repulsive and excessive, though no more and no less than the tears of a little boy standing in front of his burst balloon. The censors watch out for the former but not for the latter because they conceive their task poorly and know nothing about esthetic morality, the only one that should count.

So the filmmaker must show, as honestly as possible, what happens *before* and *after* love, that is, at the moment when the two partners show themselves to us as human beings entirely apart, and then joined in a perfect harmony of bodies and souls. For years French cinema rejected this truth, substituting the kind of insinuating jokes and cheap vulgarities which make for success in our boulevard theaters. *Et Dieu créa la Femme* is to be defended because it was the first real effort to present love truthfully in a film. The defect of Vadim's first film (which I mention here because Malle has avoided it) was to remove himself from the carnal aspect in favor of an insidious, hence less pure, eroticism: a show of panties, positions composed entirely for the camera, a sea-drenched dress, the heroine's antisocial aggressivity, and so on. Malle, admirably seconded by Louise de Vilmorin, has succeeded in making a perfectly familiar and almost banal movie, a film of absolute modesty, its integrity unassailable.

During the second half of the film—which is to the act of love what the holdup in *Rififi* was to stealing—Jeanne Moreau is either in a nightgown or completely nude without any of those special indirect effects, such as having her silhouette cut off by a light, the kind that was constantly inflicted on us in Martine Carol films.

Les Amants synthesizes the daring of a timid man: it is fresh and natural, not slick or artificial. As opposed to Vadim's films, this one is deliberately nontopical; it has no particular lesson or point—love is eternal. It deals less with women today than with women in general, those of Flaubert and those of Giraudoux. *Les Amants* may be the first film *à la Giraudoux*.

—1958

Le Feu Follet

The public came to the rendezvous that Louis Malle arranged with his *Feu Follet (Will-o'-the-wisp)*. This film is like those I used to look for in the "arts" columns—simple, personal, sincere.

Nonetheless, I have heard more intelligent arguments advanced by its detractors than by its admirers. *Le Feu Follet* is one of those films about which everything anyone says is true: yes, it is sincere;

yes, cunning; yes, it is unadorned; but it lacks rigor, etc. Now, if he had sunk into indifference, Malle's adversaries would have talked about stupidity or clumsiness—but never of posturing.

Now, in fact, and if we are careful to analyze our own intentions, criticizing a film amounts to criticizing the maker, and I can no longer do that. I believe firmly that a filmmaker's entire work is contained in his first film; not that it can all be foreseen, but it can afterward be verified. All of Louis Malle, all his good qualities and faults, was in *Ascenseur pour l'Echafaud*. Starting from there, we can say that *Vie Privée* was a "less good" *Ascenseur* and that *Feu Follet* is a "better" *Ascenseur*.

The only important complaint I wish to lodge about *Le Feu Follet* is that the main character is touching from the outset instead of growing so as the film goes along. In *A Bout de Souffle (Breathless)*, and in all of Jean-Luc Godard's films, generally, the emotion is both more powerful and purer because it is arrived at *despite* something. If Maurice Ronet had sometimes been aggressive or hateful, our attention would have been deeper, and the film, instead of simply moving us, would have been shattering.

This does not prevent the film's underlying principle from seeming valid and logical to me. We follow a desperate person throughout the film, the minutes pile up, and strong emotion is generated, almost simply, by accumulating neutral closeups. All comedians know how to get laughs through repetition; even more interesting, there is also a pathos of repetition. By using it, Louis Malle has succeeded in making his best film yet.

—1964

JEAN-LUC GODARD

Tous les Garçons S'appellent Patrick

In 1930, *A Propos de Nice* represented the avant-garde. In 1958 it is *Tous les Garçons s'appellent Patrick (All Boys Are Called Patrick)* by Jean-Luc Godard with a scenario by Eric Rohmer.

We know how Jean Vigo described his first film at the Vieux-Colombier: "In cinema, we treat our spirits with a refinement that the Chinese customarily reserve for their feet." The camera pedicures usually operate today in short subjects or in subsidized productions; a small crew and the absence of actors encourages their obsessed madness.

I love Alain Resnais' moving camera shots; I detest those that are acclaimed to be "à la Resnais." I love the flashes of madness of Franju, and I detest the brain waves that are "worthy of Franju." So, what is being done in short subjects in 1958? Two artists, Resnais and Franju, each flanked by a half-dozen slavish imitators, who have no personality of their own, who only caricature the form of the former, and the obsessions of the latter.

Still, a few names have emerged: Agnès Varda, Jacques Rivette, Henri Gruel, Jacques Demy, Jean-Luc Godard . . . all influenced by the singular Louis Lumière.

Shot at one-quarter speed with a thousand meters of film, *Tous les Garçons s'appellent Patrick* is a witty and sophisticated conversation in the form of a "News of the Week" of love. It exhibits maximum strength in its pace, and minimum sloppiness in its form.

Patrick is energetically on the make in all directions, but the ambiguity that results from trying to be everywhere at once does him in. First, he comes on strong with Véronique; then, he turns up his nose at Charlotte. In the end, Patrick (Jean-Claude Brialy), as the love-them-and-leave-them lover who is finally humbled, is the hero of an adventure that is lived out in the utmost freedom, ease, casualness, and something that even approaches grace.

—1958

Vivre Sa Vie

Let everyone live his life as he chooses, as long as he's getting along. So what about the new wave? What about it? Pierre says something good about Georges who is mad about Julien's work; he supervises Popaul who coproduces with Marcel to whom Claude gave a rave review!

Never mind. Today I am going to sing the praises of Jean-Luc, who makes films just as I do, except he makes twice as many.

When I was a film critic, I wanted above all to *convince*, probably because, having no idea of the real problems a filmmaker faces, I was instinctively trying to convince myself first of all about what was good and what was not.

I shall never try to communicate in writing to those who do not feel the *physical* joy and the *physical* pain which certain moments of *A Bout de Souffle (Breathless)* and *Vivre sa Vie (My Life to Live)* caused me.

The sheer unreality, deliberate or not, of certain cinematic styles can be seductive but it leaves us ambivalent. The most powerful reality, on the other hand, can seduce us momentarily but leave us ultimately hungry. A film like *Vivre sa Vie* pulls us continuously to the ends of the abstract and then to the limits of the concrete; the movement is undoubtedly what creates its emotion.

Cinema that moves us, that's what interests and fascinates us, no matter whether emotion is created scientifically as Hitchcock or Bresson create it, or whether it is simply born out of the artist's ability to communicate emotionally, as with Rossellini and Godard.

There are films one can admire and yet that do not invite you to follow . . . why pursue it? These are not the best films. The best films open doors, they support our impression that cinema begins and begins again with them. *Vivre sa Vie* is one of those.

—1962

JACQUES RIVETTE

Paris Nous Appartient

Every month the death throes of the "nouvelle vague" are announced. But there are twenty-four "first films" in 1960, and the number will reach thirty-two in 1961 and go even higher in 1962. Jacques Rozier, Jean-Louis Richard, Eric Rohmer, Marcel Bluwal, Alain Cavalier, André Versini, Bernard Zimmer, Lola Keigel, Jabely, Jacques Ertaud—you'll become familiar with the names of these young filmmakers who are just finishing their first movies in the first six months of next year, and others will be added to the list before the end of 1962: Alain Robbe-Grillet, Marcel Ophuls, Francis Blanche, François Billetdoux, Paul Gegauff, Jean-François Hauduroy, Jean Herman, Serge Bourguignon, and many others.

Out of all of them, we reserve a special mention for Jacques Rivette. The release of *Paris nous appartient (Paris Belongs to Us)*, his first film, is a score for every member of the team—or of our Mafia, if you prefer.

The shooting of *Paris nous appartient* was started three and a half years ago, in the early summer of 1958. The screenplay had been around for several months but no producer was interested so Rivette decided to jump into the stream. He borrowed 80,000 francs from *Cahiers du Cinéma* to buy several cases of film. The camera and laboratory were on credit; technicians and actors were hired as partners, "with full participation."

The undertaking seemed doomed from the outset, yet it was not entirely foolish. Two years before, Rivette had made a twenty-minute movie in Claude Chabrol's apartment for the price of the film. Afterward, producer Pierre Braunberger saw *Le Coup du Berger*, took it over and assumed the costs of finishing it. This little film has since been sold all around the world.

We thought that if *Le Coup du Berger* had been an hour longer, it would have been a perfectly respectable full-length film, made for ten times less than the average French movie.

The example of *Le Coup du Berger* made me decide to shoot *Les Mistons*, and Claude Chabrol to be adventuresome enough to make a full-length film from *Le Beau Serge;* and at the same time it moved the most prestigious short-subject filmmakers, Alain Resnais and Georges Franju, to try their first full-length film. It had begun.

And it had begun thanks to Rivette. Of all of us he was the most fiercely determined to move. He had arrived from the provinces—a point he has in common with Balzac—with *Aux Quatre Coins*, a little 16 mm. film, in his suitcase. In Paris he made *Quadrille*, with Jean-Luc Godard, and *Le Divertissement*. Influenced by him, I made my own decision and shot a sketchy short piece, without any interest even at that time, called *Une Visite* in Doniol-Valcroze's apartment. Out of friendship, and just for the practice, Rivette agreed to be my chief cameraman. We were all admirers of Edouard Molinaro, who had succeeded in having his 16 mm. production shown commercially, and Alexandre Astruc, who refused to show his, but the master of 16 mm. was Eric Rohmer beyond any argument. Two films by Rohmer, *Bérénice*, based on a story by Edgar Allan Poe, and even more *La Sonate à Kreutzer*, both shot in 16 mm. with the sound recorded on a tape recorder, are wonderful. I have seen them often and I went to see them again quite recently just to be sure: they compare well with the best professional films in 35 mm. that have been made in the past five years.

A fifteen-minute 16 mm. film costs between 30,000 and 40,000 francs; I have never understood why, when producers are hesitant about signing up a newcomer, they don't have him make a sequence in 16 mm. I often send overanxious assistants or apprentices who only want "to sit in a corner and watch, without causing any disturbance" back to practice with 16 mm. You can learn more by making a film in 16 mm. and editing it yourself than by acting as somebody's apprentice or assistant.

Of all our band of fanatics, Rivette was the most fanatical. The day that *Carrosse d'Or* opened, he stayed in his seat from two o'clock in the afternoon till midnight. But that didn't stop him from going, the next day, to find out all about laboratory costs and how to rent portable cameras.

One day, he had the brilliant idea of creating "Cinéastes Associés." An average French film cost 100 million francs; we felt that we could shoot one for a fifth of that. So we went to producers to propose that they finance five films. Alain Resnais, who was very taken with the idea, was going to direct the first (to be based on *Les Mauvais Coups* by Vailland), and Rivette would be his assistant. Alexandre Astruc would direct the second and I would be his assistant. Jacques Rivette would make the third, I the fourth, etc.

But, I repeat, it was Rivette who took the initiative, who threw himself into the task, who worked and made us work. Under his direction, we composed an original scenario: *Les Quatre Jeudis.* Jean-Claude Brialy was to be the star; he was our friend and our hope, though he had never made a film or played a part. But every evening at nine o'clock he evoked the spell of the curtain rising to reveal the other actors; and he was gripped by an incredible tragicomic delirium, possibly the mark of genius.

The scenario of *Les Quatre Jeudis,* labored over so meticulously by Rivette, Chabrol, Charles Bitsch and me, is still asleep in some producers' files.

Our mistake was to believe that producers were interested in making inexpensive films. In fact, since for the most part they are simply intermediaries between the banks and the distributors, their margin of profit is proportionate to the cost of the film. Once again, we received a polite, even slightly bemused reception but, "Don't bother to shut the door, we'll take care of it."

In July 1958, Rivette's problem when he began to make *Paris nous appartient* was to find enough money by each Sunday to begin work again on Monday. And what work it was! A mighty river of a film, thirty characters, thirty locations, night and dawn scenes. And he did all this without a secretary, without a manager, without a car, on "petty cash," and at a time of year when everybody was leaving on vacation.

When Chabrol began shooting *Les Cousins,* a few boxes of film passed from his movie to Rivette's. Three months later, with *Paris nous appartient* still not finished, I began *Les quatre cents Coups.* Rivette finished shooting at the same time I did, but all he had was the picture. He had too many outstanding debts against the film to attempt the dubbing and editing, even on credit.

At the Cannes Festival in 1959, Chabrol and I decided to become co-producers of *Paris nous appartient*. The editing, the dubbing, the sound track, everything has now been finished for several months, and the film will be released in France in art and avant-garde houses. It will also be released soon in Germany, Belgium, and Canada.

Rivette was more of a cinema nut than any of us, and his film proves that he is more of a moviemaker than any of us as well. Leaving aside the conditions under which it was shot, *Paris nous appartient* is the most "directed" of all the films that came out of the *Cahiers du Cinéma* team. It is a film in which technical difficulties aren't dodged but faced squarely, one by one, with stubborn pride, integrity, and the confidence of an old hand.

Even though he has not written much, Jacques Rivette has influenced all the young critics by the self-assurance of his judgments; and while he has not made many films, today he offers a movie begun in 1958 that is a standard for all our attempts.

Quoting Péguy, Rivette reminds us at the beginning of his film that Paris belongs to no one. But cinema belongs to everyone.

—1961

JACQUES ROZIER

Adieu Philippine

What director ever declared that what he was interested in was the counterfeit, or said: I have tried in this film to express the phoniest imaginable emotions in the least sincere possible manner?

Certainly none. Everyone lays claim to truth, everyone wants to express his own truth. Nine times out of ten the arguments of a film's admirers and its disparagers can be expressed by "It's truthful. . . . That's the way it is," or "What do you know about it? You've never seen it," or "You can't possibly talk about such and such since you've never been there."

Everyone is interested in youth, everyone is preoccupied with it, everyone has his own idea about it. Every scriptwriter will tell you that the most difficult dialogue to write is for children or adolescents because if you only hit it *close* it borders on blasphemy. The older you get, the more difficult it is to draw a portrait of youth that seems authentic. One can avoid the issue by stylization, like Renoir in *Le Caporal épinglé* or Castellani in his *Romeo and Juliet*, but if one goes that route, one must also renounce the general truths that André Cayatte in *Avant le Déluge*, Marcel Carné in *Les Tricheurs*, and Clouzot in *La Vérité* attempt. These films had great success with parents, though the young quite rightly did not recognize themselves in them.

If for no other reason, the new wave had to come in order to portray characters fifteen and twenty years old—a gap of only ten years between them and the directors, just right for the directors to have gained some perspective without losing along the way the accuracy of tone that is an end in itself, as in certain Raymond Queneau novels.

Jacques Rozier's first film, *Adieu Philippine*, is the clearest success of this new cinema where spontaneity is all the more powerful when it is the result of long and careful work. There is even something of genius in the balance between the insignificance of the events filmed and the density of reality that confers sufficient importance on them to fascinate us.

Dealing with the theme of boredom, one must dredge through the past, peel off one's skin, reveal one's inner core, embroider with a bewildering exactness of tone on an empty canvas, a Mediterranean gaiety that is fed by a perfectly managed improvisation. Why Mediterranean? The rest of us younger French filmmakers, how can we help feeling hopelessly Nordic when we see Marco Ferreri's *L'Infedelta Coniugale (The Marriage Bed)* or *Il Sorpasso* by Dino Risi? They are so alive that in spite of their pessimistic endings they inspire in us an irresistible urge to sing in the rain. Now French cinema has finally found an Italian temperament in Jacques Rozier. In fact, *Adieu Philippine* does not resemble any film made in France, though it does bear comparison with the best films of Renato Castellani, particularly the unforgettable *Due soldi di speranza*, which fascinated us by the way it dealt with the ordinary matters of everyday life.

This is the deciding factor between cinema that holds to the "norm" and cinema that exaggerates. Louis Lumière is of the first group, a filmmaker who uses the least number of elements to arouse our emotions. Exaggerated cinema resorts to phony violence, erotic scenes, and theatrical dialogues to hide its lack of talent.

You will not find a single unusual frame in *Adieu Philippine*, not a single camera trick, and neither will you discover a single false note nor any vulgarity. Nor will you find "poetic moments"; the film is an uninterrupted poem. Its poetry could not emerge clearly from looking at rushes; it arises from any number of perfect harmonies between images and words, sounds and music.

The treatment of sound in *Adieu Philippine* is perfect. It is first of all a film of emotions, a film of personalities. It is not because these personalities are those of "the common people" that we are touched, but because all of it is filmed with intelligence, love, an enormous scrupulosity and delicacy.

Even in a completely successful film, there are moments which dominate the whole by their utter perfection. So let us predict that the filmmaker who composed the scene of the wasps on the beach will go far.

—1963

PIERRE KAST

Vacances Portugaises

The characters in Pierre Kast's *Vacances Portugaises* are intellectuals; we seldom see such people in films, and very, very seldom do we see them in any convincing way. Like everybody else, intellectuals become entangled in love affairs, but they talk about it more, and often with great clarity. Such a film, sincere and sensitive, delicate and insightful, with emotional integrity and extraordinary authenticity of tone, should have intellectuals as its primary audience. Apparently not, though; they seem to prefer even bad Westerns.

—1964

ALAIN RESNAIS

Muriel

Alfred Hitchcock was very happy to learn that he was a silhouette in *L'Année Dernière à Marienbad (Last Year at Marienbad)* (in the form of a life-size photo mounted on plywood standing in front of an elevator in the hotel). When he learned that Resnais' new film was called *Muriel,* Hitch asked me to tell Resnais Muriel's real story:

"Two fellows are walking in the street when all of a sudden they see an arm in the gutter. 'But that's Muriel,' cries the first. The other shrugs his shoulders. 'How do you know?' A little farther on, they come on a leg, and the first man recognizes Muriel again, but the second is still skeptical. A second leg a few yards farther on still does not convince him. They turn a corner and there, next to the gutter, is a head. 'There, what did I tell you?' cries the first. 'Now, you can see that it's Muriel.' The second fellow, succumbing to the evidence, runs over, picks up the head, hugs it in his arms, and cries, 'Muriel, what is it? Is something wrong?' "

A fair exchange. Hitchcock's presence has much more importance in *Muriel;* not only his image (the subject of a gag in the same spirit) as well as numerous allusions and references—but also, one could say, his "in depth" influence on many levels that makes *Muriel* (among other fascinating things) one of the most effective tributes ever rendered the "master of suspense."

The film's critical reception was very severe: the critics were disarmed and unjust at the same time. Resnais is the most professional of French directors and one of those rare filmmakers who is an artist.

There are any number of ways of constructing a screenplay, and many ways of filming it. It is evident that Resnais envisages all of them, makes his choice, and carefully manages every detail of the enterprise, unlike so many directors who work haphazardly, building their plots any old way, filming confused ideas confusedly.

I have already seen *Muriel* three times without liking it completely, and maybe not liking the same things each time I saw it. I know that I'll see it again many times. Certainly the critics are right to be demanding with a man of Resnais's importance, a man esteemed and recognized throughout the world—but the shots leveled at *Muriel* were rarely aimed at the heart of the subject, but rather at its extremities.

I had planned to analyze the plots of two recent French films with some severity to show the negligence with which they are constructed, but I began a new film a week ago and I am filled with humility. You arrive with ten ideas in your head every day, you film three and reject the others, and you think you have done all right. You had wanted to shoot a film, and you realize that all you are doing is patching, dithering, puttering. You had hoped that the film would be a train rolling steadily on its tracks; instead it's a drifting ship that needs constantly to be brought back on course.

Film criticism, like cinema itself, is going through a crisis. It is normal that critics cannot agree on their appreciation of the production; it is not normal that they cannot even manage to describe it.

How can Georges Charensol on page 6 of *Les Nouvelles Littéraires* review a book about Mallarmé and on page 12 declare that he understood nothing about *Muriel?*

Muriel is an archetypically simple film. It is the story of several people who start each sentence with "I . . ." In *Muriel,* Resnais treats the same subject that Renoir treated in *La Règle du Jeu* and Chabrol in *Les Bonnes Femmes:* we act out "Punch and Judy" as we wait to die.

—1964

JEAN-PIERRE MOCKY

Les Vierges

If you like films, you simply want to know who *filmed* a particular movie. We've given up the pretentious "written and directed," as if it were a novel we were talking about. This is particularly true with a movie like *Les Vierges*, which has a credit list of four screenwriters, though it is an open secret that the basic work was done anonymously by Jean Anouilh.

There are two kinds of films that are made up of separate playlets. There are those that come right out and say so and those that try to give the impression of unified work by sticking a few transitions into the plot.

In *Les Vierges*, the connecting material is extremely weak; the playlets simply succeed one another; they open and close in an obvious way, and are uneven in mood, inspiration, and felicity. The first part is the best, a little heavy but a strong attempt to clarify, as Mocky contended. This is a man's film, a film about girls as seen by a man who is both obsessed sexually and a puritan, two hardly incompatible conditions.

In the first and best of the four sketches, Mocky looks not at a young female virgin but a male one, a virtuous groom who is clearly going to be a disaster as a husband. The rest is less successful but interesting nevertheless, despite some bewildering sentimental concessions. Why bewildering? Because they contradict the overall spirit of the whole, the spirit of Mocky himself, which we know quite a lot about after *Un Couple et les Snobs*.

Mocky is not the only French filmmaker to have recently discovered the brutal truth: The more like me my film is, the less the public is going to like it. (This realization provokes a variety of reactions ranging from embarrassed denial to reluctant change. If you change your mind, you may come away scarred, or a Sergeant York, a daredevil.)

I haven't answered a particular question (not that anyone's asked me, anyhow) and that is, Is this Mocky's best movie? It doesn't make any difference; the important thing is that it is not an indifferent film. Its outstanding quality is a curious mixture of falsity and truth, sincerity and pretense.

What are its good qualities? As is often true with Mocky, we have a chance to see unknown actors, well chosen and employed. Also, there is a cleanness of execution that is admirable. There is nothing in the images except what Mocky wants there and wants us to see. Everything is clean, naked, precise, direct.

If he'd had a well-constructed screenplay, Mocky would have made a much more disciplined film because he understands that one must always remove rather than add in cinema. With his native originality, if self-criticism is allowed to sink in, he will make progress and become an important film personality.

—1965

CLAUDE BERRI

Le Vieil Homme et l'Enfant

"My dear Marshal . . . On this beautiful feast day of Joan of Arc, I take up my pen to tell you . . .

"Today is the feast day of Saint Philip and I am sending you . . .

"My dear Marshal . . . On your birthday, I address you . . .

"My dear Marshal . . . I wish you a Happy New Year and good health. . . ."

Like all the French of my generation, I spent the better part of my schooldays during the German Occupation writing letters to Marshal Pétain. It was obligatory, it was enjoyable, and it was rewarded—usually with an extra vitamin cookie.

I believe that only the best letter from the class was actually sent to the Marshal; the others were graded as French homework.

From October to July, our big hit was *Maréchal, nous voilà*, which regularly won first place on our Hit Parade:

> Dear Marshal, here we are!
> Standing before you, Savior of France,
> We swear, all of us your boys,
> To obey and follow your lead.
> Dear Marshal, here we are!
> You have restored our hope,
> The Fatherland will be born again,
> Marshal, dear Marshal, here we are!

For twenty years I have been waiting for the *real* film about the *real* France during the *real* Occupation, the film about the majority of Frenchmen, those who were involved neither in the collaboration nor the Resistance, those who did nothing, either good or bad, those who survived like characters in a Beckett play. To compare our hexagon (the shape of France) to a game of chess, the movies always offered us the point of view of a rook or a bishop, never of the pawns. Recently, *Paris brûle-t-il? (Is Paris Burning?)* tried to pass off a counterfeit on us, but it only amused a few generals' widows. Now Claude Berri's first film, *Le Vieil Homme et l'Enfant (The Two of Us)*, makes the long wait worth it.

I am no longer a film critic, and I realize that it's presumptuous to write about a film one has seen only three times—but it's really like a dress rehearsal, simply some impressions, and a great pleasure that I long to share.

During the Occupation of the "Free Zone," a small Jewish boy is given a false name and placed in the home of a retired worker who lives near Grenoble, a man who is fiercely, stubbornly, and imperturbably anti-Semitic.

The film chronicles the stay of young Langmann (who has become young Longuet) in the village, the school and in the old man's house. The old man takes the boy into his confidence: "The enemies of France, mark me, are fourfold: the English, the Jews, the Freemasons, and the Bolsheviks."

There were several ways Berri could have constructed his film. It could have been heartbreaking, à la de Sica; pseudopoetic, à la Bourguignon; thematic, à la Cayatte. In all three cases, it would have been odious. Instead it is alive and droll, free of presuppositions, distrusting of all humanisms—an "abhumanist" film, as Jacques Audiberti (whom we miss more each day) would have said.

I do not think that Claude Berri was aware of avoiding the traps that various conventions were laying for him. I think his very strong instinct naturally indicated to him the zigzag path he followed, because it was the only path that resembles real life. Michel Simon (the old man) adores animals, but he takes the little boy into his affections only because he has at last found someone to listen. He detests Jews, but he admits they have never done anything to him personally. ("That would be the last straw.")

The little boy enjoys his situation wildly, he doesn't whine, he doesn't cry at night in bed, and he loves his Pépé more and more.

The setting contains all the little details that are tied to the period of the Occupation: heads shaved because of lice, rationing, the obligatory *Maréchal, nous voilà*, the shaven head of a young mother after the Liberation (the mark of the collaborationist). Everything winds down with the departure of the boy, whose parents have come for him. Berri had the tact, the intelligence, the sensitivity, and the intuition not to clear up the misunderstanding. Michel Simon watches the boy leave sadly, but he will never know that he was "one of them."

If we get such intense pleasure from watching this film, it is because we are led from one surprise to another. We never anticipate the next scene. When it happens, we approve, we recognize its reality and, at the same time, are struck with the madness it reveals. If we think about it, we observe that films which present only dishonest circumstances—exceptional people in exceptional situations—are in the long run reasonable and boring; whereas, films that seek to conquer truth—real people in real situations—give us a sensation of madness. This is true from Jean Vigo all the way to Claude Berri, through Sacha Guitry and Jean Renoir. These names do not occur to me by chance: thirty-five years after *Boudu sauvé des Eaux*, thirty-two years after *L'Atalante*, thirty years after *Drôle de Drame* and *Quai des Brumes*, fifteen years after *La Poison*, all those who see Michel Simon as one of the greatest actors in the world will applaud the return of Père Jules, the bargeman of *L'Atalante*.

So, Michel Simon plays Pépe, the old man. "And how about the boy?" you may ask. He is fine, thank you. Children who play comedy are sometimes considered monsters, false comedians whom we should mistrust. Claude Berri was right on target when he sensed that he should balance his explosive tandem harmoniously by juxtaposing the childish side of Michel Simon and the precocious and tranquil gravity of the young star. Because of that, we have one of those emotional stories that are truer and stronger than any love story. It happens each time someone succeeds in creating a situation between two persons of the same sex without falling into the double trap of endemic antagonism or a cloudless friendship.

There's glory in store for Berri, but some abuse too. You don't make such an explosive film with impunity, even if the packaging is likable, without awakening the vigilance of those who want to stop us walking thin lines. A delightful anti-Semite, a charming, double-crossing schoolmistress, an authentic T.S.F., a conformist F.F.I., a typical small village, a little Jewish boy, Edouard Drummont, who adores his *café*, . . . all this is going to bring Claude Berri to the

same scaffold they hung Ernst Lubitsch from twenty years ago, when
he was found guilty of making audiences burst into uproarious laughter
in *To Be or Not to Be*, simply by repeating the words "concentration
camp" twenty times: "So, they call me Concentration Camp Ehrhardt? Ha, ha, ha . . ." "Yes, they call you Concentration Camp
Ehrhardt. Ha, ha, ha . . ."

If Berri has to face the judges who condemned Lubitsch, and I
had the chance to be his lawyer, I would state that his comic and
daring film moved me from beginning to end, that it showed me
that men are worth more than the ideas they hold, that cinema was
waiting for this new *Réflexions sur la Question Juive* (Reflections on
the Jewish Question), and that I cannot wait for Jean Renoir to come
back to France and see *Le Vieil Homme et L'Enfant*. He will be as
delighted as he is each time he sees an offspring of *Toni*.

—1967

Le Cinéma de Papa

After *Le Vieil Homme et l'Enfant*, which I adored, *Le
Cinéma de Papa* is probably Claude Berri's best film. If its title gives
the impression that it is a film about films, the truth is that *Le Cinéma*
is really concerned with the most basic elements of life itself, precisely
those things that current films mostly avoid: the struggle to earn a
living, money problems, daily bread, the search for a trade, the birth
of a vocation, the alternation of good and bad luck.

The humanity of Charlie Chaplin's films is made of the same stuff:
the necessity of three meals a day, to find work, to be happy in
love. These are the best themes, the most simple and universal. Curiously, to the degree that cinema becomes more intellectual, they are
the most ignored.

Berri's films never whine; his characters never accuse anyone else
of being to blame for their troubles; they believe in chance and luck,
but even more in energy. I find this same energy in Berri himself,
in his work, in his personality, in his life. Cinema requires poetry,
sensitivity, intelligence, and whatever, but even more imperatively it
needs *vitality*.

Berri isn't one of those directors who are in love with cinema; he doesn't refer to other films but to life itself. He draws from the source. Like Marcel Pagnol and Sacha Guitry, who were seriously underestimated in their time, Claude Berri first of all has stories to tell. He feels them so strongly that he quite naturally invents and discovers the best forms to communicate them.

When he told me about his plan to shoot *Le Cinéma de Papa*, I told him to have someone screen *Le Roman d'un Tricheur* and *Le Schpountz* for him. But since he prefers good meals and conversations with friends, he never took the time, and he was right, because his storyteller's instinct led him to the best solution of the problems the film posed.

I want to draw your attention to an especially original aspect of *Le Cinéma de Papa*. We know that by definition artists are, if not antisocial, generally asocial. Before they criticize society at large, they have already been at odds with their families who did not understand them, or who oppressed them. Their vocation is often born of a wound. In *Le Cinéma de Papa*, and in all Berri's films, it is just the opposite; the basis of his credo could be "My family, I love you." When you come out of this movie, you are sure that Claude Berri is not scarred in the way of artists who are cut off from their families. Here is a filmmaker who loves his parents. It makes his film even more unusual.

—1971

GÉRARD BLAIN

Les Amis

As an actor, Gérard Blain had the reputation of being pigheaded, and the reputation was certainly justified. His trouble was that they make very few adventure films in France, and no Westerns or motorcycle films. If John Garfield had been born in Paris, he would have had the same career and employment problems as our friend Gérard.

Les Amis, in which he doesn't act although he wrote and directed it, proves that Blain had good reason to be difficult and demanding in his work. This potential filmmaker now shows himself to be a potent filmmaker indeed, because he is utterly logical. Logic—the logic of the whole, of its style and the execution of its intention—makes up the only trait common to good filmmakers in my opinion.

Les Amis tells the story, with great logic, of course, of an emotional liaison between a rich, married man and a poor, handsome young man. The two protagonists are well chosen and are *pointed in the right direction* (I don't like the word "directed" used about artists, or civilians for that matter), and their laconic restraint points up the ordinariness of situations that might be supposed to be exceptional.

The plot of *Les Amis* has the frankness not of a confession, but of experience. There is nothing shamefaced about it, nothing cynical. On the screen, you will see what is natural, from the first frame to "The End." Gérard Blain had the courage to do without oratorical hedges; he offers no "alibis" for his characters. For example, the hero—who likes and idealizes young blond women—has a homosexual adventure, not because of the war in Indochina, but simply because his older partner brings him the security, comfort, and tender attention he craves.

When his "godfather" asks him why he wants to become a film actor, the young man might have answered, "Because I want to bring joy and beautiful dreams to those who suffer." But none of that. He answers quite sweetly that he wants to "be famous and earn a lot of money."

The whole film proceeds with simplicity and logic: there are no embellishments, no decoration, not a single unnecessary shot. In this regard, I call your attention to the automobile accident, the best one ever filmed in my opinion.

Thanks to its absolute correctness of tone, its warm irony, and the precision of its intention, *Les Amis* has just been added to the list of "first films" that were also revelations: *Adieu Philippine* by Jacques Rozier, *Le Signe du Lion* by Eric Rohmer, *Le Vieil Homme et l'Enfant* by Claude Berri, *More* by Barbet Schroeder, *L'Enfance nue* by Maurice Pialat.

—1972

LASZLO SZABO

Les Gants Blancs du Diable

Films are as fragile as babies; it is not enough just to bring them into the world. For example, do you know or have you seen or will you ever see the films of Philippe Garrel: *Marie pour Mémoire, La Concentration, Le Lit de la Vierge, La Cicatrice Intérieure,* or *L'Athanor?* They are beautiful and inspired films, their titles move us to dreams, but these masterpieces were abandoned at birth by the mercenary producers who financed them, and passed directly from the studios where they were made to the paradise of the Cinéma- thèque.

I hope Laszlo Szabo will have better luck and that his first feature- length film, *Les Gants blancs du Diable,* will live a normal public lifespan. I hope so, and I believe so because his film comes along at this very moment to bring back the violent charm of the most commer- cial films in the world, the series of productions the American movie companies made between 1940 and 1955. It is exactly what he wanted to accomplish.

The gamble (and it is one) doesn't have the best odds in the world, and Laszlo Szabo is not the first European filmmaker to cast longing glances at Stuart Heisler and *Kiss Me Deadly.* We've seen it before; we all know that the crime film almost never returns the love French filmmakers bring to it. The fact is that the action of the crime novels takes place in an imaginary country. If one accepts this idea, he will admit perhaps that *La Belle et la Bête (Beauty and the Beast)* by Jean Cocteau to this day remains the best French equivalent to the world of William Irish or David Goodis.

You should see *Les Gants blancs du Diable;* it is precisely the bridge between Cocteau and Goodis, or between Godard (of *Made in USA*) and Hawks (of *The Big Sleep*). Shot in 16 mm. color with a budget that was surely lower than a single day's shooting of *Le Casse* (drawn from Goodis' novel *The Burglar*) or *La Course du Lièvre à travers les Champs* (from Goodis' novel *Friday the Thirteenth*), Szabo's film takes us to the imaginary country of crime novels—into that closed world that must at all costs remain shadowy by not allowing the images of sky or sun that overwhelm almost all contemporary color films to intrude. It must be pointed out that Laszlo Szabo was in on the start; he is a strange and poetic actor who has been used mainly by Godard since *Le Petit Soldat.* If Jean-Christophe Averty, with his special-effect machines, injected Laszlo Szabo's silhouette electronically onto the images of *The Maltese Falcon*, no one would be the wiser.

Like many actor/directors, Szabo has an ideal cast, ranging from Bernadette Lafont to Georgette Anys, and at the same time he has given Jean-Pierre Kalfon, Yves Alfonso, Serge Marquand, Jean-Pierre Moulin their best roles to date. The Karl-Heinz Schaefer music is the finest I have heard in any recent film; it moves hand in hand with the *Johnny Guitar* style of color in this film, an approach to color that really knows how to frighten us with its yellows, greens, reds.

Szabo's future now depends on the public that may look at the photographs at the entrances of the theaters and say, "Hey, this doesn't look like a bad movie; do you want to go?"

—1973

CLAUDE SAUTET

Vincent, François, Paul et les Autres

I happened to work with Claude Sautet once during the time when he seemed to have given up directing to become a "patcher-upper" of screen plays. After several successful patch jobs—God, what jargon—Sautet was able to raise his prices and become a consultant. From then on, it was "Doctor Sautet" who was called to the rescue when a script had broken down. Among the solutions Claude used to propose, one came up fairly often: the slap. The director in trouble would say to Sautet: "Then she tells him she won't see him any more; he tells her to go to hell . . . he won't take it . . . and then . . . I don't know." Then Sautet would suggest: "So, he walks across the room, he walks up to her, and wham! he belts her one."

I worked for three or four days with Claude Sautet on a screenplay that had come apart (the director's name isn't important). We had barely met before that and those few days of working together gave us an opportunity to get to know each other better. Often we were in agreement on how to solve the problems and, as a result, we came to realize that we had similar ideas. From there to finding each other intelligent and likable was only a step, and after that, for our own enjoyment we continued to exchange ideas over a meal from time to time.

Later, thanks to the kind insistence of Jean-Loup Dabadie, who had adapted *Les Choses de la Vie* without a director or producer having been chosen, Sautet ended by admitting that he should return to directing. He has been inspired ever since: *Les Choses de la Vie,*

Max et les Ferrailleurs, César et Rosalie, and today *Vincent, François, Paul et les Autres* are the result. The common denominator in these four films is Jean-Loup Dabadie, a true cinema writer, quite simply an excellent writer in any case, a musician of words that sound like what they are, modest and mischievous, scrupulous and inspired, a daring young man on the flying typewriter, and trained in Sautet's school.

Sautet is the least frivolous man I know. His fierce seriousness reminds me of Charles Vanel; both to my mind are the kind of head-lumberjack who could grab an axe out of the hands of an awkward worker and show him how to cut down five trees in an hour. Sautet is stubborn, shy, sincere, strong. And he is French, French, French. *L'Avant-Scène* asked me to review *Vincent, François, Paul et les Autres,* and I am keeping the promise by drawing a portrait of Claude Sautet because, if describing films says a lot about those who made them, discussing a filmmaker tells a lot about his movies, too.

Vincent, François, Paul et les Autres is French, French, French, even though Claude Sautet is one of those directors who learned his craft by watching American directors, mainly Raoul Walsh and Howard Hawks. The first time we lunched together, Sautet expressed his admiration for Raoul Walsh's maxim: "Cinema is action, action, action . . . but it must all be in the same direction!" I thought about that conversation when the aged director of *Her Man,* Tay Garnett, said to me last month, "I have the impression that young French directors understand what we learned fifty years ago, that a film is 'run, run, run.'"

To love American cinema is fine; to try to make French films as if they were American is something else again, very much open to argument. I am not going to attack anybody for it, having myself fallen into that trap two or three times. Jean Renoir learned a lesson from Stroheim and Chaplin when he was making *Nana* and *Tire au flanc,* that is to say, he reinforced the French side of his films while he absorbed the Hollywood masters. In the same way, Claude Sautet understood, after the unavoidable detour through the crime films, that he should, in Jean Cocteau's words, be "a bird who sings in his own genealogical tree."

Vincent, François, Paul et les Autres seems to me to be Sautet's best film and, by the same token, the best film from the Dabadie-Sautet team. Its subject can be summed up in one word: life. It is a film about life in general, and about what we are. Pascal, who said, "What interests man is man," would love this film. Some people who have seen it have been overwhelmed, and have said to me, "It is very beautiful but it is terrible; it's like being hit over the head." I didn't see it that way; I found it optimistic and exalting. I believed I could hear Claude Sautet whispering in my ear—though I could be wrong—"Life is hard in little things but it is good overall." That's the message I thought I heard, and I certainly approve because it goes to the heart of things. We rail about everyday problems, problems in the family, material goods, troubles of the heart and feelings. Still, when a doctor comes along and says, "The old carcass is holding up but it's cracked, you'll have to be careful of it," our poor life suddenly becomes worth its weight in gold and things assume their proper value. Life goes on, like everything, under the sign of Relativity.

Usually in films, at least most films, the actors are engaged to play roles in which any resemblance to real persons is purely coincidental. What struck me in *Vincent, François, Paul et les Autres* is how extraordinarily the people we see on screen match the words they speak; it's as if the real subject of the film were their faces.

Messrs. Montand, Piccoli, Reggiani, Depardieu: the film is a story about your forehead, your nose, your eyes, your hair, and, in a short time, I have come to know all about you because you have just made a great documentary film before going back to your make-believe, to your actor's craft, which I certainly respect and have no wish to denigrate. Misses Stéphane, Ludmilla, Antonella, Marie, Catherine and the rest, I confess to being disappointed because I wanted the film to last fifty more minutes so that I could learn more about you. Still, things being as they are, I feel sure that you are proud of this film as you have every right to be. Every one of you would deserve to be the life partner of any one of those men, but today love, and even passion, is divided into sections and we are always confronting the temporary while everything in you, and us, cries out for the permanent.

Every beautiful film is dedicated almost imperceptibly to someone and it seems to me that this one might be dedicated to Jacques Becker. It would have touched him profoundly, as it touches everyone who values people over situations, all who think that men are more important than what they do.

Vincent, François, Paul et les Autres is life; and Claude Sautet is vitality.

—1974

JACQUES DOILLON

Les Doigts dans la Tête

A hasty response I wrote to an inquiry from *Le Figaro* about "The New Wave Fifteen Years After" may give the impression that I am hostile to political cinema on principle. The reality is very different, but it is true as I watch certain films that I am shocked by a kind of artificial political layer on the surface which I sometimes feel has become as obligatory as the shot of the inside of the automobile through the windshield. Propaganda by the left is still propaganda, and, when politics is ingested gratuitously, unnecessarily, into a screenplay, dragged in by the hair, clearly intended to "cover" the filmmaker, the film's authenticity is hurt. The actors begin to speak like the daily papers and the director slips into an imitation of Cayatte without even realizing it: programmed characters, situations that are so predictable they seem as if they'd been sewn in with white thread; what you get is a computer film—what André Bazin called cybernetic cinema.

Les Doigts dans la Tête (Fingers in the Head) is a good example of the opposite sort of film. The feeling and social meaning are combined as harmoniously as in *Toni*, which I thought of often as I watched it. It may seem odd to compare Jean Renoir's tragic news item, filmed in broad daylight, with Jacques Doillon's comedy that was shot within the four walls of a maid's bedroom, but the two films are animated by the same spirit. They are alive and warm. Though social criticism is present in both of them, it is completely integrated, and logical and exact.

Because he meets a young Swedish girl who is as at home in today's world and with today's accepted ideas as a fish in water, a young baker's apprentice loses, in the course of a few days, both his money and his girl. There is no need to agonize over what *Les Doigts dans la Tête* is all about; it is a funny and truthful film, a film that sings with genuineness.

As I watched the film, I was just as interested, surprised and amused as my neighbors were, but I couldn't help thinking that the comedy was going to veer off into a bloody event. I was expecting a corpse before the end. You'll see that though I was mistaken, I wasn't far off—but *Les Doigts dans la Tête* is one of those films that, without ever falling into an arbitrary sort of fantasy, surprises us from start to finish, and yet whose integrity we salute in the end. All the most beautiful films have this sort of logic.

I appreciated at the same time that *Les Doigts dans la Tête*, though its conception includes a way of filming bits of real life, is truly *directed*, and turns away from mere techniques of reportage. Thirty years after neorealism, and fifteen years after the new wave, we are beginning to be able to differentiate the films that don't age well from those that hold their own. We can see that those that have style resist the years. In 1938, one could play the Renoir of *La Marseillaise* and *La Grande Illusion* against the Gance of *Napoléon* and *J'Accuse* (or vice versa), but today we can see clearly that they were both great directors, that their films were great films, and that it is the others in between who have aged. In a recent interview, André S. Labarthe and Janine Bazin remarked that of all the kinds of movies that they had analyzed on their program "Cinéastes de notre temps," it was *cinéma-vérité* which appeared most dated and old-fashioned. I believe the same fate awaits certain contemporary films which—under the pretext of not hiding any part of reality—are shot in the streets with portable cameras carried on the shoulders, with a zoom lens that kills proportion and rhythm, with traffic noises drowning the actors' words. If we add color, which pushes a film toward the cult of the documentary if it isn't carefully controlled, we get a kind of cinema that could be called "pure recording." It brings to the screen the pseudoinformative insipidity of television, and ends by making us nostalgic for the big studios, the star system, and all the artifices that keep *Sunrise, Big Sleep, Rear Window, Singin' in the Rain,* and others from ever seeming old-fashioned.

Les Doigts dans la Tête is filmed in black-and-white, without zoom shots, framed as seriously as *La Maman et la Putain,* directed without special effects, but *directed,* surely.

Its strong point is the acting, which is quiet and natural, so natural that one cannot resist wondering afterward whether the dialogue was in the script or improvised. I am fairly sure that 90 percent of it was written and that the actors, Christophe Soto, Olivier Bousquet, Gabriel Bernard, Roselyne Villaume, and Ann Zacharias (the marvelous Swedish girl) deserve even more praise for giving the impression that they said what came into their heads.

Les Doigts dans la Tête also demonstrates that the influence of Bresson can be, is beginning to be, constructive. Actors, whether amateurs or professionals, may let themselves be led down the antitheatrical path that the author of *Lancelot* proclaims the only proper way, provided that it doesn't lead them to become sententious. On this subject, it is interesting to note that every three years some film comes along—*Adieu Philippine, Jeanne d'Arc, Bande à Part, Ma Nuit chez Maud, Les Doigts dans la Tête*—which gives us the impression that the highest degree of authenticity in acting has now been reached. Happily, this is only an impression. The quest for authenticity in art is like climbing a ladder with no end.

—*December 1974*

INDEX

Note: Main references to films, filmmakers and actors are indicated by page numbers in italics